# CAMBRIDGE

Official Cambridge Exam Preparation

# COMPLETE

## PRELIMINARY

Student's Book with answers

Second edition

**B1** WITH ONLINE PRACTICE

Emma Heyderman and Peter May

For the revised exam from 2020

**Cambridge University Press**
www.cambridge.org/elt

**Cambridge Assessment English**
www.cambridgeenglish.org

Information on this title: www.cambridge.org/9781108525244

© Cambridge University Press and UCLES 2019

This publication is in copyright. Subject to statutory exception
and to the provisions of relevant collective licensing agreements,
no reproduction of any part may take place without the written
permission of Cambridge University Press.

First published 2010
Second edition 2019

20 19 18 17 16 15 14 13 12 11 10 9 8 7 6 5

Printed in Poland by Opolgraf

*A catalogue record for this publication is available from the British Library*

ISBN 978-1-108-52524-4 Student's Book with answers with Online Practice

The publishers have no responsibility for the persistence or accuracy
of URLs for external or third-party internet websites referred to in this publication,
and do not guarantee that any content on such websites is, or will remain,
accurate or appropriate. Information regarding prices, travel timetables, and other
factual information given in this work is correct at the time of first printing but
the publishers do not guarantee the accuracy of such information thereafter.

# Contents

| | |
|---|---|
| **Map of the units** | 4 |
| **Introduction** | 6 |
| **Preliminary content and overview** | 7 |
| | |
| **1  My life and home** | 8 |
| **2  Making choices** | 16 |
| *Vocabulary and grammar review Units 1 and 2* | 24 |
| **3  Having fun** | 26 |
| **4  On holiday** | 34 |
| *Vocabulary and grammar review Units 3 and 4* | 42 |
| **5  Different feelings** | 44 |
| **6  That's entertainment!** | 52 |
| *Vocabulary and grammar review Units 5 and 6* | 60 |
| **7  Getting around** | 62 |
| **8  Influencers** | 70 |
| *Vocabulary and grammar review Units 7 and 8* | 78 |
| **9  Stay fit and healthy** | 80 |
| **10  Looks amazing!** | 88 |
| *Vocabulary and grammar review Units 9 and 10* | 96 |
| **11  The natural world** | 98 |
| **12  Express yourself!** | 106 |
| *Vocabulary and grammar review Units 11 and 12* | 114 |
| | |
| **Grammar reference** | 116 |
| **Phrasal verb builder** | 141 |
| **Irregular verbs** | 143 |
| **Writing bank** | 144 |
| **Speaking bank** | 152 |
| **Extra resources** | 162 |
| **Answer key** | 163 |

# Map of the units

| Unit title | Reading | Writing | Listening |
|---|---|---|---|
| 1 My life and home | **Part 5:** 'Emilia's home' – living on a boat<br>Reading for understanding of vocabulary | **Part 1:** An email<br>Planning a reply | **Part 2:** Listening for specific information<br>Two candidates doing Speaking Part 1 |
| 2 Making choices | **Part 6:** 'Would you choose to study at a college or university like this?'<br>Reading for detailed understanding of words and sentences | A post about what you used to do ten years ago<br>**Part 2:** An article on what makes a great place to work<br>Using a mind map to plan an answer | Emily talking about her work experience in Mexico<br>**Part 1:** Seven short texts about daily life<br>Two candidates doing Speaking Part 3 |
| *Vocabulary and grammar review Units 1 and 2* ||||
| 3 Having fun | **Part 3:** 'Sand sculptures'<br>Reading for detailed understanding | **Part 2:** A story about a day out<br>Planning paragraphs | **Part 4:** Marc Pasqual – an Instagram photographer<br>Talking about a skiing holiday<br>Two candidates doing Speaking Part 2 |
| 4 On holiday | **Part 1:** Identifying text purpose | **Part 1:** An email<br>Suggesting where to go in a city and what to do | Discussing a quiz<br>**Part 3:** 'A bushcraft skills course'<br>Some friends discussing their next holiday |
| *Vocabulary and grammar review Units 3 and 4* ||||
| 5 Different feelings | **Part 4:** 'How I dealt with stress'<br>Identifying the topic of a paragraph<br>Identifying linking words (*this, then, do, also, however*, etc.) | **Part 2:** A story<br>Using adjectives to describe feeling | **Part 2:** Listening for facts, opinions or feelings<br>Two candidates doing Speaking Part 4 |
| 6 That's entertainment! | **Part 2:** 'Turn off the TV and go out!'<br>Selecting events from an entertainment guide | **Part 2:** An article about a celebration in your country<br>Using the correct style for an article | Eliza and Bella planning a night out<br>**Part 1:** Seven short texts about daily life<br>Two candidates doing Speaking Part 3 |
| *Vocabulary and grammar review Units 5 and 6* ||||
| 7 Getting around | **Part 1:** Identifying text purpose | **Part 1:** An email<br>Useful email expressions | **Part 4:** Olivia talks about extremely heavy snow while travelling in Italy<br>Identifying distracting information<br>Mia and Owen discuss getting to the station on time<br>A candidate doing Speaking Part 2 |
| 8 Influencers | Famous families<br>**Part 6:** An article about Emma Watson, a famous influencer | **Part 2:** An article about a person you admire<br>Using correct spelling and punctuation | **Part 3:** 'How to become famous on YouTube'<br>Completing notes<br>Carter and Will discuss presenters for a YouTube channel<br>Three candidates doing Speaking Part 1 |
| *Vocabulary and grammar review Units 7 and 8* ||||
| 9 Stay fit and healthy | **Part 3:** Evie Scott talks about exercise at work<br>Identifying opinion and attitude | **Part 2:** A story about feeling nervous<br>Using a range of past tenses to explain what happened | **Part 2:** People talking in six different situations<br>Identifying the situation and what you need to listen for<br>Two candidates doing Speaking Part 4 |
| 10 Looks amazing! | **Part 2:** 'Our top picks at the street food market'<br>Selecting places to eat | **Part 2:** An article | **Part 1:** Seven short texts about daily life<br>Listening carefully for information<br>Two candidates doing Speaking Part 2 |
| *Vocabulary and grammar review Units 9 and 10* ||||
| 11 The natural world | 'Scientists use robot chick to study penguins'<br>**Part 5:** 'Working on the Galápagos Islands' | **Part 1:** An email<br>Checking your work for mistakes | **Part 4:** Looking for the Iberian lynx<br>Identifying expressions with similar or different meanings<br>Two candidates doing Speaking Part 4 |
| 12 Express yourself! | **Part 4:** 'Can you live without your smartphone for a week?'<br>Matching sentences to paragraphs | **Part 2:** A story<br>Using a range of tenses and reported speech | Raising money for charity<br>**Part 3:** A competition to design a new app<br>Two candidates doing Speaking Part 1 |
| *Vocabulary and grammar review Units 11 and 12* ||||

| Speaking | Pronunciation | Vocabulary | Grammar |
|---|---|---|---|
| **Part 1:** Saying your name, where you live, what you do, and if you like studying English | -s endings /s/, /z/ and /ɪz/ | House and home<br>Countable and uncountable nouns | Prepositions of time<br>Frequency adverbs<br>Present simple and present continuous<br>State verbs<br>*a few, a bit of, many, much, a lot of* and *lots of*<br>Prepositions of place |
| **Part 3:** Discussing a new club for students to practise English<br>Agreeing and disagreeing<br>Making a decision | -ed endings /d/, /t/ and /ɪd/ | Life choices<br>*fail, pass, take, lose, miss, study* and *teach*<br>*do, earn, make, spend, take* and *win* | Past simple<br>Past simple and past continuous<br>*used to*<br>*So do I* and *Nor/Neither do I* |
| **Part 2:** Describing a picture<br>Explaining what you can see and where things are | -ing endings /ŋ/ | Leisure activities<br>Prepositions of place<br>Phrasal verbs<br>People's hobbies | Verbs followed by *to* or -*ing* |
| **Part 3:** Discussing where to go in a city<br>Making suggestions and giving reasons | Weak forms in comparative structures | Holiday activities<br>*travel, journey* and *trip*<br>Buildings and places | Comparative and superlative adjectives<br>*a bit, a little, slightly, much, far, a lot*<br>*(not) as … as …*<br>*big* and *enormous* (gradable and non-gradable adjectives) |
| **Part 4:** Describing personal experiences<br>Asking other people what they think | Modal verbs: weak and strong forms | Feelings<br>Adjectives and prepositions<br>Adjectives with -*ed* and -*ing*<br>Adjectives and their opposites | *can, could, might, may* (ability and possibility)<br>*should, shouldn't, ought to, must, mustn't, have to* and *don't have to* (advice, obligation and prohibition) |
| **Part 3:** Discussing plans for a festival<br>Moving on to a new subject | Contrastive stress | Television programmes<br>Going out<br>*been/gone, meet, get to know, know* and *find out* | Present perfect<br>*just, already* and *yet*<br>*since* and *for*<br>Present perfect or past simple? |
| **Part 2:** Describing what people are doing in photos<br>Adding new points, and correcting yourself<br>Describing things you don't know the name of | Word stress in compound nouns | Weather<br>Compound words | *extremely, fairly, quite, rather, really* and *very*<br>*too* and *enough*<br>The future<br>Prepositions of movement |
| **Part 1:** Answering general questions<br>Talking about your daily routine and what you like | Conditional sentences: contracted words | Phrasal verbs<br>Describing people<br>Adjective prefixes and suffixes<br>Adjective order | Zero, first and second conditionals<br>*when, if, unless* + present, future |
| **Part 4:** Discussing sport, fitness and health<br>Showing agreement and polite disagreement | Word stress: agreeing and disagreeing | Illnesses and accidents<br>Sports<br>*do, go* and *play* | Relative clauses<br>(defining and non-defining)<br>Past perfect |
| **Part 2:** Describing everyday objects in photos<br>Explaining what things are made of or used for | Connected speech: linking sounds | *course, dish, food, meal* and *plate*<br>Shops and services | Commands and instructions<br>*Have something done* |
| **Part 4:** Discussing ways to help the environment<br>Giving examples | Word stress in longer nouns<br>Word stress in passive forms | The environment<br>Noun suffixes | The passive: present simple and past simple<br>Comparative and superlative adverbs |
| **Part 1:** General questions<br>Talking about habits and routines | Intonation in direct and indirect questions | Collocations: using your phone<br>*ask, ask for, speak, talk, say* and *tell*<br>Negative prefixes | Reported speech and reported commands<br>Reported questions<br>Indirect questions |

# Introduction

**Who this book is for**

*Complete Preliminary* is a stimulating and thorough preparation course for learners who wish to take the **B1 Preliminary exam** from **Cambridge Assessment English**. It helps them to develop the necessary reading, writing, listening and speaking skills for the exam as well as teaching essential grammar and vocabulary. For those who are not planning to take the exam in the near future, the book provides skills and language based around engaging topics, all highly relevant for learners moving towards a B1 level of English.

**What the Student's Book contains:**

- **12 units for classroom study**. Each unit contains:
  - an authentic exam task taken from each of the four papers (Reading, Speaking, Writing and Listening) in the **Preliminary exam**.
  - essential information on what each part of the exam involves, and the best way to approach each task. Exam advice boxes before exam tasks explain how to do this.
  - a wide range of enjoyable speaking activities designed to increase learners' fluency and ability to express themselves.
  - a step-by-step approach to doing Preliminary Writing tasks.
  - grammar activities and exercises for the grammar learners need to know for the exam. When you are doing grammar exercises, you will sometimes see this symbol 👁. These exercises are based on research from the **Cambridge Learner Corpus** and they deal with the areas which often cause problems for students in the exam.
  - vocabulary activities and exercises for the vocabulary you need to know for the exam. When you see this symbol 👁 by a vocabulary exercise, the exercise focuses on words which Preliminary candidates often confuse or use wrongly in the exam.
- **Six unit reviews**. These contain exercises which revise the grammar and vocabulary in each unit.
- **Speaking and Writing banks**. These explain the possible tasks students may have to do in the Speaking and Writing papers, and they give you examples and models together with additional exercises and advice on how best to approach these Speaking and Writing exam tasks.
- A **Grammar reference section** which clearly explains, unit by unit, all the main areas of grammar which you will need to know for the **B1 Preliminary exam**. There are also practice exercises for all grammar points.

**Also available:**

- **Downloadable audio online** containing all the listening material for the 12 units of the Student's Book plus material for the Speaking Bank. The listening material is indicated by coloured icons 🎧 in the Student's Book.
- A **Teacher's Book** containing:
  - **Step-by-step guidance** for teaching the activities in the Student's Book.
  - A number of suggestions for **alternative treatments** of activities in the Student's Book and suggestions for **extension activities**.
  - **Photocopiable recording scripts** from the Student's Book listening material.
  - **Complete answer keys** including recording scripts for all the listening material.
  - **12 word lists** (one for each unit) containing vocabulary found in the units.
  - **Access to extra photocopiable materials online** to practise and extend language abilities outside the requirements of the **B1 Preliminary exam**.
- A Student's **Workbook** containing:
  - 12 units for homework and self-study. Each unit contains further exam-style exercises to practise the reading, writing and listening skills needed in the **Preliminary exam**. In addition, they provide further practice of grammar and vocabulary, which also use information about common Preliminary candidate errors from the Cambridge Learner Corpus 👁.
  - A **'Vocabulary Extra'** section, which contains twelve pages of further revision and practice of the essential Preliminary exam vocabulary contained in the Student's Book units.
  - **Downloadable audio online** containing all the listening material for the Workbook.
- A **Test Generator** containing:
  - A **Grammar and Vocabulary Test** at standard and plus levels of each of the 12 units in the Student's Book.
  - Three **Term Tests** including grammar, vocabulary and Preliminary Writing, Speaking, Listening and Reading exam tasks.
  - An **End of Year Test** including grammar and vocabulary from all 12 units, with Preliminary Writing, Speaking, Listening and Reading exam tasks.

# B1 Preliminary content and overview

| Part/Timing | Content | Exam focus |
|---|---|---|
| **1 Reading** 45 minutes | **Part 1** Five very short texts: signs and messages, postcards, notes, emails, labels, etc. followed by five three-option multiple choice questions.<br>**Part 2** Five descriptions of people to match to eight short texts.<br>**Part 3** Longer text with five four-option multiple choice questions.<br>**Part 4** Gapped text where five sentences have been removed. Candidates must select the five correct sentences from a list of eight.<br>**Part 5** Four-option multiple choice cloze text with six gaps. Candidates select the word which best fits each gap.<br>**Part 6** An open cloze text consisting of a text with six gaps. Candidates think of a word which best suits each gap. | **Parts 1–4** and **Part 6**: Candidates are expected to read for the main message, global meaning, specific information, detailed comprehension, understanding of attitude, opinion and writer purpose and inference.<br>**Part 5**: Candidates are expected to show understanding of vocabulary and grammar in a short text, and the lexico-structural patterns in the text. |
| **2 Writing** 45 minutes | **Part 1** An informal email. Candidates write an email of about 100 words in response to a text.<br>**Part 2** An article or story. There is a choice of two questions. Candidates are provided with a clear context and topic. Candidates write about 100 words. | Candidates are mainly assessed on their ability to use and control a range of Preliminary-level language. Coherent organisation, spelling and punctuation are also assessed. |
| **3 Listening** approximately 30 minutes | **Part 1** Short monologues or dialogues with seven three-option multiple choice questions with pictures.<br>**Part 2** Six short unrelated dialogues with six three-option multiple choice questions.<br>**Part 3** Longer monologue. Candidates complete six sentences with information from the recording.<br>**Part 4** Longer interview. Six three-option multiple choice questions. | Candidates are expected to identify the attitudes and opinions of speakers, and listen to identify gist, key information, specific information and detailed meaning, and to identify, understand and interpret meaning. |
| **4 Speaking** 12 minutes | **Part 1** A short conversation with the interlocutor. The interlocutor asks the candidates questions in turn, using standardised questions.<br>**Part 2** An individual long turn for each candidate. A colour photograph is given to each candidate in turn and they talk about it for about a minute. Each photo has a different topic.<br>**Part 3** A two-way conversation between candidates (visual stimulus with spoken instructions). The interlocutor sets up the activity.<br>**Part 4** A discussion on topics related to the collaborative task in Part 3. The interlocutor asks the candidates the questions. | Candidates are expected to be able to ask and understand questions and make appropriate responses, and to talk freely on topics of personal interest. |

# 1 My life and home

## Starting off

**1** Work in pairs. Look at the pictures and answer the questions.

1 What are these four parts of a home called?
2 Are any of these like your home? How are they similar or different?
3 Which is your favourite place in your home? Which is your least favourite? Say why.
4 What changes would you like to make to your home? Why?
5 When you go away, what do you miss about your home?

## Listening Part 2

**1** Work in pairs. Tell your partner about these things.
- the building where you live
- the street where your home is
- a place where you would like to live

**Exam advice**

- Before you listen, quickly read the first line of each question and underline the key words.
- Don't choose an answer until you've heard the whole text for that question.

**2** You will hear people talking in six different situations. In pairs, look at questions 1–6. For each question, discuss who you will hear in the conversation and what the situation is.

*1 two friends, a flat they would like to live in*

1 You will hear two friends talking about the kind of flat they would like to live in.
   They agree that it should
   A be on one of the higher floors.
   B have at least three bedrooms.
   C be close to public transport.

2 You will hear a man telling his friend about changing job.
   How does he feel?
   A He finds it hard to do his new job well.
   B He still misses his old colleagues.
   C He thinks the staff at his new firm are unfriendly.

3 You will hear a woman talking about a trip to the beach.
   What did she like best about it?
   A swimming in the sea
   B going on a free boat trip
   C playing a sport

4 You will hear two friends talking about the town where they live.
   They agree that
   A there's too much traffic.
   B some parts of it are dangerous.
   C it's smaller than they would like.

5 You will hear a man talking to a friend about shops.
   What does the man think about the small shop?
   A There aren't enough assistants.
   B The prices there are reasonable.
   C It sells a wide variety of items.

6 You will hear two friends talking about their homes.
   The woman says her room would be better if
   A it was quieter.
   B it was a lot bigger.
   C it was sometimes warmer.

**3** For each question in Exercise 2, choose the correct answer. Listen again and check your answers.

**4** Think of the three best and worst things about the place where you live. Use the ideas below, or your own. Work in small groups and discuss your ideas.
- how big or small it is
- interesting places to visit
- the people who live there
- traffic and public transport
- how safe it is
- things for people to do in their free time

## Grammar
### Prepositions of time

▶ page 116 Grammar reference
Prepositions of time

**1** Exam candidates often make mistakes with prepositions of time. Choose the correct option in *italics*.
1 I sometimes leave work *in / on* the evening.
2 *On / In* summer, they must come to Poland.
3 I'll see you *on / at* 4 o'clock.
4 We usually go to the beach *at / in* the morning.
5 I go shopping *in / on* the days when there are not too many people.

**2** Complete the table with the phrases from the box. Then add more phrases to the table.

> 5 o'clock   2020   bedtime   half past four   July
> 25 May   my birthday   night   Sundays   the afternoon
> the holiday   ~~the weekend~~   weekdays   winter

| at | in | on |
|---|---|---|
| (with times of the day, e.g. *2.15*, and expressions like *the weekend*) | (with parts of the day, years, months and seasons) | (with days and dates) |
| *the weekend* | | |

**3** Discuss when people do the activities in the box. Say when you do them. Use prepositions of time.

> do exams   eat in a restaurant   get a bus
> go shopping   socialise   watch TV

*Some people go by bus very early in the morning. I get the bus at 8.15.*

My life and home

# 1

## Grammar
### Frequency adverbs

▶ **Page 116 Grammar reference**
Frequency adverbs

**1** Read the text about Julian. In pairs, discuss how similar his daily habits are to yours.

*On weekdays, Julian always starts work at 6 am, so he usually gets up at 5 am and has a quick breakfast at 5.15. He takes the bus to work at 5.40 most days but sometimes he walks. Julian's lunchtime is usually before midday, when the café often gets busy again. He normally has dinner at six and he goes to bed at about 10 every evening.*

**2** Work in pairs and answer the questions.
1 Which is correct: frequency adverb + *be*, or *be* + frequency adverb?
2 Do frequency adverbs like *often*, *sometimes* and *rarely* go before or after other main verbs?
3 Where do we usually put longer frequency expressions like *every day* or *most days*?

**3** Complete the sentences with the words in brackets.
1 I listen to music on the radio. (occasionally)
   *I occasionally listen to music on the radio.*
2 I check my phone for messages. (every two hours)
3 I'm late for my English lessons. (never)
4 I write emails to friends. (sometimes)
5 I don't have lunch at home. (always)
6 I'm sleepy in the morning. (almost every day)
7 I go out on Monday nights. (hardly ever)
8 I stay in bed late. (most weekends)

**4** Write sentences 1–8 in Exercise 3 so they are true for you. Then work in pairs and compare your sentences.

> I rarely listen to music on the radio.

> Really? I listen to music on the radio all the time.

**5** Work in groups. Discuss how often you do the things in the pictures. Use expressions like *every day*, *once a week* and *twice a month*. Decide who does each thing most often.

> I chat with my best friend every evening.

> I tidy my flat once a week.

### Reading Part 5

**1** Work in pairs. Describe the pictures on page 11. Answer the questions.
- Which place would you like to have a holiday in? Which would you like to live in all the time? Why?
- Do you know of other unusual places to live?

**2** Read the text without filling in the gaps. Answer the questions.
1 What kind of text (e.g. story, article) is it?
2 Which photo matches the text?
3 Which <u>four</u> of these points are in the text?

- Emilia does lots of interesting things.
- Her education takes place on the boat.
- Living on a boat has some disadvantages.
- She never feels afraid when she's on the boat.
- She sometimes meets her friends.

> **Exam advice**
> • Read the text to get a general idea of the type of text, its topic and the main points.
> • Look at the words before and after each gap.
> • Try each of A, B, C and D in the gap. Which has the right meaning <u>and</u> fits the grammar of the sentence?

10

**3** Read the article again and choose the correct word for each space (A, B, C or D). Use the questions in *italics* to help you.

## Emilia's home

Most people live in flats or houses, but right now biologist Emilia Ruiz is waking up somewhere in the Pacific Ocean, because her home is a 20-metre boat. She has **(1)** ............... the last two years sailing with her colleagues Ryan and Charlie, who are also scientists.

Emilia's work **(2)** ............... of studying large sea creatures such as whales and dolphins as they cross the oceans, so she often travels very long distances and has **(3)** ............... friends all over the world. She is doing a Master's degree online and her studies are going well.

Her way of life, though, is sometimes uncomfortable. Space on board her boat is limited and bad **(4)** ............... that lasts days is common, **(5)** ............... in winter. Storms at sea can be frightening, although modern boat equipment usually helps sailors **(6)** ............... them and Emilia nearly always feels safe. She contacts friends by social media and whenever they get together they have great fun in the places they visit.

1 *Which word do we use with a period of time?*
 A passed  B used  C taken  D spent
2 *Which verb is followed by 'of'?*
 A includes  B consists  C requires  D involves
3 *Which verb often goes with 'friends'?*
 A added  B formed  C caught  D made
4 *Which noun often goes with 'bad'?*
 A temperature  B forecast  C weather  D climate
5 *Which adverb means 'especially'?*
 A particularly  B extremely  C completely  D absolutely
6 *Which verb means 'keep away from'?*
 A prevent  B control  C avoid  D remove

**4** Work in groups. Discuss what you would or wouldn't like. Give reasons.

- often going to different places
- rarely seeing friends
- never having to travel to work or university
- making new friends around the world
- having very little space at home
- living close to nature all the time

**5** Work in pairs. Imagine a typical day in Emilia's life. Use frequency adverbs to describe it.

My life and home  11

# 1

## Grammar
### Present simple and present continuous

▶ **Page 117 Grammar reference**
Present simple and present continuous

▶ **Page 118 Grammar reference**
State verbs

**1** Match the extracts from the article on page 11 with the uses of the present simple and present continuous (a–e).

1 Most people **live** in flats or houses. *e*
2 Emilia Ruiz **is waking** up somewhere.
3 She often **travels** very long distances.
4 Her studies **are going** well.
5 Emilia's work **consists of** studying large sea creatures.

a something that happens regularly
b something in progress, but not at the present moment
c verbs not normally used in the continuous
d something happening at the present moment
e something that is generally true

**2** Complete the email with the the present simple or present continuous form of the verbs in brackets.

Hi David,

I **(1)** *'m writing* (write) to you from the lovely holiday home my friends and I have rented, right next to the sea. I **(2)** .................... (sit) in my bedroom right now, which **(3)** .................... (have) a big window, and I **(4)** .................... (look) out across the waves at a little island. I **(5)** .................... (love) it here, and in the evening I sometimes **(6)** .................... (stay) here and watch the sun go down.

Every day, we **(7)** .................... (go) for a walk along the top of the cliffs. The weather **(8)** .................... (get) hotter every day. It was 35°C yesterday! But we always **(9)** .................... (leave) the house early in the morning while that cool wind from out at sea **(10)** .................... (blow).

We **(11)** .................... (have) a really good time here, and I **(12)** .................... (not want) to go home!

Bye for now,

Molly

**3** Make questions using the present simple or the present continuous. Add or change words if necessary.

1 what / 'habit' / mean?
2 any buses / stop / in your street?
3 who / watches / the most / TV / in your house?
4 you / prefer / to get up / early or late?
5 everyone / talk / to / their partners / at the moment?
6 what colour clothes / you / wear / today?
7 anyone / sit / behind / us / in class right now?
8 what / you / sometimes / forget / to do?

**4** Work in pairs. Ask and answer the questions in Exercise 3.

> What does 'habit' mean?

> It means something you often do.

**5** Do the task below.
- Write three questions using the present continuous about what your partner is doing, thinking or feeling now, e.g. *Are you feeling good?*
- Write three questions using the present simple about what your partner likes, wants or prefers, e.g. *Do you prefer weekdays or weekends?*
- In pairs, ask and answer the questions.

**6** /P/ /s/, /z/ and /ɪz/
Try saying these words. Which ones end with /s/? Which ones end with /z/? Which ones end with /ɪz/?

changes  chooses  does  finishes  forgets  goes
likes  lives  loves  passes  plays  practises
prefers  sees  speaks  studies  thinks  uses
walks  wants  washes  wears  works

**7** Work in pairs. Think of a close friend or family member. Tell your partner these things about them. Remember to pronounce the final 's' of verbs correctly.
- facts, e.g. *She lives in ..., she belongs to ...*
- things he or she often does, e.g. *He often plays ...*
- something your friend is doing around now, e.g. *She's learning Spanish.*
- what you think your friend is doing right now, e.g. *He's walking home.*

**8** Now ask your partner more questions about the friend or family member.

> Where does she work?

> Is he learning to drive this year?

12

## Vocabulary
### House and home

**1** Which of these does your home have?

> a balcony   a bathroom
> a bedroom   a dining room
> a garage   a garden   a hall
> a kitchen   a living room   stairs

**2** Look at the places in Exercise 1. Where can you find the things in the box?

> armchair   bath   blankets
> chest of drawers   cooker
> cupboards   cushions
> dishwasher   duvet   fridge
> microwave   mirror   pillow
> rug   sink   sofa   taps
> toilet   towels   wardrobe
> washing machine

### Countable and uncountable nouns

▶ Page 118 Grammar reference
Countable and uncountable nouns

**3** Choose the correct option in *italics*. Then check with the extract from the Cambridge Learner's Dictionary.

I am looking for new *furniture* / *furnitures* for my bedroom.

> **furniture** noun [U]
> objects such as chairs, tables and beds that you put into a room or building
> **Common Learner Error**
> Remember you cannot make *furniture* plural. Do not say 'furnitures'.

**4** Look at the first line of the dictionary extract again. What tells you the noun *furniture* is uncountable? What letter do you think there is for a countable noun?

**5** Think about the kitchen in your home. Write three countable and three uncountable things you can find there. Tell your partner.

## Grammar
### *a few*, *a bit of*, *many*, *much*, *a lot of* and *lots of*

▶ Page 118 Grammar reference
*a few*, *a bit of*, *many*, *much*, *a lot of* and *lots of*

**1** Look at what Giles says about his free time. Choose the correct option in *italics*.

> I don't have much time to watch TV these days. There aren't many programmes I like, and as I've got university exams quite soon, I usually have a lot of work to do in the evenings. After that, I often like to do a bit of exercise. At weekends, I like to invite a few friends to my house. We cook some food, have dinner together and talk a lot. That's lots of fun!

**Rules**

1 We use *a few* for small numbers with *countable* / *uncountable* nouns.
2 We use *a bit of* for small amounts with *countable* / *uncountable* nouns.
3 With *countable* / *uncountable* nouns in questions and negative sentences we use *much*.
4 With *countable* / *uncountable* nouns in questions and negative sentences we use *many*.
5 We use *a lot of* or *lots of* for large amounts or numbers. We use them with *countable* or *uncountable* nouns.
6 If there is no *noun*, we use *a lot* instead of *a lot of*.

**2** Choose the correct option in *italics*.

1 I put *a bit of* / *a few* make-up on, but not *many* / *much*.
2 It doesn't take *many* / *much* time to wash those clothes and it only takes *a lot of* / *a few* hours to dry them.
3 I've got *a bit of* / *a few* video games but I can't buy any more because they cost *much* / *a lot of* money.
4 Those new light bulbs don't use *many* / *a lot of* electricity, so *lots of* / *much* people are buying them.
5 I don't use *much* / *many* shampoo, just *a bit* / *a few*. My hair always goes dry if I use *a lot* / *a lot of*.
6 There isn't *much* / *a lot* space in my bedroom so I don't keep *a bit of* / *many* things there.

**3** Work in pairs. Ask your partner what he or she likes and doesn't like doing at home. Use expressions from Exercise 1. Tell the class about your partner.

> Do you watch much TV?

> No, I don't watch a lot of programmes.

My life and home   13

# Speaking Part 1
## Prepositions of place

▶ page 119 Grammar reference
Prepositions of place

▶ Page 152 Speaking bank
Speaking Part 1

**1** Exam candidates often make mistakes with prepositions like *at*, *in* and *on*. Choose the correct option in *italics*.

1. Sometimes we play cards *on / at* his house.
2. He sometimes goes running *at / in* the park.
3. We usually stay *in / at* home watching TV.
4. There's a window *on / in* the left of my bed.
5. I normally spend my day *in / at* the beach.
6. I have some photos *in / on* the wall.

**2** Work in pairs. Tell each other about your apartment or house. Describe each room and what's in it. Draw a picture of your partner's home. Show it to your partner.

**3** Complete the gaps with *at*, *in* and *on*.

............... college
work
university

............... a city
a country
a company

............... the coast
a hill
an island

**4** Put the words in order to make questions. Then match the questions with the answers.

1. your / what's / name? *What's your name?*
2. live / where / do / you?
3. Recife / do / what / do / you / in?
4. lessons / having / you / English / like / do?
5. English / future / use / the / in / you / will?

a Yes, I need to speak it well at work because we do a lot of business abroad.
b In Recife, a big city on the north-east coast of Brazil.
c Rafael Santos.
d I work in an information technology company there.
e Yes, I always enjoy them a lot!

**5** Work in pairs. Ask another student the questions in Exercise 4. Use the correct prepositions in your answers.

**6** Complete the dialogue with the correct form of the verbs in brackets and prepositions of place and time. Listen and check.

**Hugo:** Where **(1)** *do you come* (you / come) from, Sara?

**Sara:** I live **(2)** ............... Vigo, a city in Galicia. That's **(3)** ............... north-west Spain, **(4)** ............... the Atlantic coast.

**Hugo:** Do you work or **(5)** ............... (you / be) a student?

**Sara:** I'm a second-year student **(6)** ............... the University of Vigo. I'm studying economics.

**Hugo:** How **(7)** ............... (you / get) there **(8)** ............... the mornings?

**Sara:** The university isn't in the city so I usually take the bus, but **(9)** ............... summer I often ride there on my bike.

**Hugo:** And where **(10)** ............... (you / like) to go **(11)** ............... the evenings?

**Sara:** Sometimes I go out with my friends, but most evenings I stay **(12)** ............... home studying. I've got exams soon!

> **Exam advice**
> - In the Speaking exam, be friendly and polite when you meet the examiners and the other candidate.
> - Speak clearly and loudly enough for the examiners and your partner to hear you.
> - Give longer answers by adding details such as places and times of day.

**7** Work in new pairs. Ask and answer the questions from the dialogue in Exercise 6.

# Writing Part 1

▶ Page 145 Writing bank
An email

**1** Work in pairs. Look at the exam task and answer the questions.

1. Who has written to you?
   *Alex, your English-speaking friend.*
2. What do you have to read?
3. What kind of text must you write?
4. What news does Alex tell you first? How do you feel about this?
5. What does Alex ask you next? What information must you give?
6. What does Alex ask you in the fifth sentence?
7. What does Alex ask you last?

Read this email from your English-speaking friend Alex, and the notes you have made.

---

To:

From: Alex

Many thanks for inviting me to come and stay with you for a couple of weeks. I asked my boss for some more time off work and she said yes! —— *Brilliant!*

Which month would be best for me to come? —— *Say when and why.*

We've never really talked about your home. What's it like? —— *Describe.*

I'll start planning my trip today. What should I bring with me? —— *Suggest ...*

See you soon!

Alex

---

Write your email to Alex, using **all** the **notes**.

- You **must** answer this question in the exam.
- Read the instructions and the email in the question. Note who you have to write to and which points you must include.
- Note down ideas and plan your reply. Use a paragraph for each point.

**Exam advice**

**2** Read this reply and answer the questions.
1. How many main paragraphs does Frankie use?
2. Which paragraph deals with each of the notes?
3. How many sentences does Frankie write about each of the notes?
4. In Frankie's email, find prepositions of place, prepositions of time and frequency adverbs.

---

From: Frankie

To: Alex

Hi Alex,

I'm so happy you can spend a fortnight at my place. I'm really looking forward to it!

Summer is lovely here. I'm usually away in August, so July would be the perfect time to come and visit.

I live in a three-bedroom flat on the fifth floor in a quiet neighbourhood. It's comfortable, with modern furniture, big windows and a large balcony where I sometimes have barbecues at weekends.

It hardly ever rains in July, so I'd recommend bringing just light clothes, plus your swimming costume. There's lots to do here and I'm sure we'll have a fantastic time.

See you in the summer!

Frankie

---

**3** Plan your own reply to Alex. Use each of the notes as a heading and write your own ideas below them.

| Brilliant! | Say when and why | Describe your home | Suggest |
|---|---|---|---|
| it's great that ... | | | |

**4** Write your email.
- Begin and end in a friendly way.
- Use paragraphs, one for each of the notes.
- Write at least one sentence about each of the notes.
- Use frequency adverbs and prepositions of place / time.

**5** Check your partner's email. Has your partner:
- organised the email like Frankie's?
- written about all four notes on Alex's email?
- written about 100 words?

My life and home 15

# 2 Making choices

## Starting off
### Life choices

1 Work in pairs. Match the photos to the words in the box. Then put these events into the order someone might do them.

> apply for a job
> get some work experience
> quit your job    retire early
> take a gap year

2 In pairs, ask and answer these questions.
- How often do people in your country decide to do the activities in Exercise 1?
- Why do people make these choices?
- Is there anything in Exercise 1 that you haven't done but you would like to do? Why?

## Reading Part 6

1 Work in pairs. Read the article about four different universities. Then answer the question in the title. Do not complete the gaps for now.

### Would you choose to study at a college or university like this?

At Worcester University, England there are students (1) ............... take very few exams. Those studying an English degree only have (2) ............... hand in essays in their third year.

A small number of students who (3) ............... studying at Cleveland Institute of Music, USA can live at a local retirement home. The students don't pay rent in exchange for spending time (4) ............... the elderly people living there and playing concerts.

At Mondragon University, Spain, students studying Leadership and Innovation set up (5) ............... own companies and try to earn enough money to pay for their next year at university.

Students at Deep Springs University, USA live on a large animal farm in the middle of the Californian desert. Classes are very small, usually between four (6) ............... 12 students on each course.

2 What type of word is missing in each gap (1–6) in Exercise 1 (a verb, a preposition, etc.)?

3 Read the text in Exercise 1 again and write the word which best fits each gap.

16

4  Work in pairs. Look at the title of the article below and the photos. What do you think the article is about?

5  Read the article and check your ideas. Do not complete the gaps for now.

## Follow your interests with one of these unusual qualifications!

People who know they want **(0)** ...to... be doctors study medicine and future lawyers study law. But what **(1)** ........................ those who don't know what they want to be but know what they enjoy? Equestrian Psychology is perfect for horse lovers who **(2)** ........................ keen to understand this animal's behaviour. There's even an opportunity to take part in **(3)** ........................ exchange programme with universities in Australia, Hungary or Canada. An option for water sports fans is a degree in Surf Science and Technology. Students do subjects such **(4)** ........................ geography, surf culture and how to be safe in the water. Back on land, someone who likes plants can apply for a degree in Floral Design and learn how to arrange flowers for a living. And finally, people **(5)** ........................ enjoy making friends or family members laugh should consider a degree in Stand-Up Comedy. Apart **(6)** ........................ regular classes, they also have the chance to perform in comedy clubs.

**Exam advice**

- Without filling in any of gaps 1–6, quickly read the text to find out what it's about.
- For each gap, look at the sentence and decide what kind of word (e.g. a preposition) is missing.
- Read the sentence again and think of the word which best fits the gap.

6  Read the article and think of the word which best fits each gap. Write one word in each gap.

7  What makes a good college or university? Make notes on the ideas below.

| accommodation | classrooms and facilities |
| fees and other costs | journey and location |
| teachers and courses | timetable and exams |

8  Work in groups. Tell each other your ideas.

Making choices 17

# 2

## Vocabulary

*fail, pass, take, lose, miss, study* and *teach*

**1** Exam candidates often make mistakes with *fail, pass, take, lose, miss, study* and *teach*. Complete the definitions with the words from the boxes.

> fail   pass   take

1 We have to ....*take*.... an exam at the end of this course. (= do an official test)
2 I hope I ..................... the exam and get a good mark. (= be successful in an exam)
3 I'm studying a lot because I don't want to ..................... my exam. (= not be successful in an exam)

> lose   miss

4 I don't want to ..................... my music lesson. (= not go to something which happens or arrive too late to get on a bus, a train, etc.)
5 I often ..................... my keys. (= not be able to find something or someone)

> learn   study   teach

6 I want to ..................... how to ride a horse. (= get new knowledge or skills)
7 A colleague is going to ..................... me how to change the tyre on my car. (= give new knowledge or skills)
8 My brother would like to ..................... biology at university. (= go to classes, read books, etc. to try to understand new ideas and facts)

**2** Choose the correct option in *italics*.

1 Do you ever *take* / *make* exams?
2 Do you ever *miss* / *lose* your mobile, keys or bag?
3 What subject(s) did your favourite teacher *teach* / *learn* you?
4 Would you like to *take* / *learn* a new sport, language or musical instrument?
5 Is it sometimes OK to *miss* / *lose* lessons or work?
6 What kinds of subjects do people in your country *learn* / *study* at university?
7 Would you like to be a school teacher or university lecturer? What subject would you like to *teach* / *learn*?
8 Do you think that people who never *fail* / *pass* exams are more intelligent than others? Or have they just got better memories?

**3** Work in small groups. Ask and answer the questions in Exercise 2.

## Grammar

Past simple

▶ Page 120 Grammar reference
Past simple

**1** Work in pairs. Before university, Emily went to Mexico City to do some work experience. Discuss the differences you think she found between her life in Canada and in Mexico.

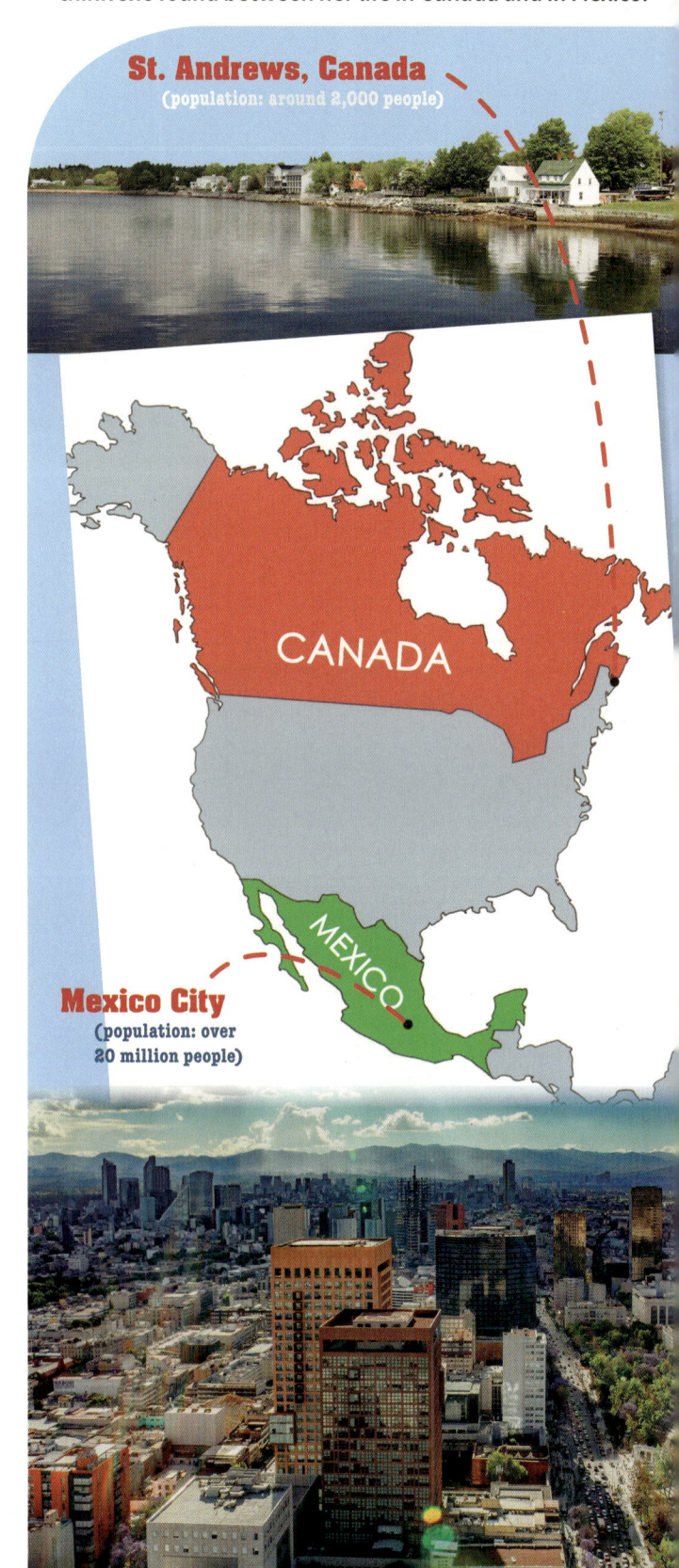

**St. Andrews, Canada**
(population: around 2,000 people)

CANADA

MEXICO

**Mexico City**
(population: over 20 million people)

18

**2** Listen to Emily talking about her experience. Make notes on how the city, shops and entertainment were different.

**3** Work in pairs. Write the interviewer's questions, using *you* and the past simple.

1 where / go? *Where did you go?*
2 why / decide / to work abroad?
3 how / find / a place in the laboratory?
4 where / stay?
5 speak / Spanish / before / go?
6 how / feel / when / first / arrive?
7 like / the city?
8 enjoy / the experience?

**4** Listen again and complete Emily's answers.

1 I ....*went*.... to Mexico for nine months.
2 I .................. to get some work experience and improve my Spanish.
3 My dad .................. an agency and they .................. me a place.
4 I .................. with Alicia and her family.
5 Yes, I did. I .................. French and Spanish at school.
6 When I .................., I .................. scared.
7 I .................. it a lot.
8 Oh yes, I did. I .................. working in the laboratory.

**5** Look again at Emily's answers. Underline the regular past simple forms. Circle the irregular past simple forms.

**6** /p/ /d/, /t/ and /ɪd/

Listen to the sentences. How do we pronounce these regular past simple *-ed* endings? Choose the correct option.

1 I want**ed** to improve my Spanish.   /d/ /t/ /ɪd/
2 I stay**ed** with Alicia and her family.   /d/ /t/ /ɪd/
3 I lik**ed** the city a lot.   /d/ /t/ /ɪd/

**7** Complete the table with the past simple form of the verbs from the box. Listen and check.

| arrive   contact   decide   enjoy   help   invite |
| like   love   need   ~~stay~~   study |
| want   watch   work |

| /d/ | /t/ | /ɪd/ |
| --- | --- | --- |
| stayed | | |

**8** Work in pairs. Student A, ask the questions from Exercise 3. Student B, read Emily's answers from Exercise 4. Then change. Remember to pronounce the regular past simple endings correctly.

**9** Exam candidates often make spelling mistakes with the past simple. Underline and correct one spelling mistake in each sentence.

1 My friends and I plaied football yesterday.
2 In our first English lesson our teacher teached us some new words for sports.
3 When I went to university, I studyed very hard.
4 Last weekend, I founded a very good restaurant in my town.
5 When I arribed at work, my colleagues weren't there.
6 My friend Sara bringed her dog to class one day.
7 I'm reading a book that my English teacher recommend to me.
8 We puted all our things in the car and we set off on holiday.

**10** Complete Zak's review with the past simple form of the verbs in brackets.

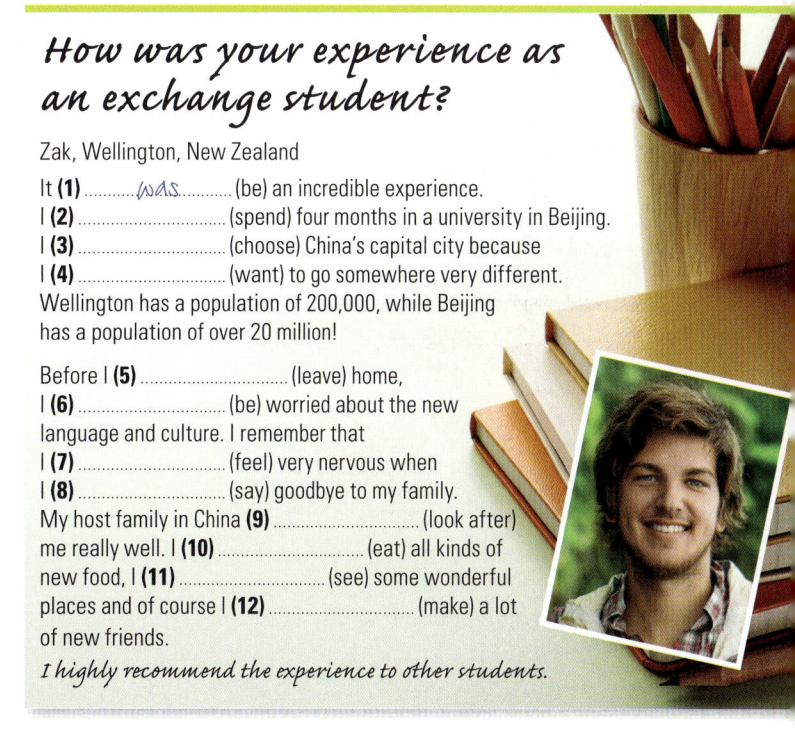

### How was your experience as an exchange student?

Zak, Wellington, New Zealand

It (1) ....*was*.... (be) an incredible experience.
I (2) .................. (spend) four months in a university in Beijing.
I (3) .................. (choose) China's capital city because
I (4) .................. (want) to go somewhere very different. Wellington has a population of 200,000, while Beijing has a population of over 20 million!

Before I (5) .................. (leave) home,
I (6) .................. (be) worried about the new language and culture. I remember that
I (7) .................. (feel) very nervous when
I (8) .................. (say) goodbye to my family.
My host family in China (9) .................. (look after) me really well. I (10) .................. (eat) all kinds of new food, I (11) .................. (see) some wonderful places and of course I (12) .................. (make) a lot of new friends.
I highly recommend the experience to other students.

**11** Work in pairs. Think of a new place you went to. Ask and answer the questions.

- Where did you go?
- Why did you go there?
- How did you feel?
- What did you think of it?

Where did you go?

I visited Madeira.

Making choices   19

# 2

## Grammar

### Past simple and past continuous

▶ **Page 120 Grammar reference**
Past simple; Past continuous

**1** Work in pairs. Look at the picture. What happened to Emily when she was walking to work?

**2** Listen and check. What do you think happened next?
🎧 07

**3** Listen to the rest of Emily's story. Were you right?
🎧 08

**4** Look at the extracts from Emily's story. Answer the questions.

1. Suddenly a woman <u>appeared</u> from nowhere and she <u>started</u> screaming at the dogs. The dogs <u>ran</u> off.
   Did the three actions happen at the same time? What happened last?
2. The sun was shining and I was feeling good.
   Do we know when the sun started shining? Do we know if the sun stopped shining?
3. I was walking to work with Alicia when we <u>saw</u> a group of dogs.
   Did Emily and Alicia see the dogs before they started walking to work?

**5** Complete the rules with *past simple* or *past continuous*.

### Rules

- We use the **(1)** *past simple* to talk about actions or situations in the past (often one action happened after the other).
- We use the **(2)** ............... to talk about an activity that was already happening at a moment in the past. We don't say if this activity finished or not.
- We often use the **(3)** ............... and the **(4)** ............... together to show that an action happened in the middle of an activity.
- We generally use *when* to introduce the action in the **(5)** ............... .
  *I was walking to work with Alicia **when** we saw a group of dogs.*
- We can use *when*, *as* or *while* to introduce the activity in the **(6)** ............... .
  ***As/When/While** I was walking to work, I saw a group of dogs.*

**6** Alicia goes to Canada to stay with Emily. Complete Emily's blog with the past simple or past continuous form of the verbs in brackets. Listen and check.
🎧 09

One morning, Alicia **(1)** ...*woke up*... (woke up) early and **(2)** ............... (go) to the kitchen where I **(3)** ............... (talk) loudly to my flatmate. We **(4)** ............... (stop) talking and I **(5)** ............... (say), 'Look outside! There's 20 cm of snow on the ground. We'll have to ski to the town centre.' Alicia **(6)** ............... (feel) excited and nervous at the same time. Snow in Mexico City is very rare and she **(7)** ............... (not know) how to ski. I **(8)** ............... (help) her to put on the skis. As we **(9)** ............... (set off), one of the neighbours **(10)** ............... (shout), 'Everything is closed, even the shops!' We **(11)** ............... (take off) our skis and **(12)** ............... (start) throwing snowballs.

**7** Work in pairs. Choose a title from the box and prepare a description of an unusual day. Think about who you were with and what exactly happened. Use the past simple and continuous.

> Bad weather stops everything!
> I'm the boss for a day!
> Famous visitor arrives in town!   No electricity all day!

**8** Work in groups. Tell each other about your unusual day.

## Listening Part 1

**1** Read the questions and underline the key words. These are underlined for you in question 1 as an example.

1 What do the people need to bring for the cycling trip?

A  B  C

2 What time does Stuart need to be at work?

A  B  C

3 Where does Jack live?

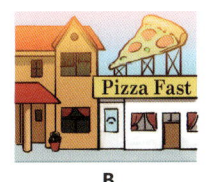

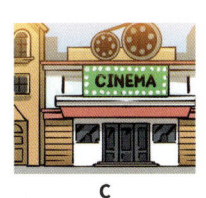

A  B  C

4 Where did the man find his football boots?

A  B  C

5 What did Julia eat before she came home?

A  B  C

6 What are the two friends going to buy Paul for his birthday?

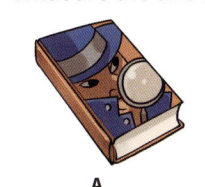

A  B  C

7 What is the weather forecast for tomorrow?

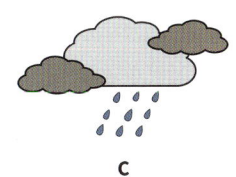

A  B  C

**2** Work in pairs. Look at the pictures for questions 1–7. What can you see in each one?

> **Exam advice**
> - Before you hear each recording, underline the key words in each question so that you know exactly what to listen for.
> - The first time you listen, try to tick the correct box. Then, as you listen for the second time, check your answer.

**3** Listen and note the important words you hear next to the pictures. Listen again and choose the correct answer.

## Grammar
*used to*

▶ Page 121 Grammar reference
*used to*

**1** Read Marina's blog post. Which verb does Marina use to talk about things that happened in the past but don't happen now?

> **Was your life easier ten years ago? Were you still at school? Did you use to hang out with your classmates, for example?**
>
> Yeah! Ten years ago, I was at secondary school and I was still living at home. My classmates used to be my best friends so I didn't need to make an effort to meet new people. I used to have quite a lot of free time. Although I used to help around the house I didn't use to think much about what food to buy and cook. My dad used to do most of that because my mum used to work nights. Now, I usually spend a lot of my free time shopping, cooking and cleaning. In many ways, life used to be much easier. Perhaps I should move back home!  *Marina, Bologna, Italy*

**2** Answer the questions.

1 Does *used to* change when we change the subject pronoun (*I/you/he/she*, etc.)?
2 How do you make negative sentences and questions with *used to*?
3 What verb form generally follows *used to*?

**3** Write a post saying whether your life was easier ten years ago. Use *used to* and *didn't use to*.

*I think my life was easier ten years ago because I used to live at home ...*

Making choices

# 2

## Vocabulary

*do, earn, make, spend, take* and *win*

**1** Complete the sentences with *do, earn, make, spend, take* or *win*.

We asked our readers to tell us what was important to them in their job and they said …

1 It's easy to meet new people and ……make…… friends.
2 I …………………… a reasonable salary.
3 It doesn't …………………… a long time to get to the office.
4 I …………………… most of my time working in a team.
5 I can …………………… regular breaks during the day and holidays during the year.
6 My company pays for us to …………………… courses.
7 My boss encourages me to …………………… my best.
8 I can play football on the company team. We even …………………… matches!

**2** Work in groups. Talk about what's important to you in your job. Use verbs and expressions from Exercise 1.

## Speaking Part 3

▶ Page 159 Speaking bank
Speaking Part 3

**1** Tanya and Gareth's boss would like to introduce one of these social activities at work. Listen and answer the questions.

> a quiz night    a weekend trip
> a team meal    yoga and relaxation
> a running group    a cooking class

1 Which of the activities does Tanya suggest?
2 Which of the activities does Gareth suggest?
3 Which activity do they both choose?

## *So (do) I* and *Nor/Neither (do) I*

▶ Page 121 Grammar reference
*So (do) I* and *Nor/Neither (do) I*

**2** Underline the words that Tanya and Gareth use to agree. When do we use *nor* and *so*?

1 **Gareth:** I'm not sure about that one.
   **Tanya:** Nor am I.
2 **Tanya:** I still think a team meal is the best option.
   **Gareth:** So do I. Let's go for that.

**3** Complete the sentences. Listen and check.

1 <u>Shall we</u> …………………… with the quiz night?
2 <u>How</u> …………………… a team meal?
3 <u>Good</u> ……………………. Let's talk about another one.
4 <u>I don't</u> ……………………. Some of us hate running.
5 <u>I'm not</u> …………………… about that one.
6 …………………… <u>go for that</u>.

**4** Match the underlined phrases from Exercise 3 with these uses.

- Suggesting *Shall we …?*
- Agreeing
- Disagreeing
- Deciding

> **Exam advice**
> - Listen carefully to the examiner's instructions. Then look at the pictures.
> - Talk about the different things in the pictures by making suggestions and replying politely to your partner's suggestions.

**5** Read the instructions for the Speaking Part 3 task. Do the task. Talk for at least two minutes.

> A language school would like to organise a new club for students to practise their English outside class. Here are some activities they could do there.
> Talk together about the different activities the students could do at the clubs. Say which will be the most popular.

22

# Writing Part 2

▶ Page 148 Writing bank
An article

**1** Read the task below and answer the questions.
1 What do you need to write?
2 What information do you need to include?

> You see this advert for a writing competition in an English language magazine.
>
> > **Articles wanted!**
> > What makes a great place to work?
> > Is it the people who work there, the facilities or is it something else?
> > What kinds of social activities should a great place to work offer?
> > Write an article answering these questions and you may be our lucky winner!
>
> Write your article.

**2** Work in pairs. Make a list of things that make a great place to work.

*staff, facilities …*

**3** Complete the mind map with your ideas from Exercise 2. Add reasons. You may need to add some more shapes and lines to the map.

Mind map — A GREAT PLACE TO WORK:
- staff — *get on well with colleagues*
- social activities — *a fair boss who encourages us*
- facilities — *a large, bright office with space is more pleasant to work in*
- working day

**4** Read Charlotte's answer below. Does she mention any of your ideas from Exercise 3?

> In my opinion, a great place to work is where staff enjoy being at work because they get on well with each other. Their boss is fair as well and encourages everybody to do their best. A great office is large and bright and there is enough space for everyone. In my last job, we used to start work at 9.30 but I believe that starting earlier is much better.
>
> I also feel a good work place needs social activities to help the staff make friends. In some companies, staff do fun things like sports competitions or camping trips, while at my job, there isn't anything.

**5** Look at the questions. Read Charlotte's answer again and decide if she completed the task well.
1 Does the article include all the information for the task?
2 Is the answer written in paragraphs?
3 Are the ideas connected with words like *and*, *because* and *while*?

> **Exam advice**
> - Read the instructions and the text in the task. Decide what information you need to include.
> - Think about the topic and your reader. Note down some ideas and decide how many paragraphs you will write.
> - Make a plan for each paragraph. Then write your article.

**6** Use your ideas from Exercise 3 to write your article. Then use the questions from Exercise 5 to check your writing.

Making choices

# 1 Vocabulary and grammar review

## Grammar

**1** Complete the email with *at*, *in* or *on* in each gap.

Hi everybody,

Well, here I am **(1)** ___in___ New Zealand, staying with a very friendly family **(2)** ............... the town of Westport. It's quite a big house and my bedroom is **(3)** ............... the second floor. I like it because there are lots of cupboards to put my things **(4)** ............... and the bed is much bigger than the one **(5)** ............... my room **(6)** ............... home!

**(7)** ............... the evenings and **(8)** ............... weekends, the family sometimes take me out, though most of the time we just stay **(9)** ............... and watch TV. I usually go to bed quite early, sleep well and get up **(10)** ............... about 7.30 **(11)** ............... the morning.

I'm enjoying myself a lot here, but I'm looking forward to being home again **(12)** ............... August 15th.

Write soon!

Aiden

**2** Choose the correct option in *italics*.

1 I have a big family and there's always a lot of (housework) / *houseworks* to do.
2 We've got *a few / a bit of* time before the film starts. Let's get a drink.
3 It's very dark and cold here in winter, so I don't go out *a lot / a lot of*.
4 The living room is very big but there's not *many / much* furniture in it.
5 These days, Max spends a lot of *time / times* at the sports club.
6 I haven't got *much / many* work to do, so I'll go out soon.
7 Paula isn't very well, but I think she can eat *a few / a bit of* food now.
8 We sometimes invite *a bit of / a few* people to have dinner with us.

**3** <u>Underline</u> and correct one mistake in each sentence.

1 We don't <u>eat always</u> in the dining room.
   *We don't always eat in the dining room.*
2 Hello, I call to ask if you want to go out somewhere tonight.
3 Why do you stand here in the rain at this time of night?
4 I'm tired usually in the morning.
5 I'm never believing anything that newspaper says.
6 I every day water the plants on the balcony.
7 How do you often have a bath?
8 I get normally home at about half past five.

## Vocabulary

**4** Label the photos with words from Unit 1.

1 a r m c h a i r
2 s _ _ _ 
3 f _ _ _ _ _ 
4 c _ _ _ _ _ 
5 d _ _ _ _ _ _ _ _ 
6 m _ _ _ _ _ _ _ _ 
7 d _ _ _ _ 
8 c _ _ _ _ o _ d _ _ _ _ _ _ 
9 w _ _ _ _ _ _ _ 
10 w _ _ _ _ _ _ m _ _ _ _ _ _

24

# Vocabulary and grammar review 2

## Vocabulary

**1** Choose the correct option in *italics*.

1 I was late for the dentist because I *lost* / (missed) the bus.
2 My teachers used to say that we had to study hard and *do* / *make* our best.
3 My grandfather taught me to be positive. I *learned* / *studied* a lot from him.
4 The English test was very easy so I think I'll *pass* / *fail* it.
5 Being happy at work is important but *earning* / *winning* a reasonable salary is too.
6 When Helen moved to a new city, she soon *did* / *made* a lot of new friends.
7 My brother is nervous because he's *taking* / *passing* his driving test today.
8 My brother *did* / *made* engineering at university.

## Grammar

**2** Correct one mistake with a verb in each sentence.

1 A TV company <u>choosed</u> this street to make a film because it is the oldest in the city.
2 I think I lefted my bag at your house last night.
3 Our teacher was kind. She teached us very well.
4 I woke up very early because I was planing to go to the lake.
5 My dad only payed €75 for his mobile phone.
6 While my sister was riding her bike, she felt and injured her leg.
7 When I was younger, I prefered to take the bus everywhere.
8 I met Holly a very long time ago. We were studing at the same university.

**3** Complete the sentences with the past simple or past continuous form of the verbs in brackets.

1 Anita ....*fell*.... (fall) asleep when she ....*was doing*.... (do) her homework.
2 When I got to class, some of my friends ................ (chat) and the lecturer ................ (write) on the board.
3 Yesterday, when we ................ (have) lunch, the phone ................ (ring).
4 While I ................ (buy) some milk in the supermarket, I ................ (see) a famous TV actor.
5 At first I ................ (think) English ................ (be) difficult but now I love it.
6 It ................ (begin) to rain as I ................ (walk) to the beach.
7 When my best friend ................ (sit) on the table, it ................ (break).
8 Last night we ................ (watch) a short film in English and I ................ (understand) everything.
9 Last weekend I ................ (go) to my cousin's party. I really ................ (enjoy) myself.
10 I ................ (feel) tired after the long journey, so I ................ (go) to bed.

**4** Complete the sentences with the words in the box. There are three extra words that you do not need.

> didn't   gave   give   use   ~~used~~   used
> wasn't   weren't

1 When my mum was younger, she ....*used*.... to play basketball for her school team.
2 I didn't ................ to have lunch at school. I went home instead.
3 I remember our maths teacher well. He used to ................ us a lot of homework.
4 Before Eva bought an alarm clock she ................ to be late for everything.
5 My grandparents ................ use to watch TV because they didn't have one.

Vocabulary and grammar review 25

# 3 Having fun

## Starting off
### Leisure activities

**1** Complete the leisure activities with the verbs from the box. Which activities can you see in the photos?

> ~~doing~~  going  playing  posting
> riding  taking  visiting  watching

1 ......*doing*...... sports
2 ........................ photos
3 ........................ dancing
4 ........................ a bike, a motorbike or a horse
5 ........................ a film or play
6 ........................ a musical instrument
7 ........................ messages on social media sites
8 ........................ an art gallery or museum

**2** Work in pairs. Discuss how you like to spend your free time. Put the leisure activities in Exercise 1 in order.

**3** Work in small groups. Discuss the questions.
- Which other leisure activities do people enjoy in your country? Why?
- Are these activities difficult to learn? Why / Why not?
- How much time a week do you spend doing your favourite leisure activity?

## Listening Part 4

**1** Work in pairs. Discuss the questions.
- What do the photos show? Do you think they are interesting?
- What kind of person do you think the photographer is?

**2** Look at questions 1–6. Decide what kind of information (an opinion, a reason, advice or feelings) you need to listen for in each one.

> **Exam advice**
> - Before you listen, look at each question and decide what kind of information you need.
> - Listen for details about this information and choose the best answer.

## 3

**3** For each question, choose the correct answer.
You will hear a radio interview with the Instagram photographer Marc Pasqual.

1 Marc became a full-time Instagram photographer because he wanted to
   A start travelling to other countries.
   B do a different kind of photography.
   C make more money.

2 Marc thinks he is good at photography because he
   A plans all his photos very carefully.
   B sees details that others often miss.
   C was taught it very well.

3 What mistake does Marc say he made when he began?
   A He didn't spend enough money on special apps.
   B He didn't put enough selfies on Instagram.
   C He didn't post photos online often enough.

4 What does Marc most enjoy about being a photographer?
   A Remembering everywhere he has been.
   B Being able to do his job on his own.
   C Communicating online with other photographers.

5 In the future, Marc wants to
   A become the employee of a big company.
   B do a degree at university.
   C study the history of photography.

6 Marc advises new Instagram photographers to
   A add some information to their online photos.
   B put their best photos onto other social media sites.
   C upload their photos only on Saturdays or Sundays.

**4** Work in groups. Discuss the questions.
- What kind of photos do you like the most / least?
- Is there a hobby that you would like to turn into a job?

## Vocabulary

### Prepositions of place

**1** Listen to Kirsty talking on the phone. Draw these objects on the picture. Check your answers on page 162.
- Kirsty's racket
- her tennis balls
- her trainers
- her T-shirt

**2** Write sentences describing where the objects from Exercise 1 are. Use the prepositions from the box.

> above   behind   in   in front of   inside   near
> next to   on   on the right   opposite   under

*Kirsty's racket is in front of the wardrobe. It's on the floor.*

Having fun 27

# 3

## Reading Part 3

1. Work in pairs. Look at the picture. What do you think it shows? Do you like it?

2. Read the text quickly. What is the writer's main purpose?
   - A to explain how to become an expert at making sand sculptures
   - B to describe a particular sand sculpture that she made
   - C to give some advice about making sand sculptures
   - D to encourage more people to make sand sculptures

3. Read the text again and answer the questions.
   1. Why did Ariana decide to start making sand sculptures?
   2. How did Ariana feel when her first sand sculpture failed?
   3. In the final paragraph, what does Ariana say annoys her?

> **Exam advice**
> - Quickly read the text to get the general idea of what it is about.
> - For each question, decide what the text says about it before you look at options A–D.
> - Choose the option that is most similar to what the text says.

4. Read the text and the questions below. For each question, choose the correct answer.

   1. Why did Ariana decide to start making sand sculptures?
      - A She has always been good at other kinds of art.
      - B She saw some sculptures that her friends had already made.
      - C She wanted to do a new outdoor activity with her friends.
      - D She was impressed by some objects that were made out of sand.

   2. What did Ariana realise when she started making her first sculpture?
      - A She wasn't very patient.
      - B She thought it would be easier.
      - C She knew straight away it wouldn't be a success.
      - D She disliked people watching her make the sand sculpture.

   3. How did Ariana feel when her first sculpture failed?
      - A She felt like giving up her new hobby.
      - B She was embarrassed because of how it looked.
      - C She regretted ignoring some useful advice.
      - D She was angry with herself for wasting four hours.

   4. In the final paragraph, what does Ariana say annoys her?
      - A people damaging her sculptures
      - B the sea covering her sculptures
      - C the weather destroying her sculptures
      - D people believing it is only a hobby for children

## SAND SCULPTURES

My name's Ariana and I live on the coast of Portugal where there are lots of beautiful sandy beaches and warm sunny days. It's the perfect location for my favourite hobby – making sand sculptures. It's always great fun and it costs nothing. For fairly basic sculptures like the ones I make, all you really need is a safe place to build it, something to dig with, and a large bucket. I'd never actually thought of making sand sculptures before until my friends and I discovered some fantastic ones that were along the shore near where I live. I couldn't believe that such beautiful model buildings, incredible creatures, and some amazingly realistic faces of famous people were all made out of sand. From that moment, I knew that this was something I just had to do even though I'd never considered myself to be an artist or very creative.

In fact, anyone can create a sand sculpture, but it's much harder than it looks as I soon discovered. The first sand sculpture I ever made was of a two-metre-long dolphin. I was making brilliant progress on it until quite suddenly the head started to break off!

I tried everything to try and fix it, but it was hopeless. Soon the whole thing was a big pile of wet sand on the beach. Some people sunbathing nearby seemed to think this was extremely funny, but that just made me want to keep trying even more. I wished I'd listened to an expert on YouTube who recommends digging up wet sand and using it to build the sand sculptures because it sticks together better. So, I did that for my next sculpture of a camel. And I managed to complete it in four hours, though they don't always take me that long to make.

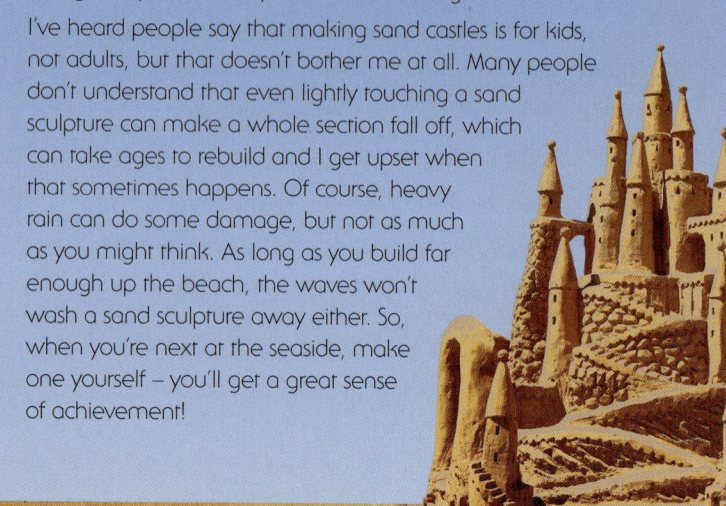

I've heard people say that making sand castles is for kids, not adults, but that doesn't bother me at all. Many people don't understand that even lightly touching a sand sculpture can make a whole section fall off, which can take ages to rebuild and I get upset when that sometimes happens. Of course, heavy rain can do some damage, but not as much as you might think. As long as you build far enough up the beach, the waves won't wash a sand sculpture away either. So, when you're next at the seaside, make one yourself – you'll get a great sense of achievement!

**5** Work in pairs. Discuss the questions.
- Would you like to build sand sculptures? If so, what kind?
- Which of the activities below do you enjoy doing?
- Which would you not like to do? Why?

> flying a kite   sailing   sunbathing
> swimming in the sea   windsurfing

## Grammar
### Verbs followed by *to* or *-ing*

▶ Page 122 Grammar reference
Verbs followed by *to* or *-ing*

**Rules**
- We can use either *-ing* or *to* (+ the infinitive) after verbs such as *start, begin, like, love, hate, prefer* and *continue* with little difference in meaning.
- Its head **started breaking** off. / Its head **started to break** off.
- With other verbs, only one form is possible.

**1** Look at the underlined verbs. Which are followed by a verb ending in *-ing*? Which are followed by *to*? Complete the table.

1 Some people sunbathing nearby seemed to think it was funny.
2 … that just made me want to keep trying
3 I wished I'd listened to an expert on YouTube who'd suggested digging up wet sand.
4 I managed to complete it in four hours.

| verb + *-ing* | verb + *to* |
|---|---|
| keep | seem |

**2** Complete the table with the verbs in the box. Can you add more verbs?

> admit   afford   agree   avoid   decide   enjoy   fancy
> feel like   finish   hope   learn   mind   miss   practise
> promise   want   would like

**3** Some verbs can be followed by *-ing* or *to*, but with a change of meaning. Look at sentences 1–4.
Which two are about:
- something the speaker has to do?
- a memory of something in the past?

1 I remember just chatting to her.
2 I must remember to get a map.
3 Don't let me forget to take my sunglasses.
4 I'll never forget flying over that beach.

**4** Underline the mistakes and correct them.
1 I forgot asking you about your family.   *to ask*
2 I hope see you soon!
3 I really enjoyed to help at a music festival.
4 Do you fancy to come out with us?
5 When we finished to eat I went home.
6 I'll never forget to visit New York last year.

**5** Complete questions 1–6 with the correct form of the verbs in brackets.
1 Where do you fancy *going* (go) this evening?
2 What kind of music do you enjoy ........ (listen) to at home?
3 What are you planning ........ (do) at the weekend?
4 Do you remember ........ (go) away on holiday when you were younger?
5 Do you ever forget ........ (bring) anything to your English lesson?
6 What would you like ........ (do) tomorrow?

**6** /P/ *-ing* endings /ŋ/
Listen to the sentences. Then answer the questions.
1 How do we pronounce *-ing*?
2 Is there a /g/ sound when we say *-ing*?
3 Is this part of the word stressed?

**7** Work in pairs. Ask and answer the questions from Exercise 5.

**8** Tell your partner about the things below. Remember to pronounce *-ing* correctly.

Something you …
1 are learning to do
2 can't afford to buy
3 decided to do last week
4 must remember to do tomorrow
5 will finish doing soon
6 shouldn't forget to do next weekend

> I'm learning to play the drums.

Having fun   29

# 3

## Vocabulary
### Phrasal verbs

▶ **Page 123 Grammar reference**
Phrasal verbs

> **phrasal verb:** *noun* [U] a phrase which consists of a verb plus a preposition or adverb or both. The meaning of this phrase is different from the meaning of its separate parts: **look after** (be responsible for), **hang on** (wait) and **run out of** (use all of) are all phrasal verbs.

**1** Complete these short conversations with the three phrasal verbs from the dictionary extract.

1. **A:** 'The bus leaves in ten minutes so we'd better go now.'
   **B:** 'Can you .................... a moment? I'm nearly ready.'
2. **A:** 'I don't think I can afford to go out this evening.'
   **B:** 'Don't worry. If you .................... money, I'll lend you some.'
3. **A:** 'I'm going away but I can't take the dog and the cat with me!'
   **B:** 'I'll .................... them if you like.'

**2** Match the phrasal verbs in the article to meanings 1–9.

### CHOOSE YOUR HOBBY

Which kind of hobby would be good for you? If you find group activities exciting and you'd like to <u>join in</u>, why not <u>put your name down</u> for something like white-water rafting or rock climbing? Or, if you love animals, you could <u>take up</u> horse-riding. It can be a bit expensive, though, so before you <u>sign up for</u> 20 or 30 lessons you need to be sure you won't <u>give up</u> a couple of weeks later! Cycling may be cheaper, and of course you can <u>set off</u> on the road whenever you like and <u>go on</u> cycling all day if you want. Or how about a creative hobby such as painting, photography or playing a musical instrument? That's something you can <u>look forward to</u> doing whenever you have a spare moment, and once you find out which you like best you'll probably never <u>go off</u> it.

1. take part in an activity with other people  *join in*
2. stop doing something before you have completed it
3. feel happy about something that is going to happen
4. start doing a hobby
5. stop liking
6. continue
7. arrange to do an organised activity
8. register to do something
9. start a journey

**3** Answer the questions about the phrasal verbs in Exercise 2.

1. Which two of the phrasal verbs have three words?
2. Sometimes the object of a phrasal verb can come between the verb and its adverb, e.g. *My friend <u>picked me up</u> in her car.* Which phrasal verb in the text is separated by an object?

**4** Work in pairs. Complete the sentences with the correct form of phrasal verbs from Exercise 2. Listen and check.

**Chris:** Hi, Ava. Are you and Megan going away on holiday soon?
**Ava:** Yes, on Saturday. We want to **(1)** *set off* very early in the morning.
**Chris:** Are you going to the coast?
**Ava:** No, we **(2)** .................... beach holidays a long time ago. There are always too many people. We've decided to **(3)** .................... skiing instead. We're off to the Alps.
**Chris:** Do you know how to ski?
**Ava:** Err, not really. That's why I'm going to **(4)** .................... my name .................... for lessons.
**Chris:** I tried skiing once but I found it really difficult. After three days I **(5)** .................... and went home!
**Ava:** Well, the lessons **(6)** .................... until late afternoon every day, so I hope I can improve quickly. I'm really **(7)** .................... trying, anyway!
**Chris:** Yes, I'm sure you'll have a great time.

**5** Tell your partner about an activity, sport or subject you found difficult at first.

- When did you take it up?
- Did you ever feel like giving up?
- Do you look forward to playing/doing it now?
- Do you want to go on doing it?

30

**People's hobbies**

6 **Work in groups. Follow the instructions.**
  1 Match the hobbies in box A with the pictures.
  2 Match the hobbies with the people and equipment in box B.

  *chess: picture 4, chess player, board, pieces*

  **A**

  camping  chess  cooking
  cycling  music  painting  photography

  **B**

  backpack  bike  board  brush  camera  chess player
  cook  cooker  cyclist  helmet  instrument  musician
  oven  paint  painter  photographer  pieces  tent

7 **Work in pairs. Which other words go with the hobbies?**

  *chess: indoor game, black and white squares, queen, move*

8 **Choose an interesting hobby. Describe it to your partner and try to persuade them to take it up.**

  You find somewhere safe and dry, put up your tent and sleep in a sleeping bag. You light a fire to cook your food or use a little gas cooker. You can go where you like when you like, and it's healthy because you're outdoors in the fresh air!

Having fun  31

# 3

## Speaking Part 2

▶ Page 154 Speaking bank
Speaking Part 2

**1** Work in groups. Look at the photos.
- What are these activities called?
- What do you know about each activity?
- Which activity do you think is most fun? Why?

**2** Listen to Eduardo describing one of the photos. Which photo is it? Tick (✓) the things he talks about.

activities ☐   people ☐
clothes ☐   place ☐
colours ☐   time of day ☐
equipment ☐   weather ☐
objects ☐

**3** Listen again. Complete the sentences.

1 In the picture I ...... *can see* ...... two people.
2 The woman on the left ............................ a green jacket.
3 It ............................ they're cooking some vegetables.
4 ............................ they are backpackers.
5 ............................ there's a high mountain and a forest.
6 It ............................ winter because there's snow.
7 Although the weather ............................ dry, I think it's probably very cold there.

**4** Answer the questions.

1 Why do we say *look like* in Question 3 but *look* (without *like*) in Question 7?
2 Which prepositions of place does Eduardo use in sentences 1–7?

> **Exam advice**
> - Listen carefully to the instructions and then study your photo.
> - Talk about everything you can see (the place, people, objects, colours, clothes and weather).
> - Use prepositions of place (e.g. *next to, opposite*) to say where things are.

**5** Work in pairs. Using expressions from Exercise 3, take turns to describe one of the other photos for one minute.

**6** Discuss the questions with your partner.
- Did you both speak for at least a minute?
- Did you follow the exam advice?
- How could you improve the description?

**7** Work in pairs. Look around your classroom and describe these to your partner.
- a part of the room (where it is and what size it is)
- three objects in the room (where they are and what they look like)
- another pair of students (where they are, what they are wearing and what they are doing)

## Writing Part 2

▶ Page 150 Writing bank
A story

**1** In Writing Part 2, you can choose to write a story. Look at this task and answer the questions.

1 Do the instructions give you the first line of the story?
2 Should you write in the first person (I) or the third person (he/she/it)?

- Your English teacher has asked you to write a story.

> • Your story must begin with this sentence:
> *I had a really great day out.*

**2** The story below has three paragraphs. Decide which paragraph:

a describes the main events  2
b sets the scene for the action
c describes the writer's feelings after the main event
d tells us how the writer felt during the action
e introduces the story (saying who did what, where and when)

**3** Plan your own story for the task in Exercise 1. Make notes before you write. Use the ideas below.

- Use your imagination to invent a completely new story.
- Write about something that has happened to you, or someone you know.
- Use an idea from a film, TV programme or book, but change it a bit.
- Plan your story in two or three paragraphs.

> **Exam advice**
> • Read the instructions. If you are given the first sentence, you must use it.
> • If there's a name or pronoun (e.g. *I* or *she*) in the sentence, use it in your story.

**4** Write your story in about 100 words.

## Snow Biking

[1] I had a really great day out last week. The weather was good and my brother and I went high up into the mountains. There, we hired bicycles with huge, thick tyres. We were going snow biking!

[2] We set off down the mountain, following the steep, narrow track round trees and rocks and doing some exciting jumps. It was great fun and although I fell off twice, I didn't hurt myself because I landed in deep, soft snow. We carried on for hours, enjoying the cool, fresh air.

[3] Afterwards, we sat in a nice little café. We felt tired but very, very relaxed!

Having fun

# 4 On holiday

## Starting off
### Holiday activities

**1** Work in pairs. Look at the photos of the holiday activities. What do they show? Which would you like to do? Use the words in the box to help you.

> buy gifts/souvenirs   go sightseeing   go snorkelling
> go snowboarding   hang out with friends   hire a bike
> look around a market   take photos

*I'd like to hire a bike because I love cycling. What about you?*

*I'd prefer to go snorkelling.*

**2** Listen to Joe asking Sonia about her last holiday. Where did she go? What did she do?

**3** Work in groups. Discuss the questions.

When you go on holiday, do you prefer to …
1 go somewhere in your own country or go abroad?
2 do lots of different activities or hang out by the pool or beach?
3 go on a tour with a guide or make your own plans?
4 send messages to your friends or post something general for everyone to see?

34

## Reading Part 1

**1** Work in pairs. Look at this first question from Reading Part 1. What do you have to do in this part?

> **Boat trip**
> Due to bad weather, this has been put off until the same time tomorrow morning. Lunch will still be provided.

The notice for the boat trip is telling customers …
- A the refreshments have changed.
- B the time has changed.
- C the day has changed.

**2** Look at the text in Exercise 1 again and answer these questions.
- Is it a note, an email or a sign?
- What does it say about the weather, the time, the day and the food?

**3** Read the text and underline the key words. Then find similar words in each option (A, B and C).

**4** Now choose the correct letter A, B or C.

> **Exam advice**
> - With each text, think about what kind of text it is.
> - Underline the key words in each option. Then look for words and phrases in the options and the text that have similar meanings.

**5** Look at the text in each question (2–5). For each question, choose the correct answer.

**2**
> Hi Dan
> I had loads of fun today! My friends and I went sailing before playing tennis. Then we had a barbecue on the beach and ate the fresh fish we'd caught. See you soon,
> Vicki

- A After playing tennis, Vicki went on a boat trip.
- B Vicki ate dinner on the beach before going sailing.
- C During her boat trip, Vicki went fishing.

**3**
> **From:** Dave
> **To:** Rob
> **Subject:** Snowboard
>
> Can I still borrow your snowboard for the trip? Pete says he can lend me his but I think yours is better. Let me know.

- A Pete's snowboard is not as good as Rob's.
- B Dave would rather borrow Pete's snowboard.
- C Rob would prefer to lend his snowboard to Pete.

**4**
> **Pool Rules**
> Please shower before entering
> Diving is only permitted in the deep end
> No food or drink in the pool area

- A Eating and drinking is not allowed next to the pool.
- B After swimming, please use the showers provided.
- C Diving is forbidden in all parts of the pool.

**5**
> Jane,
> Please check I'm up before you leave for work. I don't want to miss the bus for the trip and I'll need to make some sandwiches.
> Claire

Claire is asking Jane to …
- A make her some sandwiches for her trip.
- B make sure she is awake by a certain time.
- C drive her to the bus stop.

**6** Work in small groups. Choose one of the holidays in the photos. Plan your holiday together.
- Where are you going? In which season and how long for?
- What are you going to see and do there?
- Where will you stay? Where will you eat?

**7** Present your holiday to the class. Listen carefully to each presentation. Decide as a class which is the most attractive holiday.

On holiday 35

# 4

## Vocabulary
### travel, journey and trip

**1** Exam candidates often make mistakes with *travel*, *journey* and *trip*. Choose the correct option in *italics*.

1  I often go on business *journeys / trips*.
2  I'd love to win a *trip / journey* to Australia and stay in a five-star hotel.
3  Last summer, we *tripped / travelled* around my country.
4  I've just got back from holiday. It was a wonderful *travel / trip*.
5  I'm really afraid of flying so I often get very nervous about the *travel / journey*.

**2** Look at this extract from the *Cambridge Learner's Dictionary* and check your answers from Exercise 1.

> **travel, journey or trip?**
> The noun **travel** is a general word which means the activity of travelling.
> *Air travel has become much cheaper.*
>
> **travel** verb to make a journey
> *I travel abroad a lot on business.*
>
> Use **journey** to talk about when you travel from one place to another.
> *He fell asleep during the train journey.*
> *Did you have a good journey?*
> ~~Did you have a good travel?~~
>
> A **trip** is a journey in which you visit a place for a short time and come back again.
> *a business trip*
> *a three-day trip to Spain*

**3** Work in groups. Ask and answer questions to find someone who …
- would like to travel around the world.
- went on a trip abroad last summer.
- often gets bored on long journeys.
- prefers travelling by train to travelling by car.
- doesn't like travelling.

> Would you like to travel around the world?
>
> Yes, I would.
>
> Where would you like to go?

## Grammar
### Comparative and superlative adjectives

▶ **Page 124 Grammar reference**
Comparative and superlative adjectives

**1** Work in pairs. Read these facts. Decide if they are true or false. Then check your answers on page 162.

a  The population of Canada is <u>larger than</u> the population of Tokyo.
b  <u>The longest</u> country in the world is Brazil.
c  Rain is <u>more common</u> in Rome <u>than</u> in Paris.

**2** The sentences in Exercise 1 compare things. Complete the rules with the correct sentence letter.

> **Rules**
> 1 We generally use comparative adjectives (e.g. *larger than*) to say that something has more size, height, etc. than another: sentences ..*a*.. and ........ .
> 2 We generally use superlative adjectives (e.g. *the longest*) to say that within its group, something has the most size, height, etc.: sentence ........ .

**3** Exam candidates often make mistakes with comparative and superlative adjectives. Complete the table.

|  | adjective | comparative | superlative |
|---|---|---|---|
| **regular** | deep | (1) ............... than | the deepest |
|  | safe | (2) ............... than | the safest |
|  | noisy | (3) ............... than | the (6) ............... |
|  | big | (4) ............... than | the (7) ............... |
|  | beautiful | more beautiful than | the (8) ............... |
| **irregular** | good | better than | the (9) ............... |
|  | bad | (5) ............... than | the (10) ............... |
|  | far | farther / further than | the farthest / the furthest |
| **more/less** |  | more | the (11) ............... |
|  |  | less | the (12) ............... |

**4** <u>Underline</u> and correct the mistake in each sentence.

1  I don't like living in the countryside even if it is more safe than cities.
2  That's the worse joke I have ever heard in all my life.
3  In the centre is the bigest market in Europe.
4  Portugal is the hotest country I have ever visited.
5  This town is more quiet than the town I used to live in.
6  My best friend is taler than me and better looking too!

**5** Look at the sentences in Exercise 4 again. What are the spelling rules for regular comparative and superlative adjectives?

36

**6** Complete each sentence with the comparative or superlative form of the adjective in brackets. Then choose the correct option (A, B or C).

## The biggest... The fastest...

1. North America is ……bigger…… (big) than
   A Asia.   B Africa.   C South America.

2. What is ……the largest…… (large) country in the world?
   A Russia   B Canada   C China

3. What is ……………………… (dangerous) creature in the world?
   A the snake   B the mosquito   C the shark

4. An African elephant is ……………………… (light) than a
   A blue whale.   B brown bear.   C giraffe.

5. A howler monkey is ……………………… (noisy) than
   A a parrot.   B a lion.   C a lion and a parrot.

6. What is ……………………… (slow) fish in the world?
   A the sea horse   B the tuna   C the shark

7. Great white sharks are ……………………… (fast) than
   A tunas.   B killer whales.   C dolphins.

8. Where is ……………………… (busy) train station in the world?
   A New York   B London   C Tokyo

9. Y40 Deep Joy is ……………………… (deep) diving pool in the world. It's in
   A Italy.   B Sydney.   C Argentina.

10. Antarctica is ……………………… (dry) than
    A Australia.   B Europe.   C any other place in the world.

**7** Listen to Abby and Lucas discussing the quiz and check your answers.

**8** /P/ **Weak forms in comparative structures**
Listen to the extracts. Are the underlined syllables stressed or not stressed?

- I wouldn't like to share my home with a howler monkey.
  They're much loud<u>er</u> th<u>an</u> parrots or lions.
- Great white sharks can swim at 40 kilometres per hour,
  so they're fast<u>er</u> th<u>an</u> dolphins, which can swim at 30 kilometres per hour.

**9** Work in pairs. Take turns to read the sentences in Exercise 8 with the correct stress.

On holiday

# 4

## a bit, a little, slightly, much, far, a lot

▶ **Page 125 Grammar reference**
*a bit, a little, slightly, much, far, a lot*

**10** Complete the sentences with the comparative form of the adjective in brackets. Use *a bit, a little, slightly, much, far* or *a lot*.

1. Mount Everest, in the Himalayas, is around 8,850 metres high. K2, also in the Himalayas, is around 8,611 metres high. (high)
   *Mount Everest is slightly higher than K2.*

2. An African elephant's brain weighs over 5kg. A human adult's brain weighs about 1.3 kg. (heavy)
   An African elephant's brain is ................................................. .

3. Arica, in Chile, gets 0.76 mm of rain per year. Death Valley in Arizona, USA, gets less than 50 mm per year. (dry)
   Arica is ................................................. .

4. 84 million people travel through Atlanta International Airport, USA, each year. 67 million people travel through London's Heathrow Airport. (busy)
   Atlanta International Airport is ................................................. .

5. Cherrapunji in India gets 11,777 mm of rain every year. Tutendo in Colombia receives 11,770 mm per year. (wet)
   Cherrapunji is ................................................. .

6. Cheetahs can run at 120 kilometres an hour. Elephants can run at about 20 kilometres an hour. (fast)
   Cheetahs can ................................................. .

## (not) as … as

▶ **Page 125 Grammar reference**
*(not) as … as*

**11** Read part of a blog about Shanghai, in China, and then answer the questions.

> One of my favourite cities in the world is Shanghai, in China. It isn't the capital – that's Beijing. Shanghai is <u>not as polluted as</u> Beijing, even though Shanghai is bigger and more people live there. It's an international city. It's <u>as international as</u> many other large cities in the world like New York or London, so it has a lot to offer.

1. What expression do we use to say things are the same?
2. What word do we add to say things are different?
3. Does the form of the adjective change?

**12** Write down an example of each thing in the box.

> your favourite city    your favourite museum
> your favourite celebrity    your favourite activity

**13** Work in pairs. Compare your favourite things in Exercise 12. Say which you think is better. Use *as … as*.

> What's your favourite museum?

> I love going to art museums like the Louvre in Paris.

> I don't! They're not as interesting as science museums. The one in Munich is the largest in the world and it's amazing!

## Vocabulary
### Buildings and places

**1** Work in pairs. Look at the photos. Do you know what these places are? Use some of the words in the box.

> art gallery   bookshop   bridge   cinema
> department store   factory   fountain   library
> market   monument   shopping centre   sports centre
> stadium   town hall   youth club

> I think the stadium is in Barcelona. What do you think?

**2** Which of the things in Exercise 1 do you have in your town or city? Which do you like most?

**3** Write the opposite of each adjective.

> cheap   clean   dangerous   dull   ~~empty~~
> interesting   low   near   old   quiet   ugly   wide

1 crowded *empty*    5 dirty         9 safe
2 narrow             6 beautiful    10 expensive
3 high               7 lively       11 noisy
4 modern             8 boring       12 far

**4** Work in groups. Ask and answer questions about where you do these activities.

> get fit   get some peace and quiet   go shopping
> have a good time   stay dry when it's raining   take photos

> We often go to the market, but we rarely go to the shopping centre because it's too crowded and noisy.

## Grammar
### *big* and *enormous*

▶ **Page 125 Grammar reference**
Gradable and non-gradable adjectives

**1** Match descriptions 1–3 with the photos A–C in Exercise 1. Then answer the questions.

1 The Statue of Liberty was a gift from France in 1886 and, at 93 metres, it's <u>quite tall</u>. Visitors need to climb 354 stairs to get to the top.
2 The Mall of the Emirates is <u>very large</u>. Apart from hundreds of shops and restaurants, there's a games centre, a cinema and a theatre, and two hotels. You can also go skiing.
3 The Camp Nou (or 'New Ground') football stadium is <u>absolutely enormous</u>. It is the biggest stadium in Europe and 99,354 people can watch football there.

- Which of the underlined adjectives can we use with *very*, *extremely* and *quite*? (These are called **gradable** adjectives.)
- Which of the adjectives can we use with *absolutely* or *totally*? (These are called **non-gradable** adjectives.)

**2** Write the gradable adjectives for these non-gradable adjectives. (Sometimes, more than one answer is possible.)

1 enormous *big*    5 terrible
2 tiny              6 exhausting
3 boiling           7 fascinating
4 freezing          8 fantastic

**3** Exam candidates often make mistakes with non-gradable adjectives. Choose the correct option in *italics*.

1 It's a(n) *very / absolutely* wonderful place.
2 It was a(n) *quite / extremely* good movie. You should see it.
3 That dog is *very / absolutely* enormous.
4 The weather is *absolutely / quite* hot here.
5 This food is *very / absolutely* nice.

**4** Listen to Ani and write her answers to the questions. Then listen again and check.

1 Where do you come from?
2 What do you like about living there?
3 What would you change about where you live?

**5** Work in pairs. Ask and answer the questions in Exercise 4, trying to use *very*, *quite*, *absolutely* and *extremely* with gradable and non-gradable adjectives.

On holiday

# 4

## Listening Part 3

**1** What can you see in the photo? Would you like to do a bushcraft course? Why / Why not?

> **Bushcraft** describes the skills we need to stay alive in the wild, for example how to hunt for animals, look for drinking water or build a fire.

**2** Read these notes about a bushcraft skills course. Decide what information you think is missing from each space (number, date, noun etc.).

### BUSHCRAFT SKILLS COURSE

**SATURDAY MORNING**
- meet your guide outside the (1) ..........................
- learn how to use equipment
- make a (2) .......................... to sleep in
- prepare food for lunch, e.g. (3) .......................... you have caught

**SATURDAY AFTERNOON**
- visit the river

**OTHER EXAMPLE ACTIVITIES INCLUDE HOW TO**
- make drinking water
- predict the weather with (4) ..........................

**FURTHER INFORMATION:**
Email address: (5) ..........................@bushcraftskills.com
Phone number: (6) ..........................

**Exam advice**
- Before you listen, read the notes carefully. Think about what kind of words are missing.
- Write down the answers exactly as you hear them.

**3** For each question, write the correct answer in the gap. Write one or two words or a number or a date or a time. You will hear a woman talking to a group of people about the bushcraft courses she organises.

**4** Work in groups. Discuss the questions.
- How could these skills help you in your everyday life?
- What other skills would you like to learn?

## Writing Part 1

▶ Page 145 Writing bank
An email

**1** Read the Writing Part 1 task. Answer the questions.
1 What do you need to write?
2 What information should you include?

Read this email from your English-speaking friend Stevie, and the notes you have made.

> **From:** Stevie
>
> How are you? Did I mention that I'm thinking of taking some time off next year to travel? Well, I'd love to visit your country as part of this trip. — *Great idea!*
>
> I'd also love to see your city. What's it like? — *Describe it.*
>
> I'm not very keen on crowds of tourists, so when is the best time to visit? — *Tell Stevie.*
>
> Where else should I go in your country while I'm there? — *Recommend.*
>
> Please write back soon.
>
> Best wishes,
>
> Stevie

Write your email to Stevie, using **all** the **notes**.

**2** Read Bandile's answer. Which city is he writing about?

> Hi Stevie,
>
> You should definitely visit my country. There's so much to experience in South Africa, from absolutely amazing wildlife to history and culture.
>
> I live in Johannesburg, which is the most visited city in Africa. One of the best things about my city is the weather because the sun even shines in winter. Tourists mainly come in our summer, which is between December and February, so if you want to avoid them, come in March.
>
> You should also go to Kruger National Park, stay on a campsite and explore it with a guide. You might see an elephant or a lion!
>
> Bye for now,
>
> Bandile

**3** Read Bandile's email again. Answer the questions.

1. Does the email answer all the parts of the question?
2. Is the answer well organised?
3. Does the email open and close in a suitable way?
4. Are the ideas connected with words like *and*, *because*, *so* and *which*?
5. Is there a variety of vocabulary and grammar (adjectives, comparatives and superlatives etc.)?
6. Is the email about 100 words?

**4** Write your own answer to the task in Exercise 1. You can use the underlined expressions from Bandile's email.

**5** Work in groups. Read each other's emails to see if you have answered all the questions in Exercise 3.

> **Exam advice**
> - In preparation for the exam, it is useful to write rough drafts. Your teacher and other students can then help you to improve your work before you write your final draft.
> - In the real exam you won't have time to write a rough draft. Just make notes before you start writing.

**6** Write the final draft of your email.

## Speaking Part 3

▶ Page 159 Speaking bank

**1** Listen to a group of friends talking about their next holiday. Which type of holiday do they choose?

**2** Work in pairs. Answer these questions about the conversation.

1. Does each member of the group take turns to speak?
2. Does each member make a suggestion and then give reasons for their suggestion?

**3** Complete the sentences. Then listen again and check.

1. Why ___don't___ we all go to Paris for our next holiday? ___S___
2. I'd _____ to go somewhere quieter. _____
3. It's one of the _____ beautiful places in the world. _____
4. Not camping again, please! We got _____ wet last time. _____
5. What _____ trying a new sport like surfing? _____
6. Let's _____ that! _____
7. There's so _____ to do. _____

**4** Decide which sentences from Exercise 3 are suggestions (S) and reasons (R).

> **Exam advice**
> - Don't talk for a long time without letting your partner speak.
> - Give reasons for your suggestions and ask the other candidate to give reasons for theirs.

**5** Do this task with a partner. Talk for at least two minutes.

> Your friend is visiting his cousin, who is working in an English-speaking country. While his cousin is at work, he's going to spend the afternoon on his own in the city.
> Here are some things he could do there.
> Talk together about the different things your friend could do in the city and say which would be most enjoyable.

On holiday 41

# 3 Vocabulary and grammar review

## Vocabulary

**1** Choose the correct option in *italics*.

1 In my English class I sit *behind / (between)* two friends, so all three of us are on the front row.
2 I live *next to / near* the place where I work and I can walk there in ten minutes.
3 I live on the third floor and my cousins live right *below / above* us on the fourth floor.
4 I couldn't see at the cinema because a tall man sat *in front of / opposite* me.
5 You can either cross the river on the bridge or take the tunnel *under / in* it.
6 We ran *between / inside* a shop when the rain started.

**2** Match the beginnings of sentences 1–8 with endings a–h.

1 I'm going to put my name ...... c ......
2 We're all really looking ............
3 People who like art often take ............
4 I love languages so I think I'll sign ............
5 I'm sure that you can deal ............
6 In the next game, you can join ............
7 It's a long walk, so I need to set ............
8 If I spend too much, I'll run ............

a up painting as a hobby.
b with any problems like that.
c down for swimming lessons.
d off very early in the morning.
e forward to surfing tomorrow.
f out of money soon.
g in and play for our team.
h up for Spanish lessons.

**3** Choose the correct option (A, B or C).

1 While I'm away, a neighbour is ............ our cat.
   A looking for
   B looking after
   C looking at

2 When I go cycling, I always wear a ............ to protect my head.
   A helmet
   B board
   C tent

3 My brother is a very good ............ . He makes some lovely meals.
   A cook
   B cooker
   C cooking

4 I want to learn the piano, or another musical ............ .
   A object
   B equipment
   C instrument

5 Mila was so busy that she had to ............ her favourite hobby.
   A give in
   B give up
   C give out

6 It's more fun to take ............ in a game than just watch it.
   A team
   B part
   C practice

## Grammar

**4** Complete the email with the *-ing* or the infinitive form of the verb in brackets.

Hi Louis,

I'm planning **(1)** ...to go... (go) away on holiday next week, but there are still so many things I need **(2)** ............ (do) before I leave! I want **(3)** ............ (take) some new clothes with me, but I can't afford **(4)** ............ (buy) expensive things. Actually I don't feel like **(5)** ............ (spend) anything at all, so I've decided **(6)** ............ (borrow) some clothes from my sister. I'm also hoping **(7)** ............ (see) my friends here before I go, so I've suggested **(8)** ............ (spend) Sunday afternoon together. And when I'm away, I must remember **(9)** ............ (send) you photos. I forgot **(10)** ............ (do) that last summer, but I promise I will this time!

See you on Friday

Aria

42

# Vocabulary and grammar review 4

## Vocabulary

**1** Complete Clara's email with adjectives in the correct form. The first letter is given and there is one space for each other letter in the word.

Hi George,

I live in Bilbao, which is a very large city in Spain. In fact, it is the **(1)** b<u>iggest</u> city in the area. Bilbao is **(2)** g _ _ _ _ – I love it! It's located on the north coast and it can be quite rainy. April is by far the **(3)** w _ _ _ _ _ month but January is the **(4)** c _ _ _ _ _ _ month. Last January was **(5)** f _ _ _ _ _ _ _ – temperatures fell to -20C! As for the city itself, Bilbao is absolutely fascinating. I love shopping and there are many places to go in the city centre. My friends love the shopping centre. It's always fun and **(6)** l _ _ _ _ _. I prefer El Corte Inglés, it's a **(7)** h _ _ _ department store. Tourists usually visit the Guggenheim Museum, but I think it's a bit **(8)** b _ _ _ _ _. Why don't you come and visit me?

Hope to hear from you soon.

Lots of love,

Clara

**2** Choose the correct option in *italics*.

1. At 250 metres below the sea, Jericho is the world's *highest* / (*lowest*) / *widest* city.
2. Gustave Eiffel was responsible for building the Eiffel Tower and the Statue of Liberty. The Statue of Liberty is slightly older *then* / *as* / *than* the Eiffel Tower.
3. One of the most popular tourist attractions in the world is Istanbul's Grand Bazaar, which is a(n) *absolutely* / *very* / *far* large market.
4. The pool at San Alfonso del Mar, Chile is *more* / *far* / *very* larger than any other swimming pool in the world.
5. Steve Fossett was the first person to *travel* / *trip* / *journey* around the world in a hot-air balloon. He took just under 15 days.
6. The world's largest *bookshop* / *department store* / *library* is in Washington DC in the USA. It has over 38 million books that only people working for the government can borrow.

## Grammar

**3** Exam candidates often make mistakes with comparative adjectives. <u>Underline</u> and correct the mistakes in the sentences.

1. My city is much <u>more better</u> than any other city in the world. *better*
2. It is more easy for you to walk to my house.
3. That's the worse restaurant we've ever been to.
4. I like living in the city much more that the countryside.
5. Those days on holiday were the happier days of my life.
6. Hotels are more cheaper here than the hotels in the city.

**4** Complete the article about a holiday with the words which best fit each gap. Use only one word in each gap.

Last August, we set off for our summer holiday on a small Greek island. I thought the journey was going to be really terrible but it wasn't as **(1)** *bad* as I'd expected. The hotel was brilliant. It was nearer to the beach **(2)** _____ the hotel we stayed in last year and the food was absolutely delicious. In fact the restaurant in our hotel was the **(3)** _____ popular restaurant in town. We tried lots of new sports. Of all the activities, I liked going snorkelling **(4)** _____ . It really was an amazing experience. The weather was boiling. I have never visited a place as hot **(5)** _____ this. I don't think I'll ever forget that holiday. That island has to be one of the most beautiful places **(6)** _____ the world.

Vocabulary and grammar review 43

# 5 Different feelings

## how emotional are you?

1. ....*sadness*....
Your favourite football team has just lost a very important match. What do you do?
*I call my friend to talk about it*

2. Somebody borrows a book from you but then loses it. What do you do?

3. You have broken a tooth, so you have to go to the dentist. How do you feel?

4. You pass your driving test. What do you do?

5. Someone you don't like wins a huge prize on the lottery. What do you say to your friends?

## Starting off
### Feelings

**1** Work in pairs. Answer the questions.
- Look at the pictures. What do they show?
- How do the pictures make you feel? Why? Choose from these words.

afraid   angry   happy   jealous   sad

> The photo of the rock climber makes me feel a little bit afraid!

**2** Which nouns express the emotions in Exercise 1?
*afraid — fear*

**3** Complete the headings in the quiz with nouns from Exercise 2.

**4** Do the quiz. Make notes on your answers.

**5** Work in small groups. Compare your answers in Exercise 4. How emotional do you think you are?

## Listening Part 2

**1** Match the feelings in the box with definitions 1–6.

> bored  confident  disappointed  embarrassed
> grateful  nervous

1 feeling or showing thanks  *grateful*
2 unhappy because something wasn't as good as you hoped, or didn't happen
3 worried about something that will or might happen
4 sure that you can do something well
5 feeling ashamed or shy
6 unhappy because something isn't interesting or you've got nothing to do

**2** Look at the exam task below. What is the situation in each question (1–6)?

**Exam advice**
- Read each question to understand what the situation is. Decide what you have to listen for (e.g. a feeling or an opinion).
- You can change your mind about an answer while you listen the second time.

**3** For each question, choose the correct answer. Then listen again and check.

1 You will hear a woman talking about taking part in a singing contest.
   After she finished singing, she felt
   A confident about winning the competition.
   B disappointed with her scores.
   C embarrassed by her performance.

2 You will hear two friends talking about camping.
   The man advises the woman to
   A pack plenty of food.
   B take some warm clothes.
   C camp close to a lake.

3 You will hear a student talking to his friend about a literature exam.
   How does he feel?
   A nervous about taking it
   B bored of revising
   C happy with his friend's advice

4 You will hear a young woman telling a friend about studying abroad.
   Who did she have most fun with?
   A other students on the course
   B people in the town centre
   C the family she stayed with

5 You will hear a man telling his friend about how he travels to work.
   Why has he decided to go by bike?
   A to save some money
   B to get more exercise
   C to help reduce pollution

6 You will hear a woman talking to a friend about shopping.
   Who annoyed her yesterday?
   A people who worked in the shop
   B other customers in the shop
   C pedestrians outside the shop

## Grammar

*can*, *could*, *might* and *may*

▶ **Page 126 Grammar reference**
Modal verbs: *can*, *could*, *might* and *may* (ability and possibility)

**1** Look at the underlined modal verbs for ability and possibility. Then answer the questions.

> So, do you think you'll try again in next year's contest?

> Yes, if I <u>can</u>. I <u>might not</u> win, but I think I <u>could</u> do better than this year.

1 Which modal verb is negative?
2 Where does *not* go?
3 What is the short form of *cannot* and *could not*?
4 What form of the verb goes after a modal verb?

**2** Exam candidates often make mistakes with modal verbs. Underline and correct one mistake in each sentence.

1 We can to go to the cinema next weekend.
2 I know it may seems strange.
3 Sorry but tomorrow I not can go.
4 What we could do?
5 We can doing a lot of sports here.
6 It's could be quite boring for you.
7 We could met at 8 o'clock near the cinema.

Different feelings  45

# 5

**3** Read the message. Then complete the rules with the underlined words.

> Hi Kylie, I'm sorry I <u>couldn't</u> meet you yesterday and I don't think I <u>can</u> go out on Thursday, either. I <u>may</u> be busy all evening on Friday, too, so Saturday <u>might</u> be better. There's a new film on at the cinema. I don't know much about it but it's got our favourite actor in it, so it <u>could</u> be really good! Let me know what you think. Lauren

**Rules**

1 We use ............... to talk about ability in the present and ............... to talk about ability in the past.

2 We use ..............., ............... or ............... for possibility in the present or future, with no real difference in meaning.

**4** Read Kylie's reply. Choose the correct option in *italics*.

> Hi Lauren, thanks for your message. I (1) *might not / couldn't* reply to you earlier because I was at work. I (2) *may / can* see you're very busy at the moment, so perhaps it (3) *can / might* be better to meet another weekend. It's a shame we (4) *can't / may* not see each other more often. You're my best friend and I know I (5) *might / can* always tell you anything. I (6) *could / couldn't* phone you in the next few days if you like.
> Love, Kylie

**5** Work in pairs.

1 Student A: think of a place, then say what you can and can't do there.
Student B: guess what the place is.

> You can eat ice cream, you can't arrive late, you can't talk during the film …

> The cinema!

2 Tell your partner about things you could, may, might or might not do next weekend.

> I could go to the park, but I may just stay in and watch TV.

## Speaking Part 4

▶ Page 161 Speaking bank
Speaking Part 4

**1** Work in groups. Discuss these questions.

1 How do you usually chat to other people? e.g. *by phone, online messaging*. Which websites or apps do you use?
2 In your country, what differences are there in the way generations a–c chat? Why?
a) children and teenagers  b) young adults
c) middle-aged and older people
3 What topics do you think generations a–c talk about most? Why?

**2** Listen to Daniel from Mexico and Wen from China talking about chatting to people. Complete the questions.

1 ............... do you most enjoy chatting ...............?
2 ............... do you ............... chat?
3 ............... can you chat ............... people?
4 ............... do you most like chatting ...............?

**3** Listen again. Complete the questions they use to ask for each other's opinion.

1 How ............... you?   4 Do you ...............?
2 ............... you?   5 What do you ...............?
3 What ............... you?

> **Exam advice**
> • Take turns with your partner and try to speak for about the same length of time.
> • Make the discussion longer by asking your partner for more information or about their opinions.

**4** Work in pairs. Ask and answer the questions in Exercise 2. Use expressions from Exercise 3 in your conversation.

## Grammar
### Modals for advice, obligation and prohibition

▶ **Page 126 Grammar reference**
Modal verbs: *should, shouldn't, ought to, must, mustn't, have to, don't have to* (advice, obligation and prohibition)

**1** Look at the people in the pictures. Underline the modals used in the advice.

*You ought to put on a new T-shirt.*   *You shouldn't go out tonight.*

**2** Read the rules. Then match pictures A–D with sentences 1–4.
1. You must get here earlier. D
2. You have to be members to come in.
3. You mustn't touch it!
4. You don't have to pay.

**Rules**
- Use *have to* when a rule or a law says it's necessary that you do something.
- Use *don't have to* when it's not necessary to do something.
- Use *must* when the speaker thinks it's necessary that you do something.
- Use *mustn't* when you're not allowed to do something.

**3** Read the comments by people about where they study or work. Choose the correct option in *italics*.
1. We *shouldn't* / (*mustn't*) talk to each other during exams.
2. It's a rule that we *ought to* / *have to* wear a suit.
3. We *don't have to* / *mustn't* go there on Saturdays.
4. Our boss says we *must* / *shouldn't* arrive by half past eight in the morning.
5. We *shouldn't* / *don't have to* take days off without permission.

**4** Complete the sentences using *must, mustn't, have to* or *don't have to*. Sometimes more than one answer is possible.
1. It's still early. We ……*don't have to*…… go home yet.
2. You look tired. You ……………………… take a break.
3. It's a secret. You ……………………… tell her what I said.
4. Great, it's a holiday! I ……………………… get up early!
5. No, you can't drive the car. You ……………………… be 18!

**5** Work in pairs. Use modal verbs to say which sentences from Exercise 3 are true for where you study or work.

> We can talk to each other in some exams.

**6** Ask your partner about other rules for their work, study or life in general.

> Do you have to write a lot of reports in your job?

> I don't have to write very many. About two a month.

Different feelings  47

# 5

### /P/ Modal verbs: weak and strong forms

**7** Read and listen to these sentences. The words in bold are stressed.
- **Leah** can **take** a **taxi**.
- **Jack** should **go** to **work**.

Now complete the rules using these words.

articles   main   modal   names   nouns   prepositions

**Rules**

In spoken English, we often stress words such as people's (1) .................... , (2) .................... and (3) .................... verbs, but use the weak form of the vowel, /ə/, in (4) .................... , e.g. *the*, (5) .................... and (6) .................... verbs.

**8** Listen and repeat the sentences. Then answer the questions.
- a I can buy another one.
- b I can't afford that one.
- c I could meet you at 5.30.
- d I couldn't live without my phone!
- e I should get up earlier on Sundays.
- f I shouldn't go to bed so late.

1 In which sentences is it easier to hear the modal verb? Do these sentences also contain *not*?
2 How is *not* written? Is it easy to hear this?
3 Which sentences have a weak form of the modal verb, which is not so easy to hear? Do these sentences also contain *not*?

**9** Work in pairs. Tell your partner about something you…
1 have to do at home.
2 mustn't do at work or college.
3 don't have to do at weekends.
4 must do this week.
5 shouldn't do but sometimes do.
6 ought to do but probably won't do.

> I have to clean the kitchen every week.

## Vocabulary
### Adjectives and prepositions

**1** Work in pairs. Discuss how you feel when people tell you to do things. Give examples.

> I feel annoyed with my boss when she says I must work harder.

**2** Look at the sentence in Exercise 1 and underline the preposition. Then underline the preposition which comes after the adjective in these sentences written by exam candidates.
1 My boss was very angry with me.
2 I never get tired of watching this film.
3 He was very sorry about what happened.

**3** Complete the table with the prepositions *about*, *of* and *with*. Then think of more adjectives for each preposition.

| | |
|---|---|
| afraid, ashamed, jealous, bored, fond | (1) .......... |
| angry, disappointed, pleased, satisfied | (2) .......... |
| sad, nervous, crazy, sure, depressed | (3) .......... |

**Note:** some adjectives can be followed by different prepositions with no change of meaning (e.g. *Ivy was getting bored **of/with** her job.*; *It was a red car, I'm sure **of/about** that.* Others take one preposition for somebody, e.g. *she's angry **with** Luca*, but another for something, e.g. *she's angry **about** the delay.*

**4** Complete the questions with the correct prepositions. Then ask your partner the questions.
1 Is there anything in the news you feel sad ................... ?
2 Is there anyone you sometimes get angry ................... ?
3 When you were small, what were you afraid ................... ?
4 What do you sometimes get bored ................... ?
5 Is there anything you sometimes feel nervous ................... ?

48

## Adjectives with -ed and -ing

▶ **Page 127 Grammar reference**
Adjectives with -ed and -ing endings

**1** Quickly read the story. Do not complete the gaps for now.

1 Why did Leo ask the airline to help?
2 What happened in the end?

**2** Complete this sentence. How does the spelling change from the word in brackets?

For many people the flight from Europe to Australia is long and ............................. (bore).

**3** The sentence could be changed like this. What -ed adjective does it use? When do we use the -ing adjective and when do we use the -ed adjective?

Many people feel <u>bored</u> on the long flight from Europe to Australia.

**4** Complete the text with the correct form of the adjectives in brackets. Use -ing if it describes something, or -ed if it tells us how someone feels.

**5** Work in pairs. Talk about the last time you were …

- surprised.
- tired.
- disappointed.

Now ask your partner to describe situations that were …

- exciting.
- interesting.
- embarrassing.

**6** Write three pairs of sentences using the adjectives from gaps 2, 8 and 10 in the text.

*It's relaxing to listen to music.*
*I always feel relaxed when I play my favourite song.*

# LOVE in the AIR

For many people, the flight to Australia is long and (1) ......*boring*........ (bore). But it wasn't for Abbie and Leo Davies – because that's where they first met.

'Abbie was sitting next to me,' said Leo. 'I felt (2) ............................. (relax) talking to her and we got on really well. We chatted all the way to Sydney and it was (3) ............................. (surprise) how quickly the time went.'

But they forgot to get each other's phone number, so after the flight Leo contacted the airline. 'To be honest, it was a bit (4) ............................. (embarrass) because the staff were quite (5) ............................. (amuse) by the situation, but anyway I gave them her seat number, and waited.'

Abbie, too, was feeling sad.

'I was (6) ............................. (annoy) with myself for not getting his number,' she said, 'though I was also a bit (7) ............................. (disappoint) he didn't ask me for mine. I thought he wasn't really (8) ............................. (interest) in seeing me again. So I was (9) ............................. (amaze) when the airline phoned to ask if I wanted to call Leo. I was so (10) ............................. (excite) that I phoned him that evening, and soon we had our first date. Now we're married and we're very happy together.'

Different feelings 49

# 5

## Reading Part 4

**1** Work in pairs. Answer the questions.
1. Which of the situations in the box are the most stressful?
2. What other causes of stress are there?
3. What happens to people when they feel stressed?

> changing job   difficulty sleeping   exams
> money worries   moving house   problems at work
> relationship problems   speaking in public

**2** Quickly read the article. What is the topic of each paragraph?

1: the effects of stress

> **Exam advice**
> - Quickly read the main text. Decide what each paragraph is about.
> - Look at the ideas before and after each gap, then look for similar ideas in A–H.
> - Look for words that often link ideas, for example *this*, *then*, *do*, *also* and *however*.

**3** You are going to read an article about dealing with stress. Five sentences have been removed from the text. For each question, choose the correct answer. There are three extra sentences which you do not need to use.

A  One I particularly like has a 'quick tips' section for stressful situations.
B  It was so funny that I felt more cheerful straight away.
C  That made me realise I couldn't go on feeling so stressed.
D  I knew I had to finish that first.
E  It recommended that everyone should laugh more often every day.
F  So I took up dancing instead.
G  People who do so often seem to be miserable.
H  If it's longer, I find it hard to concentrate on my original task.

**4** Work in pairs. Discuss the questions.
- Do you think an 'anti-stress' app could work? Why / Why not?
- Which of the other ideas in the text might help you relax? Why?
- What other ways can you think of to deal with stress?

## How I dealt with stress

**1** For months I'd been unable to relax and I felt awful. I worried about things, I wasn't sleeping well and I couldn't concentrate on my work in the office. Then my best friend told me that everyone thought I was always in a bad mood. (1) ......C......

**2** I began by making some simple changes to my routine. Each morning when I woke up I thought about things I was looking forward to so that I started the day in a more positive mood. I kept doing that until it became a habit. I also knew I should do more exercise but to tell the truth I don't enjoy doing sports. (2) ............... That really helped me to relax, particularly when I learnt to concentrate on enjoying the experience rather than letting negative thoughts go through my mind.

**3** I changed the way I worked, too. I used to answer every email as soon as it came in, but this meant that I kept stopping and starting work, and I could only make slow progress which made me feel really stressed. Nowadays, I leave most messages until later in the day and reply to any urgent ones only when I take a break. I do this every 40 minutes or so, usually for no more than ten minutes. (3) ...............

**4** I've also discovered some great anti-stress apps such as Headspace, Pacifica and Calm. Apps like these have breathing exercises, relaxing sounds such as the ocean, rain or streams, and suggestions for making changes in your daily life to help you relax. (4) ............... Some of these apps are free.

**5** Last month I read an article which said people with a good sense of humour are usually happier and more relaxed. (5) ............... Having fun with friends or watching your favourite comedy series are easy ways to achieve this. And when you aren't stressed, it can make it much easier to do your job!

50

## Vocabulary
### Adjectives and their opposites

**1** Match adjectives in box A with their opposites in box B.

**A**

~~awful~~  funny  generous  miserable
negative  nervous  simple  strange

**B**

cheerful  complicated  ~~fantastic~~  mean
ordinary  positive  relaxed  serious

**2** Work in pairs.

Tell your partner about something …
- strange that happened in a film you saw.
- fantastic that happened during your holidays.
- awful that happened at work or college.
- funny that you saw online or on TV.

## Writing Part 2

▶ **Page 150 Writing bank**
A story

**1** Read this Writing Part 2 task and answer the questions.

- Your English teacher has asked you to write a story.
- Your story must begin with this sentence:
  *Olivia read the message from her friend and smiled.*

1 Are you given a title or the first line?
2 Should you write in the first or the third person?
3 Which are the key words?

**2** Read the example answer, then answer the questions.
1 Where and when does most of the action happen?
2 Who are the main characters and what is their relationship?
3 What is the situation?
4 What problem do the characters have?
5 How is this problem solved?
6 How does the story end?

**3** Look at the story again. Find four adjectives that describe how Olivia felt.

---

Olivia read the message from her friend and smiled. She was excited because Ellie, who lived abroad, was coming to visit her this Friday!

Just as Olivia reached the airport to pick up Ellie, she received a call. 'There's thick fog here and my plane can't take off,' explained Ellie, 'I'm not sure what'll happen.'

'I'm really disappointed,' replied Olivia.

As Olivia waited at the airport she became quite miserable. But then Ellie called again. 'The sky's cleared!' she said. Three hours later, Olivia was delighted when Ellie's flight had finally landed. Ellie said, 'It's fantastic to see you!' when she finally saw Olivia.

**4** Read this Writing Part 2 task and answer the questions from Exercise 1.

- You are going to write a story.
- Your story must begin with this sentence:
  *Matthew felt excited as he waited for the train.*

**5** Think about the questions in Exercise 2 and plan your story.

> **Exam advice**
> - Decide where and when to set your story.
> - Plan the main events and think about the kind of person your main character is.
> - Try to make your story interesting for your readers.

**6** Write your story in about 100 words.

Different feelings

# 6 That's entertainment!

## Reading Part 2

**1** Tom and Ian are looking for something to do one afternoon. Read about what they like and dislike. <u>Underline</u> the key words.

Tom and Ian have a free afternoon but neither of them like crowds. They're interested in theatre and exhibitions, but they don't have much money.

**2** Read the entertainment guide on page 53 and decide on the most suitable event for Tom and Ian. <u>Underline</u> where you find the information. Then answer the questions.

1 Tom and Ian are interested in theatres and exhibitions. Why isn't D suitable?
2 Neither of them like crowds. Why isn't G suitable?

**3** Read the guide again. Decide which event would be the most suitable for the people (2–5).

> **Exam advice**
> - Underline the key words in the descriptions of people.
> - Read each of A–H to find information that matches the key words in 1–5.

2 Alice wants to take her 14-year-old cousin to see something brand new and have a meal afterwards nearby. They will go by public transport but they don't want to walk too far.

3 Jack is keen on cartoons. As he'll be alone, he would like to go somewhere where he can get to know people with similar interests and also add to his collection of old books and magazines.

4 Two friends, Patricia and Steph, would love to see a live performance in a foreign language. Whenever they go out together, they always buy something to eat during the interval.

5 Simone has offered to take her mum to see a show with music for her birthday. They would like to see an enjoyable story but her mum isn't fond of rock or pop.

## Starting off
### Television programmes

**1** Match the types of TV from the box with the photos.

> advert   cartoon   chat show   comedy series
> cooking show   quiz show   reality show   sports
> the news   wildlife documentary

**2** Listen to Clare asking Nick about TV. How much TV does Nick watch? What are his favourite types of programme?

**3** Listen again and write down Clare's five questions. Then work in groups. Ask and answer Clare's questions so they are true for you.

52

# TURN OFF THE TV AND GO OUT!

### A Beautiful Sunset ★★★
This rock band returns once again to play songs from their latest album. Expect an amazing performance from these musicians, who have sold over 80 million records. Tickets are on sale for €60, the price includes a free souvenir T-shirt. Enjoy a meal in our restaurant after the show. Public transport nearby.

*The Sports Palace*

### B Our lives, their lives
Now in its second year, this display explores the changing lives of people from around the world through photographs and cartoons, music and interviews. Some of the interviews are with grandparents who compare their lives with those of their children and grandchildren. Free entry to this popular museum which is rarely busy after 3pm. Don't miss the excellent gift shop.

*Jameson Museum*

### C Captain Rob's Adventures in 4DX
Not cheap, but this animated version of a well-known film is an experience you definitely can't get at home. The picture and sound quality is fantastic, and the 4D effects are amazing. Feel the wind and the waves, as you sail with Captain Rob. Choice of restaurants nearby. Public transport within easy walking distance.

*Filmworld 4DX*

### F In Paris ★★
Paris during the French Revolution and Marco Morelli has fallen in love with a rich young woman. However, one of the family's servants is also in love with her. This is a new version of the Italian opera with amazing singing and real classical music! Audiences of all ages will be entertained. Food and drink not permitted in the theatre.

*Elizabeth Theatre*

### D The Music Teacher
Based on a film, this musical is now showing on stage. An out-of-work guitarist tells some lies and gets a job as a teacher. He persuades some of his students to create a rock group so that they can take part in the Battle of the Bands competition. Afternoon and evening performances from €50. Refreshments available.

*Queens Theatre*

### G Big Sight
Held over three days, this comic market celebrates Japanese animation. In this huge conference centre, fans can meet other fans, buy rare comics, dress up as their favourite characters and take selfies. No admission fee, reasonably priced food but expect long queues!

*The Conference Centre*

### H Traditional Future
For less than €8, watch Anuang'a Fernando from Kenya as he uses traditional words from his country, modern music and movement to perform this work of art. Anuang'a Fernando has already performed this show in Paris and Italy. Book soon – the theatre only holds 200 people. Snacks will be available. Close to public transport.

*Drake Hall*

### E Rubbish ★
The Opera House has been turned into a big tent for *Rubbish*. Set on the streets in the 1940s, young artists do gymnastics, dance and theatre using rubbish like wheels, furniture and boxes. First performances this week! Under-15s must be accompanied by an adult but ask about family discounts at our restaurant. A two-minute walk from the underground.

*Opera House*

**4** Work in pairs. Which event would you like to attend? Why?

That's entertainment!

# 6

## Vocabulary
### Going out

**1** Look at the words in the box. Are they used to talk about a film, a play or a concert? Complete the diagram.

> acting   book early   ~~interval~~   live music
> perform   refreshments   reviews   ~~screen~~
> stage   subtitles   ticket

FILMS — screen
PLAYS
CONCERTS
(shared) interval

**2** Complete the questions with words from Exercise 1.

1. Do you usually read the ....reviews...... before you see a film or a play?
2. Do you ever watch films in English with ............................... ?
3. Think of the last time you went to see a film, play or concert. Did you have to ............................... or could you buy tickets on the door?
4. How often do you buy ............................... like popcorn at the cinema?
5. Do you prefer to listen to music at home or to go out to see ............................... ?
6. Can young people afford to go to the cinema in your town? How much is a ............................... ?
7. Would you rather see your favourite actor on the screen or on ............................... ?
8. Some people are fantastic actors. Are you good at ............................... ?

**3** Work in groups. Ask and answer the questions from Exercise 2. Remember to say why or why not.

## Grammar
### Present perfect

▶ Page 128 Grammar reference
Present perfect

**1** Listen to Eliza and Bella planning a night out together in Madrid. What do they decide to do?

**2** Listen again and complete the sentences.

1. Have you ............................... *The Lion King* <u>yet</u>?
2. I've <u>already</u> ............................... it.
3. I haven't ............................... the new Robin Hood film <u>yet</u>.
4. I've <u>just</u> ............................... how to play one of the songs.

**3** How do we form the present perfect? When do we use this tense?

**4** Complete the rules with *already*, *just* or *yet*.

> **Rules**
>
> 1 Use ............................... to talk about things that happened a short time ago.
>
> 2 Use ............................... to say something has happened, often sooner than expected.
>
> These two words normally go in the middle of the sentence, between *have* and the past participle.
>
> 3 Use ............................... in questions and negative sentences when we expect something to happen. It means 'until now'. This word normally goes at the end of the sentence.

**5** Complete the email. Use the given words and put the verbs in the present perfect tense.

> Hi Jodie,
>
> Sorry I haven't written to you for so long but I've been really busy. I've got so much to tell you. **(1)** My sister and her boyfriend / just / get married. **(2)** My brother / not find / a new job / yet. **(3)** But he / start / a course in computing. **(4)** My flatmate / just / win / a prize in a photography competition. **(5)** you / see / the new *Star Wars* film yet? **(6)** I / already / see / it / three times. It's great! What about you? **(7)** You / take / your driving test yet?
>
> Please write soon,
>
> Harry

*1 My sister and her boyfriend have just got married.*

54

▶ **Page 128 Grammar reference**
*since* and *for*

**6** Exam candidates sometimes make mistakes with *since* and *for*. Look at the sentence from Eliza and Bella's conversation and answer the questions.

We've been good friends <u>for</u> three years but we haven't been to a show together <u>since</u> last summer.

1 Which word do we use to talk about the beginning of a period of time? ..............................
2 Which word do we use to talk about the whole period of time? ..............................

**7** Complete the interview with *since* or *for*.

Interviewer: Mark, how long have you lived in Mumbai?
Mark: I've lived here **(1)** .............................. four months.
Interviewer: Have you joined any clubs or classes **(2)** .............................. you arrived?
Mark: Yes, I've been in a cycling club **(3)** .............................. March and I've started Hindi classes.
Interviewer: How long have you taken Hindi classes?
Mark: **(4)** .............................. three weeks, but I've learnt a lot **(5)** .............................. then.

**8** Work in pairs. Ask and answer the questions in Exercise 7 so that they are true for you. Then continue the conversation with some more '*How long have you…?*' questions.

> How long have you lived here?

> I've lived here all my life.

## Present perfect or past simple?

▶ **Page 129 Grammar reference**
The present perfect or the past simple?

**1** Read about Martin Garrix. What is he famous for?

Martijn Gerard Garritsen or Martin Garrix is a Dutch DJ who was born in Amsterdam **in 1996**.
**When** he was only 17, his single *Animals* became famous.
He's been a DJ **for over ten years** and he's toured with his music many times.

**2** Read the text in Exercise 1 again. <u>Underline</u> the verbs in the present perfect and circle the verbs in the past simple. Do we normally use the time expressions in bold with the present perfect or the past simple?

**3** We use some time expressions with the present perfect and others with the past simple. Complete the table with the expressions in the box.

> already    at 8 o'clock in the morning    ~~for ten years~~
> ~~in 1996~~    last year    since 2010    this week    today
> two months ago    yesterday    yet

| the present perfect | the past simple |
|---|---|
| for ten years | in 1996 |

**4** <u>Underline</u> the time expressions in the sentences. Then complete the sentences with the present perfect or past simple form of the verbs in brackets.

1 I *haven't made* (not/make) my bed <u>yet</u> today.
2 .............................. you .............................. (read) this month's *Surf* magazine yet?
3 I'm not going to the theatre. I .............................. (see) that show three months ago.
4 Our football team are playing better now. We only .............................. (win) twice last year.
5 Let's go to the beach! I .............................. (not/swim) in the sea for three months.
6 You look tired. What time .............................. you .............................. (go) to bed last night?
7 How many photos .............................. you .............................. (take) since you bought your phone?

**5** Work in pairs. You are going to interview another student in the class. Look at the example below and write some questions about the topics in the box.

> a car or motorbike    a favourite sport
> a foreign language    a free-time activity    a pet    a phone

> Have you got a mobile phone?

> Yes, I have.

> How long have you had it?

> I've had it for 6 months.

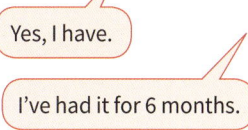

That's entertainment!    55

# 6

## Vocabulary

*been/gone*, *meet*, *get to know*, *know* and *find out*

**1** Read the texts and answer the questions.

Paul isn't at home, he's <u>gone</u> to a friends' home. His sister Sophia has just got home. She's <u>been</u> to the cinema.
1. Where's Paul now?
2. Where's Sophia now?
3. *Been* and *gone* are both forms of *go*. Which one means 'go and come back'? Which one means 'hasn't come back yet'?

Lucas has <u>known</u> his friend Nick for five years. They first <u>met</u> at university. They <u>got to know</u> each other and they became good friends. Lucas often <u>meets</u> Nick at the weekend and they go out together. Lucas sometimes <u>stays</u> at Nick's house when he misses the last bus home.
4. When and how did Lucas and Nick become friends?
5. Do they still see each other? When?
6. When does Lucas sleep at Nick's house?

Sam rents a flat from his aunt but she didn't <u>know</u> he was having a party. The neighbours phoned Sam's aunt because of the noise. When she <u>found out</u> about it, she wasn't very pleased.
7. Did Sam tell his aunt about the party?
8. Who told Sam's aunt that he was having a party?

**2** Choose the correct option in *italics*. Use the texts in Exercise 1 to help you.
1. Have you ever *been / gone* abroad? Where?
2. Imagine your flatmates have *been / gone* away for the weekend. Do you have a party?
3. Have you got a best friend? How long have you *known / met* them? How did you first *meet / know* each other?
4. Do you usually *meet / stay* with your friends at the weekend? What do you do?
5. Do you enjoy *knowing / getting to know* new people? Why (not)?
6. How often do you use the internet to *find out / know* information? Have you used it this week? What for?

**3** Work in groups. Ask and answer the questions from Exercise 2.

## Listening Part 1

**1** In Listening Part 1, you may hear someone describing clothes. Look at the pictures on page 57 and find examples of these things. Write the picture number.
1. a plain jumper — 1A, 1B
2. a pocket
3. a round neck
4. a striped jumper
5. a smart skirt
6. a V-neck

**2** Work in pairs. Read the questions carefully and <u>underline</u> the important words. Then decide what each picture shows and the difference between each one.

56

1 What would the woman like to try on?

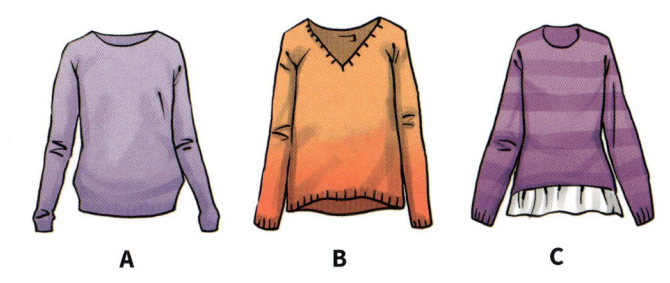

A   B   C

2 Where has Matt left his keys?

A   B   C

3 What did Karen buy last weekend?

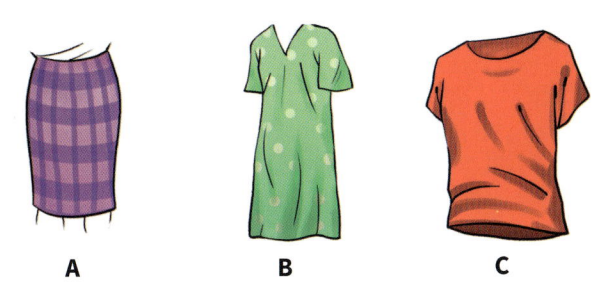

A   B   C

4 Which one is Sarah's cousin?

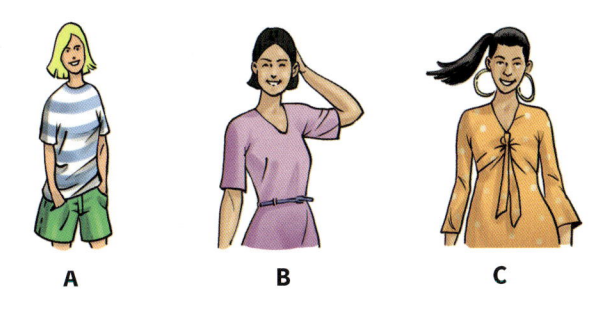

A   B   C

5 Where did the man get the trainers he's wearing now?

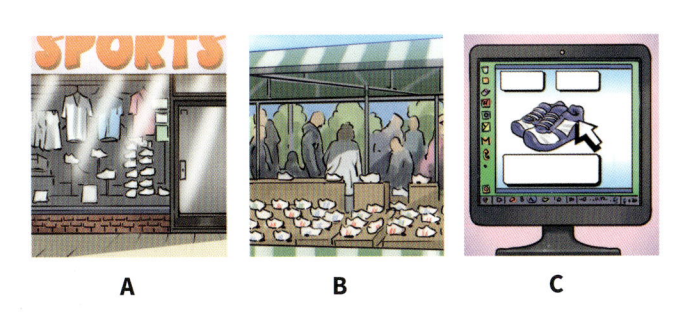

A   B   C

6 What's the latest time visitors can buy a ticket today?

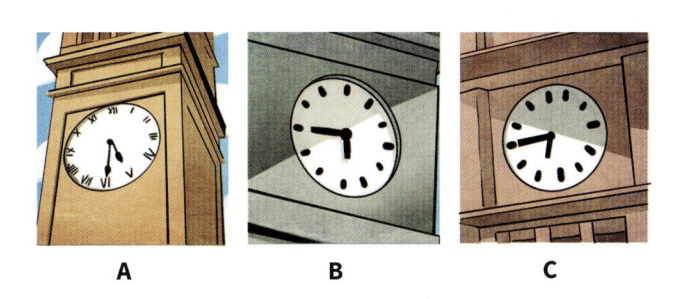

A   B   C

7 What sorts of TV programmes does the woman like watching?

A   B   C

**Exam advice**
- The pictures can tell you a lot about what you will hear. Study them carefully before you listen.
- Be careful: the speakers might mention all the things in the pictures, but only one answer is correct.

**3** Listen. For each question, choose the correct answer. Then listen again and check. (30)

**4** /P/ **Contrastive stress**

Read Connor's reply to the girl from question 7. What words do you think are stressed?

**Connor:** Oh? I didn't think you liked those sorts of programmes.

**5** Now listen to Connor saying his line in three different ways. What makes the meaning of each sentence change? (31)

**6** Work in groups. Ask and answer questions about the clothes you usually wear for these occasions. Stress the words you think are important!
- a trip to the countryside
- family celebrations
- hanging out with friends
- relaxing at home

That's entertainment!   57

# 6

## Speaking Part 3

▶ Page 159 Speaking bank

**1** Work in pairs. Read the Speaking Part 3 task below. Decide what you need to talk about.

> A university would like to celebrate its 25th anniversary with a special event. Here are some events the university could organise for past and present students.
>
> Talk together about the different events the university could organise and say which would be most popular.

**2** Work in pairs. Look at these possible events. Decide which ones you think would be good ideas for a 25th anniversary celebration.

> bike ride   concert   disco   photography exhibition
> student fashion show   talent show

**3** Look at the sentences and decide which you should or should not do in this part of the Speaking exam. Put a tick (✓) or a cross (✗) in each box in the *You* column.

|   |   | You | Noa & Greta |
|---|---|---|---|
| 1 | Listen carefully to the examiner's instructions. |   | ✓ |
| 2 | Discuss your ideas with your partner and the examiner. |   |   |
| 3 | Make suggestions and reply to suggestions. |   |   |
| 4 | Take turns to speak. |   |   |
| 5 | Talk about only one picture. |   |   |
| 6 | Agree as quickly as you can. |   |   |
| 7 | Speak for at least two minutes. |   |   |

**4** Listen to Noa and Greta doing this task. Which things from Exercise 3 do they do? Put a tick (✓) or a cross (✗) in the *Noa & Greta* column. 🎧 32

**5** <u>Underline</u> two expressions Greta uses to move on to a new picture.

**Greta:** Perhaps you're right. Shall we talk about the student fashion show?

**Noa:** OK. I think it's a great idea. Past and present fashion students could show the clothes they've designed.

**Greta:** Um … I'm not very interested in fashion, I'm afraid. We haven't talked about the bike ride yet. Do you think it's a good idea?

### Exam advice

- Keep the conversation going, for example by saying *Shall we talk about the …?*
- Talk fully about all the pictures <u>before</u> finally agreeing with your partner.

**6** Work in pairs. Do the Speaking Part 3 task below.

> A town is planning to celebrate its anniversary with a festival. Here are some activities which the festival could include.
>
> Talk together about the different activities the festival could include, and say which would be most popular.

58

# Writing Part 2

▶ Page 148 Writing bank
An article

**1** Work in pairs. Look at the photos. What can you see? What are the people doing and wearing?

**2** Discuss the questions.
1. What celebrations are there in your country?
2. What's your favourite celebration? Why?
3. What do people wear and do?

**3** Read this Writing Part 2 exam task and underline the important words.

> You see this announcement in an international English-language magazine for teenagers.
>
> **Let's celebrate!**
> Tell us about a celebration in your country.
> *What do people usually wear?*
> *What do people do?*
> *Why is it special?*
>
> **Write an article answering these questions and we will publish the most interesting articles in our magazine.**
>
> Write your **article** in about **100** words.

**4** Work in pairs. Read the first paragraphs of two articles. Which is better? Why?

> *The story began on Chinese New Year. People were wearing amazing costumes and they were dancing in the street. We left our flat and we walked to my aunt's house. She was preparing a special meal for us.*

> *My favourite celebration in my country is the Venice Carnival in February. The celebrations last for two weeks. There are dances, concerts and performances but I love the masks and costumes best.*

**5** Now read the complete article about the Venice Carnival. Do you think it is a good answer?

> My favourite celebration in my country is the Venice Carnival in February. The celebrations last for two weeks. There are dances, concerts and performances but I love the masks and costumes best.
>
> My favourite mask is made of leather, it's painted by hand and it has a very long nose. We all wear traditional costumes so Venice looks like an 18th-century city.
>
> We go for walks in our special clothes, we watch actors perform in the street and we go to dances called balls. It's a very special celebration because there is nothing like it anywhere else in the world.

**6** Answer the questions.
1. Is the text an article and not a story?
2. Is the first paragraph interesting? Does it make you want to keep reading?
3. Does the article include all the information?
4. Is it about 100 words?

> **Exam advice**
> - If you decide to write an article, write an article and <u>not</u> a story.
> - Make sure your first paragraph is interesting to make the reader want to keep reading.

**7** Use your answers from Exercise 2 to write your article.

**8** Use the questions in Exercise 6 to check your work.

That's entertainment!

# 5 Vocabulary and grammar review

## Vocabulary

**1** Choose the correct options in *italics*.

Hi Tamsin,

Sorry I've taken so long to reply. In your last email, you asked what was happening with my friends, so here's my news. Lucas was disappointed **(1)** *of / on / with* his first-year exam results at university so he's working harder now, but I think he's getting tired **(2)** *about / of / on* studying all the time. He usually goes out in the evenings, so he must be getting very bored **(3)** *with / on / about* life. Natalie is still very keen **(4)** *of / on / with* football and is quite proud **(5)** *on / with / of* the two goals she scored last Saturday. However, she can't play next week so she's sad **(6)** *about / of / with* that. Claire is crazy **(7)** *on / with / about* music and a local band has asked her to sing with them at a concert next Friday. She's really nervous **(8)** *on / about / with* singing in front of all those people, but I don't think she should be frightened **(9)** *with / of / on* doing it. I've told her that some people will be jealous **(10)** *of / on / about* her!

Well, that's all for now.

Lots of love,

Bastian

**2** This blog post contains adjectives ending in *-ed* and *-ing*. Underline and correct five more mistakes.

When I was tidying my room last Sunday, I found some surprising things. Among all the ~~bored~~ *boring* exercise books from my school days, there was something amazed – my diary, from when I was eight years old. It was really interested to read my thoughts from back then, though at times I felt a bit embarrassing, too. For example, I was still very frightening of the dark in those days. It was also funny to read how exciting I was about being nine soon – I thought I would be really grown up then.

**3** Complete the crossword with words from Unit 5.

**Across**
1 the opposite of 'generous'
5 the noun form of 'angry'
6 Some people are … of insects and spiders.
8 wanting something that another person has
9 I felt really … because I had nothing to do.

**Down**
2 the opposite of 'positive'
3 the opposite of 'happy'
4 feeling worried or anxious about something
6 a word that means 'very bad'
7 a word that means 'like a lot'

## Grammar

**4** Choose the correct option in *italics*.

1 A: Do you think Dylan and Leah are at the café?
   B: They *can / might* be there, but I'm not sure.
2 A: Do you like going to the swimming pool?
   B: No, I *can't / couldn't* swim.
3 A: I've got a bit of a headache.
   B: I think you *shouldn't / should* take an aspirin.
4 A: *Could / Might* you run for an hour without stopping?
   B: No, I'd be too tired after 30 minutes!
5 A: Are the buses to the city centre expensive?
   B: No, you *mustn't / don't have to* pay if you're under 16.
6 A: The weather's not looking very good now.
   B: You're right. I think it *can / might* rain later.
7 A: What do I need to go to the USA?
   B: You *should / have to* take your passport.

# Vocabulary and grammar review 6

## Vocabulary

**1** Complete this review by writing a word from the box in each space.

> admission   audiences   interval   live
> performances   ~~reality shows~~   reviews

### Cirque Eloize

Are you bored of watching (1) _reality shows_ on TV? Do you fancy doing something new? Why don't you go and see Cirque Eloize's new show? (2) .................... will be amazed by the acrobatics, dance and (3) .................... music. This touring show has already received very good (4) .................... in other parts of the country. There are two (5) .................... each day: one at 2.30 and the other at 7.30. Tickets are still available for many dates with reduced (6) .................... for students and over-60s. The show lasts about 85 minutes with no (7) .................... .

**2** Choose the correct word (A, B or C).

1. I think I left my keys in the front .................... of my jeans.
   - **A** pocket ✓   B bag   C coat
2. My mum often wears bright, .................... shirts and long skirts.
   - A colour   B colourful   C coloured
3. I first .................... my best friend when I moved to this town.
   - A met   B knew   C found out
4. I'd love to go to New York to get to .................... the city.
   - A find out   B know   C meet
5. I've visited Washington DC but I haven't .................... to the White House.
   - A visited   B known   C been

## Grammar

**3** Exam candidates often make mistakes with the present perfect and the past simple and their common adverbs. Underline and correct the mistakes in the sentences.

1. <u>I've</u> bought some clothes last week.
2. My grandmother has lived here since three years.
3. I haven't seen him for ages because he's gone to Argentina a few years ago.
4. We've gone to the cinema three times this month. Let's do something else.
5. Already I've been to a few shops to look for new shoes.
6. I still can't find my mobile phone. I looked for it everywhere.
7. Milan is the best place I've never been to for clothes.
8. I lost a beautiful pair of gloves which my mother has given me for my birthday.
9. We're planning to go out, but we didn't decide where to go yet.
10. There's a wonderful cinema in my town. It has opened six months ago.

**4** Complete the article about living in a big city with the word which best fits each gap. Use only one word in each gap.

> I moved to Japan when I got a job here about a year (1) _ago_. I have lived in Tokyo (2) .................... about 6 months. I have to say that I (3) .................... never lived in such an exciting city and I love it here. I've been in this flat (4) .................... September and I've known my best friend since then. We (5) .................... to know each other when I sat next to him in Japanese classes and we soon became good friends. We love going to the cinema to see new films. We've (6) .................... been to the cinema twice this weekend.

61

# 7 Getting around

## Starting off
### Weather

**1** Work in pairs.

1 Match the words in the box to the photos. Then discuss the questions.

> cold  foggy  freezing  frost  hot  ice  icy  lightning
> rainy  showers  snowy  storm  sunny  sunshine
> thunderstorm  windy

2 How do you think people experiencing this weather feel?

> They probably feel quite cold, and they might not be able to see well through the fog.

3 What kind of weather do you like most/least? Why?
4 What do you think the underlined expressions mean?
- I hope the sun will <u>come out</u> soon.  *start shining*
- I put on a jumper because it was a bit <u>chilly</u> by the sea.
- It's <u>pouring</u> outside, so take your umbrella.
- Open the window. It's <u>boiling</u> in here!
- Even in summer, it gets quite <u>nippy</u> at night.
- It was cloudy earlier, but then the weather <u>cleared up</u>.
- Because of the <u>soaring temperatures</u>, lots of people have gone to the mountains.

## Listening Part 4

**1** Look at the exam task in Exercise 2. Answer the questions.

1 What is the main speaker's name?
2 What is the topic?
3 What do you need to listen for?

**2** For each question, choose the correct answer. You will hear an interview with a woman called Olivia talking about her experience of travelling through a snowstorm with her friend Grace.

**Exam advice**
- Quickly read the instructions and the questions to get an idea of what you will hear.
- Listen for reasons why one option is correct – and reasons why the other two are wrong.

1 When it started to snow heavily, Olivia and Grace were
  A  talking about what to do next.
  B  driving along a main road.
  C  having a snack in a café.

2 How did Olivia feel as heavy snow began to fall?
  A  annoyed with Grace for getting lost
  B  sure that the snow would stop soon
  C  scared about what might happen

3 Why did the car stop moving?
  A  It had run out of petrol.
  B  The snow was too deep.
  C  They had hit another vehicle.

4 How did they try to keep warm in the car?
  A  They put on lots of clothes.
  B  They kept the heater on all night.
  C  They drank some hot liquids.

5 They were in the car nearly all night because
  A  it became impossible to open the doors.
  B  they had been told not to leave it.
  C  nobody knew where they were.

6 The following day, they travelled to a village in
  A  a rescue vehicle.
  B  an ambulance.
  C  their own car.

**3** Listen again and check.

🎧 33

**4** Work in pairs. Discuss the questions and give reasons.
- How would you feel in Olivia's situation? What would you do?
- Have you ever been stuck anywhere due to bad weather? What happened? How did you feel?

## Grammar

*extremely, fairly, quite, rather, really* and *very*

▶ Page 130 Grammar reference
Adverbs of degree

**1** Read the sentences from the recording. Then complete the rules with the underlined words.
- <u>Really</u> heavy snow started coming down.
- I was <u>quite</u> certain it wouldn't last long.
- It was <u>rather</u> annoying we'd gone the wrong way.
- It was getting <u>quite</u> difficult to see.

### Rules

1 Adverbs of degree such as *very*, *extremely* and ............................ always make an adjective stronger.

2 The adverbs *fairly* and ............................ always make it weaker.

3 The adverb ............................ usually makes it weaker, but with adjectives like *sure*, *true* and *different*, it can mean 'completely'.

**2** Discuss the questions, using adverbs of degree.
- Have you ever experienced extreme weather, e.g. really hot, very stormy weather?
- What was it like?
- How did you feel and what did you do?

> Last year we had an extremely hot summer. The temperatures were very high and I felt really uncomfortable so I went to the shopping mall. It was quite cool there!

Getting around   63

# 7

## too and enough

▶ Page 130 Grammar reference
*too* and *enough*

**1** Read what some people say about the weather. Complete the rules by choosing the correct option in *italics*.

*'In summer it's too hot to work!'*

*'We had enough time to get indoors before the storm hit our town.'*

*'It was a hot July day in the city. There were too many cars and there was too much noise.'*

*'It was winter, so it wasn't warm enough to swim in the sea.'*

### Rules

1 In the examples above, *too* means *as much as / more than* you need or want. It does not mean the same as *very*.
2 The word *too* goes *after / before* an adjective, often followed by the *-ing / to + infinitive* form of the verb.
3 We use *too much* before *countable / uncountable* nouns and *too many* before *countable / uncountable* nouns.
4 In the examples above, *enough* means *as much as / more than* you need or want.
5 The word *enough* usually goes *after / before* a noun but *after / before* an adjective, often followed by the *-ing / to + infinitive* form of the verb.

**2** Exam candidates often make mistakes with *too* and *enough*. Some of the sentences contain mistakes. Underline and correct them.

1 It was hot enough to spend the whole day in the water.
2 In the streets, there are too much cars.
3 My sister is very young to travel alone.
4 In summer it would be too hot to cycle.
5 We did not have plenty of time to see the University of Cambridge.
6 I think you are enough old to spend this summer with your friends.

**3** Work in groups. Write down six places you'd like to visit. Then discuss which is the best. Use *too* and *enough*.

> I'd love to go to the mountains, but they are too far away and we don't have enough time!

> How about the lake? That's nice, and close to here.

## Reading Part 1

**1** Look quickly at the signs and messages below. Where could you see each one?

**A** DANGER — Thin ice! Deep water!

**B** CYCLISTS
Leave bicycles in parking spaces provided on ferry
Go to passenger area
Return to bicycles when ferry reaches harbour

**C** City Centre/Airport bus service
NOTICE TO PASSENGERS
Fare £3 Coins only

**D** Sign up for our new phone contract in five days and you'll get £30 of extra credit!

**E** NO SKATEBOARDING IN PEDESTRIAN-ONLY AREAS

**2** Match the texts (A–E) with the purposes (1–5). Underline the words in the texts which tell you the purpose.

1 to give you information  *C*
2 to say what you must not do
3 to warn you of something
4 to say what you must do
5 to advertise something

64

**3** For each question, choose the correct answer.

> Decide what the purpose of each text is and where you might see it.
> *Exam advice*

**1**

**ATTENTION**
In case of fire, use this emergency exit.
Alarm bell rings when open.

A Ring the bell before opening the emergency exit.
B You must find another exit if there is a fire.
C Only go out this way if there is an emergency.

**2**

To: Lacey
From: Zara

I'm still really keen on having a holiday together, but I'm a bit short of cash right now. Would you mind if we booked for a week rather than a fortnight?

A Zara wants to have a shorter holiday.
B Zara doesn't want to go away with Lacey.
C Zara regrets paying for a two-week holiday.

**3**

**FOR SALE**
Fashionable winter jacket
(Size: medium)
Hardly ever worn
Small tear on left sleeve but now mended
£20, or make me an offer!
Contact Alex in the Research Department

A The jacket is in perfect condition.
B The seller may accept a lower price.
C Alex has worn the fashionable jacket many times.

**4**

**FOREST NATURE PARK**
- No fires or barbecues
- No camping permitted except at Forest Campsite
- No rubbish – take it all away with you!

A There is a particular location where people can camp in the park.
B Rubbish must be left in the bins provided by the park.
C Pay special attention when cooking food on fires at the park.

**5**

**February's ski trip**
Places are still available, but the University must receive all forms by January 31st.
A photocopy of your Student ID must be attached to the form, or it will not be accepted.

A All students should take their identity cards on the ski trip.
B Students must apply for the ski trip before February.
C It is now too late to book a place on the ski trip.

Getting around 65

# 7

## Grammar
### The future

▶ Page 131 Grammar reference
Future forms

**1** Listen and complete the conversation between Mia and Owen with the correct verbs. Use the short forms of *be* and *will*.

**Mia:** Look at the rain, Owen.
**Owen:** Yes, I know. I'm hoping it **(1)** *'ll stop* soon, but I don't think there's much chance of that.
**Mia:** No, the weather forecast said it's a big storm and it **(2)** ................ for hours. What time do you have to be at the station?
**Owen:** I **(3)** ................ Jason and Mark there at 8.30, in the café near the main entrance. The train **(4)** ................ at 8.45.
**Mia:** It's quite a long walk to the station, isn't it? And it's 8.15 already. Look, I **(5)** ................ you in the car.
**Owen:** Thanks!

**2** Match the verb forms in Exercise 1 with uses a–e.

a for timetables and future dates  *4 leaves*
b for decisions at the moment of speaking
c for things that aren't certain, e.g. after *I think* or *I hope*
d for future arrangements
e for predictions based on evidence, and plans

**3** Put the words in order to make questions. Then ask and answer the questions.

1 the photos / will / send / you / when / me ?
   *1 When will you send me the photos?*
2 this evening / are / where / go / going / you / to ?
3 next English test / take / your / when / will / you ?
4 the Earth / get hotter / going / is / to ?
5 will / think / cloudy / it / do / tomorrow / you / be ?

**4** Work in pairs. What would you say in each of these situations? Tell your partner, using future forms.

1 'Do you want to come to a party with me?' (Tell your friend you can't.)
   > I'm sorry but I'm going to a concert with friends.
2 'I'm having trouble with my computer.' (Offer to help your friend.)
3 'When's the first day of your holiday?' (Tell your friend which date.)
4 'The wind is getting stronger.' (Say it's likely there will be a storm soon.)
5 'Which other language do you plan to study next year?' (Tell your partner.)

## Vocabulary
### Compound words

**1** Match the words in A with the words in B to form compound words. Then match the compound words with definitions 1–8.

A

> back   camp   cross   ~~guide~~   over   sight   sign   suit

B

> ~~book~~   case   night   pack   post   roads   seeing   site

1 a book that gives information about a place  *guidebook*
2 a bag with a handle for carrying clothes, etc.
3 a place where two roads meet and cross each other
4 a bag that you carry on your back
5 a sign by the road that gives information
6 from late evening until the morning
7 a place where people can stay overnight in tents
8 visiting interesting places

**2** Use compound words from Exercise 1 to complete Lewis's blog. Then listen and check.

# Travel Blog

HOME  POST  PHOTO  CONTACT

Next week I'm going to Australia! I'm arriving in the north, so first I'm going to stay **(1)** *overnight* in Darwin. My **(2)** ................ says it's an interesting city, so I think I'll do a bit of **(3)** ................ there. Then I'm getting the train to Alice Springs, right in the middle of the country, where I'll spend the night at a **(4)** ................ . The next day I'm hoping to get a lift down the main road. I'm taking all my things in a **(5)** ................ so that I don't have to carry a heavy **(6)** ................ around. About 200 kilometres south of Alice, I'll reach a **(7)** ................ where there's a **(8)** ................ that says 'Uluru 247 km'. Uluru is also known as Ayers Rock – one of the most amazing sights in the world.

UPLOAD   LIKE ✓

**3** /P/ **Word stress in compound words**
Listen again to Lewis. Does he stress the first part of answers 2–8, or the second? Underline the correct part of each word.

**4** Tell your partner about an exciting journey you would like to go on. Use compound words from Exercise 1 with the correct stress.

> I'd love to go sightseeing in New York …

## Grammar
### Prepositions of movement

▶ Page 132 Grammar reference
Prepositions of movement

**1** Complete this phone message about travelling around a city with the missing prepositions (*in*, *off*, etc.). Then listen to check.

Hi Leon, Toby here. I'm really pleased you're coming to our new house next week. The quickest way here is **(1)** *by* train to the city centre, which takes an hour and is usually **(2)** ................ time. Then you can get **(3)** ................ the number 64 bus to Edgely, getting **(4)** ................ by the stadium. From there it's a 15-minute walk. Or, if you don't feel like walking, you could jump **(5)** ................ a taxi and ask the driver to take you to the end of Valley Road. When you get **(6)** ................ of the taxi, you'll see our place right in front of you. See you soon!

**2** Use words from the message to complete the rules.

### Rules

1 For cars, we use *get* (or *jump*, *climb*, etc.) *into* or ................ , and ................ when we leave them.

2 For most other road vehicles, plus trains, planes, boats and horses, we use ................ or *onto*, and ................ when we leave them.

3 We travel ................ bus, train, plane or boat, or in other words, ................ road, rail, air, land or sea. We also say we are *on (board)* a train, plane or ship, or *at sea*.

4 If you arrive neither late nor early, you say you are (or the bus, train, plane, etc. is) ................ time.

**3** Some of the sentences contain mistakes made by exam candidates. Underline the mistakes and correct them.
1 You can get here in plane.
2 I jumped into my car.
3 The bus drivers are on strike, so everybody has to go by car.
4 Could you come at time, please?
5 I will travel with train.

**4** Work in groups. Think of a place you like in your town or city. Describe how to get there using public transport. Use prepositions of movement.

Getting around  67

# 7

## Speaking Part 2

▶ Page 154 Speaking bank

**1** Work in groups. Describe what you can see in the photo.

**2** Listen to Lorenzo. Which of the things you said in Exercise 1 did he mention? Did he describe anything else?

**3** Listen again and complete the sentences.
1 There are some trees on the left and I can see some green fields, ........*too*........ .
2 .................................. a train .................................. into the station.
3 .................................. some people .................................. to get on it.
4 They're very close to the railway lines, on the .................................. .................................. people stand.
5 She's wearing, .................................. .................................. carrying, a large bag on her shoulder.
6 The man's wearing a suit and he .................................. has a bag on his shoulder.
7 The train has big windows but they're a bit dark and I can't see the .................................. .................................. is driving it.

**4** Write your answers from Exercise 3 next to the uses (a–d).
a adding a point *too*
b correcting yourself
c describing actions
d describing things you don't know the name of

> **Exam advice**
> - Correct yourself if you make a mistake.
> - Before the exam, practise talking about pictures for a minute. Time yourself!

**5** Work in pairs, choose one of the photos and describe it to your partner.
- Use prepositions of movement and expressions from Exercise 3.
- Use adverbs such as *quite*, *really* or *rather*.
- Speak for at least one minute.
- After you finish speaking, ask your partner if you have described everything.

## Writing Part 1

▶ Page 145 Writing bank
An email

**1** Where would you put these expressions in an email? Write *B* for beginning or *E* for end.

Lots of love, *E*
Hi,
Looking forward to hearing from / seeing you.
Well, that's all for now.
All the best,
This is just a quick message to say …
It was great to hear from you.
Give my love to everyone.
Take care,
See you soon.
Don't forget to write soon.
Sorry I've taken so long to write back.
Bye for now.
Dear,

68

## 2 Look at the exam task and answer the questions.

1 Who is the email from and what is it about?
2 Which of the expressions from Exercise 1 does Thomas use?
3 Which future forms and which adverbs of degree does he use?
4 Which of these points (a–e) should you put in your reply? What else should you include?

a It doesn't matter that the writer has been slow to reply.
b What you will do before Saturday.
c Why you want to go.
d Where you want to eat.
e Where you want to meet.

Read this email from your English-speaking friend Thomas, and the notes you have made.

To:
From: Thomas

Hi,
Sorry I've taken so long to write back but I've been very busy with work. — *No problem!*

I'm going to an international music festival with some friends on Saturday morning. Would you like to go with us? There will be bands from all over the world, — *Yes, say why.* including some that play your favourite kind of music.

We'll be there all day so we'll need to eat. Do you want to take some food or buy something there? — *Tell Thomas.*

By the way, where will you meet us on Saturday? — *Suggest ...*

All the best,
Thomas

Write your email to Thomas in about **100** words, using **all** the **notes**.

## 3 Read the reply and answer these questions.

1 Is Marco's letter the correct length?
2 Which paragraph covers each of the notes?
3 Which language points (a–d) does Marco use? Give examples.

a expressions from Exercise 1
b adverbs of degree
c future forms
d *too* and *enough*

Hi Thomas,

Don't worry about that. This month I haven't had enough time to get anything done, either!

I'd love to go on Saturday. It'll be really great to see some live Latin American music, particularly Mexican bands and musicians from the Andes.

Food at the festival will be very expensive, so I think I'd better take sandwiches and drinks. Do you think that'll be enough?

I can meet you at the festival – the 64 bus will take me straight there. How about meeting at the main gates? I'll text you as soon as I arrive.

See you soon,

Marco

---

**Exam advice**
- If you are writing to a friend, use informal language.
- Always put the opening (e.g. *Hi Sam*), the closing (e.g. *Bye for now*) and your own name on separate lines.

## 4 Plan and write your email in about 100 words. Use expressions from Exercise 1.

## 5 Work in pairs. Read and check your partner's email.

1 Where you think there are mistakes, use a pencil to write *G* for grammar, *V* for vocabulary, *WO* for word order, or *Sp* for spelling.
2 Discuss your corrections together.
3 Correct any mistakes in your email.

Getting around

# 8 Influencers

1 **Zinedine Zidane's** parents were from Algeria but he grew up in France, where he played for the international football team. Now retired from playing football, he's a coach. All four of his sons have played football for Real Madrid's youth teams.

2 American singer, songwriter and actress **Miley Cyrus** is the daughter of the country singer, Billy Ray. Her brother Trace is a singer and guitarist while her grandfather Ron was a politician.

3 **Marie Curie** was the first woman to win a Nobel prize and the only person ever to win a prize in both physics and chemistry. Marie shared her prize in physics with her husband Pierre. Thirty-two years later, her daughter and son-in-law were given a Nobel prize in chemistry.

4 **Indira Gandhi** came from a family of Indian politicians. She was the daughter of India's first prime minister and then she became India's first female prime minister. Although Indira and the social leader Mahatma share the same family name, they aren't relatives. Indira changed her surname when she got married.

## Starting off

1 Work in groups. Discuss what you know about the famous families in the photos.

2 Match the descriptions of famous families (1–4) with the photos (A–D).

3 Work in pairs. Discuss the advantages and disadvantages of being famous and of being part of a famous family.

## Reading Part 6

**1** Work in pairs. Read part of a website and look at the photo. What do you think an *influencer* is? What do you know about these influencers?

### HOW PEOPLE ARE USING SOCIAL MEDIA TO INFLUENCE THE WORLD

**INFLUENCER #1**
Tanya Burr uploads videos on make-up, fashion and cooking. Over 3.7 million people have signed up for her YouTube channel. She has also set up her own make-up company.

**INFLUENCER #2**
With more than 380,000 followers, Marc Forne is one of Spain's biggest influencers. He uploads photos of himself in different parts of the world. Companies like Calvin Klein, Inditex and Louis Vuitton provide him with clothes and luggage.

**2** Read the rest of the text quickly. Do not complete the gaps for now. In what ways is Emma Watson an *influencer*?

**INFLUENCER #3**
Are all influencers just interested in being famous and making money? Perhaps not in the case of Emma Watson. Emma (1) ............... born in Paris but brought up in England. She took up acting at an early age and starred in her first Harry Potter film (2) ............... she was just eleven years old. By the time she was 19, she was earning more money (3) ............... any other Hollywood actress.

Around that time, Emma went to university to do an English degree. She also became well known (4) ............... a speaker on how men and women should be given the same opportunities. She travelled to places like Bangladesh and Zambia (5) ............... support education for girls. Thousands of Emma Watson's fans follow her on social media, but she uses her accounts to discuss issues such as women in society and the effect of fashion (6) ............... the environment.

---

**Exam advice**
- You must complete each space with one word only and your spelling must be correct.
- If you can't fill in a gap, go on to the others and come back to it later.
- When you have filled in all the gaps, check your completed text makes sense.

**3** For each question, write the correct answer. Write one word in each gap. There is an example at the beginning.

**4** Exam candidates often make spelling mistakes. Underline the mistakes in the sentences and correct them.

1. She's clever. She's very funny to.
2. We where both young when I first met her in school.
3. He plays soccer very well, an he's the junior world champion in shooting.
4. At first I thought she was shy because she was a very quite girl.
5. I love spending time whit him. I can say that he's my best friend.
6. I like to do my homework with Daniela becouse she is intelligent.

**5** Work in groups. Discuss these questions.
- How often do you use social networks? What do you use them for?
- Do you follow anyone online? Who? Why?
- Do you think that celebrities should use social media to talk about social issues? Why? / Why not?
- What do you think of influencers? What are some of the positive and negative effects?

Influencers 71

# 8

## Vocabulary
### Phrasal verbs

**1** Look at the underlined phrasal verbs. Decide what each one means by looking at the complete sentence.

1. Zinedine Zidane's parents were from Algeria but he <u>grew up</u> in France.
2. Tanya Burr has <u>set up</u> her own make-up company.
3. Emma Watson was born in Paris but was <u>brought up</u> in England.
4. She <u>took up</u> acting at an early age.

**2** Replace each <u>underlined</u> expression with the correct form of a phrasal verb from the box, so that the meaning stays the same.

| bring up | find out | get on with |
| ~~grow up~~ | make up | run out (of) |
| set up | take up | |

1. I was born in a small village but I <u>became older</u> in Athens with my parents and two brothers. *grew up*
2. When my phone <u>doesn't have any more</u> battery, I borrow a friend's phone.
3. I'd love to <u>start</u> my own YouTube channel.
4. If I had to choose a new sport, I would <u>start playing</u> hockey.
5. I <u>have a good relationship with</u> my older sister. We often go out together.
6. If I didn't know an answer in an important interview, I would never <u>invent</u> one.
7. If I <u>discovered</u> that my boss was reading my emails, I wouldn't get angry.
8. I was <u>looked after</u> in the countryside, but now I live in a city.

**3** Rewrite four or five of the sentences in Exercise 2 so that they are true for you. Use phrasal verbs.

*1 I was born in Naples but I grew up in Rome, the capital city of Italy.*

**4** Work in groups. Compare your sentences. Find things that you have got in common.

## Grammar
### Zero, first and second conditionals

▶ **Page 133 Grammar reference**
Conditional sentences

**1** Kristian has been offered a place on a reality TV show, but he's studying at university and wants to finish his degree. What advice would you give him?

**2** Listen to the conversation and answer the questions.
1. What advice does Ella give Kristian?
2. Do you agree with this advice?

**3** Listen and complete the sentences with the correct form of the verb in brackets.
1. If I ......*take up*...... (take up) the offer, I ......*'ll have*...... (have) to give up my degree.
2. If you ............... (speak) to your tutor, I'm sure she ............... (understand).
3. And you ............... (have) to leave if you ............... (not pass) the year!

**4** The sentences from Exercise 3 are all examples of conditionals. Conditionals are often divided into different types. Match each type of conditional (sentences 1–3) with the rules (a–c).

- **Sentence 1:** Type 1 (First conditional)   Rule ...............
- **Sentence 2:** Type 2 (Second conditional)   Rule ...............
- **Sentence 3:** Type 0 (Zero conditional)   Rule ...............

### Rules

a This is used when the speaker is not thinking about a real possibility but is imagining a situation that will probably not happen.

b This expresses things which are always or generally true.

c This expresses a real possibility in the future.

**5** What form of the verb do we use in each conditional type? Do we use a comma in all conditional sentences?

*Type 0 (Zero conditional): If + present simple, present simple*

## 6 /P/ Conditional sentences: contracted words

Listen. How many words are missing from each sentence? Contractions (*I'll* etc.) are two words.

1 And if I ......*don't finish my degree,*...... what will everyone say? ......*(5 words)*......
2 If you .................................................. pass the year. ....................................
3 If I .................................................. to the university. ....................................

## 7 Listen again and complete the sentences in Exercise 6.

## 8 Complete these sentences with the correct form of the verbs in brackets.

1 If it ......*rains*...... (rain) this weekend, I'll go to the cinema.
2 I often spend the day at the beach if the weather .............................. (be) good.
3 If I .............................. (get) home late, I have to make my own dinner.
4 I .............................. (not go out) next Saturday if there is something good on TV.
5 I .............................. (buy) some crisps if I get hungry on my way home tonight.
6 If I .............................. (not sleep) well at night, I'm in a bad mood all day.

## 9 Rewrite the sentences in Exercise 8 so that they are true for you. In pairs, compare your answers.

## 10 Complete these sentences with your own ideas. Use the first or second conditional.

1 If I lost my mobile phone,
   ......*I'd go to the nearest police station*......
2 If I'm not busy on Saturday,
   ....................................................................
3 If I was an influencer,
   ....................................................................
4 If a TV channel offered me a place on a reality show,
   ....................................................................
5 If my favourite sports team
   ........................................................., I'd
   ....................................................................

## 11 Write a question for each of the sentences in Exercise 10. Then ask and answer the questions in pairs.

> What would you do if you lost your mobile phone?
>> I'd go to the nearest police station.

## *when*, *if* and *unless*

▶ Page 133 Grammar reference
Conjunctions: *when*, *if*, *unless* + present, future

### 1 Work in pairs. Josh, Hayley and Oliver are going to a conference for a week. Read their messages below and decide which person will definitely contact their friends or family.

> Good luck with your talk, Josh!
>> Thanks. I'll send you a message **if** I need anything. 😊

> Keep in touch, Hayley!
>> Don't worry! I'll let you know **when** we get there. 😊

> Safe trip, Oliver!
>> Sure! 👍 I'll call you tonight **unless** we get there really late.

### 2 Complete the rules using *if*, *unless* or *when*.

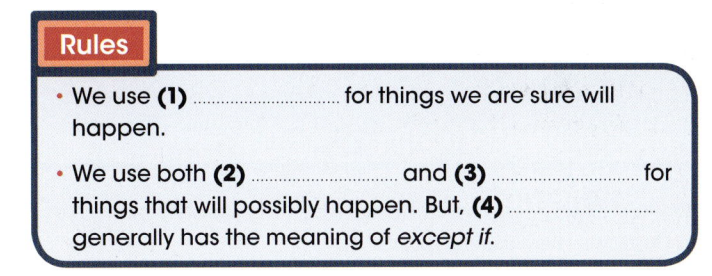

**Rules**

- We use **(1)** .............................. for things we are sure will happen.
- We use both **(2)** .............................. and **(3)** .............................. for things that will possibly happen. But, **(4)** .............................. generally has the meaning of *except if*.

### 3 Choose the best option in *italics*.

1 I'll go out *if* / *when* I finish this report on Friday.
2 I wouldn't be able to write very well *if* / *when* I broke my right hand.
3 We'll miss the bus *if* / *unless* we run.
4 Maya won't play tennis tomorrow *if* / *unless* it rains.
5 She can't hear you well *when* / *unless* you shout.
6 Jake will give us a lift *when* / *unless* he gets home.

Influencers 73

# 8

## Listening Part 3

**1** Work in pairs and answer the questions.
- How often do you watch videos online?
- Do you have a favourite video channel? Which one?
- Have you (or anyone you know) ever created your own channel? What was it about? What did you think of it?

**2** You will hear a man called Ben Richards talking about how to get famous on YouTube. Before you listen, read the information below. Decide what is missing in each space (a number, date, time, noun, etc.).

### How to become famous on YouTube ▶▶

About **(1)** ............................ hours of videos are uploaded to YouTube every minute.

Videos about **(2)** ............................ are usually more popular than all other types.

People want to find out about the video presenter, so be **(3)** ............................ .

Make at least ten videos before telling people about your **(4)** ............................ .

Make sure each new video has a **(5)** ............................ which is easy to understand.

And be patient! It may take two or three **(6)** ............................ to become well known.

### Exam advice
- There is always enough time between the six answers for you to write down the missing words.
- Be careful with spelling, especially if the word is spelt out in the recording or if it is a very common word, e.g. *day*.

**3** Listen to the talk. For each question, write the correct answer in the gap. Write one or two words or a number or a date or a time. Then listen again and check.

**4** Work in groups. Your local university wants to create a video to welcome exchange students and visiting lecturers. Talk together about the different kinds of information you could include (the place, the people, activities, etc.).

**5** Share your ideas for Exercise 4 with the whole class.

## Vocabulary
### Describing people

**1** Carter is talking to his friend Will about finding a presenter for his new YouTube channel. Listen and look at the pictures. Who does Carter choose?

A

B

C

D

74

**2** Work in pairs. Complete the mind map with words from the box.

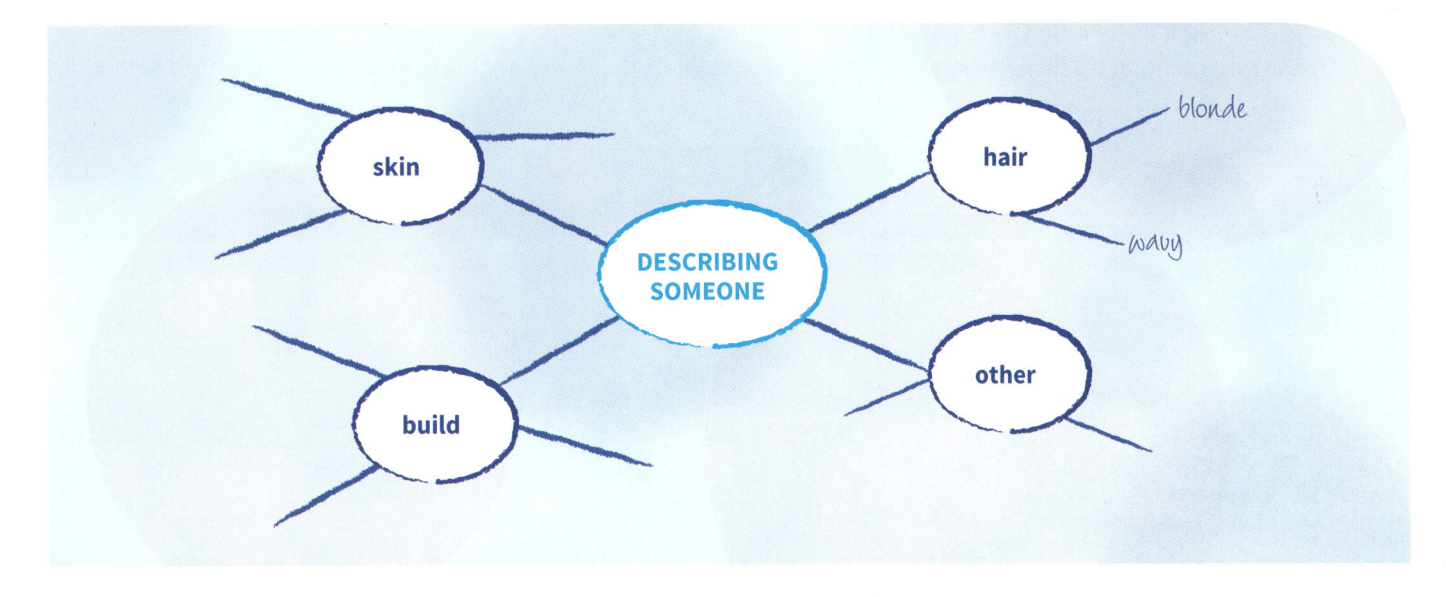

- skin
- hair — blonde, wavy
- DESCRIBING SOMEONE
- build
- other

attractive  bald  beard  beautiful  blond(e)  broad shoulders  curly  dark  fair  good-looking  grey  long  medium height  moustache  pale  plain  red  scar  short  slim  straight  wavy

**3** Write the opposites of the adjectives.

anxious  ~~easygoing~~  generous  lazy  polite  quiet  shy  stupid

1 strict  *easygoing*
2 hard-working
3 smart
4 noisy
5 mean
6 rude
7 calm
8 confident

**4** Will describes one of the people as *honest* and *reliable*. Add *un-*, *im-* or *dis-* to make the adjectives negative.

...*un*...friendly        ............honest
............patient         ............reliable
............pleasant

**5** Add *-ful* or *-less* to the nouns to make adjectives.

1 success  .....*successful*..... (someone who has a lot of success)
2 cheer ........................... (someone who is usually happy and positive)
3 beauty ........................... (someone or something who looks good)
4 help ........................... (someone who likes to help)
5 help ........................... (someone who can't help themselves)

**6** Exam candidates often make mistakes with adjective order. Read the rules and correct one mistake in each example a–f.

### Rules

1 Adjectives generally go <u>before</u> the noun and we don't normally use more than two adjectives before each noun.
   a In my tennis club, there are two coaches very nice.
   b My best friend has hair and eyes brown.
2 When there are two adjectives together, we generally put the 'opinion' adjective before the 'fact' adjective.
   c At the beginning of the film, a young handsome man is sitting in a café.
   d She is wearing a white beautiful dress.
3 When there are two fact adjectives together, we generally put those that describe shape or size before those describing colour.
   e I've made a new friend with black short hair.
   f He lives in a house with a green big garden.

**7** Work in pairs. Take turns to describe the people below. Don't say who it is. Talk about their appearance and their character. Guess who your partner is describing.

- someone else in this class
- a teacher or lecturer at this college
- a famous person

> He's almost bald, medium height and quite attractive. He's often cheerful and he's always patient.

> Is it your lecturer?

Influencers  75

# 8

## Speaking Part 1

▶ Page 152 Speaking bank

**1** Listen to three candidates doing a Speaking Part 1 test. Complete their answers.

🎧 43

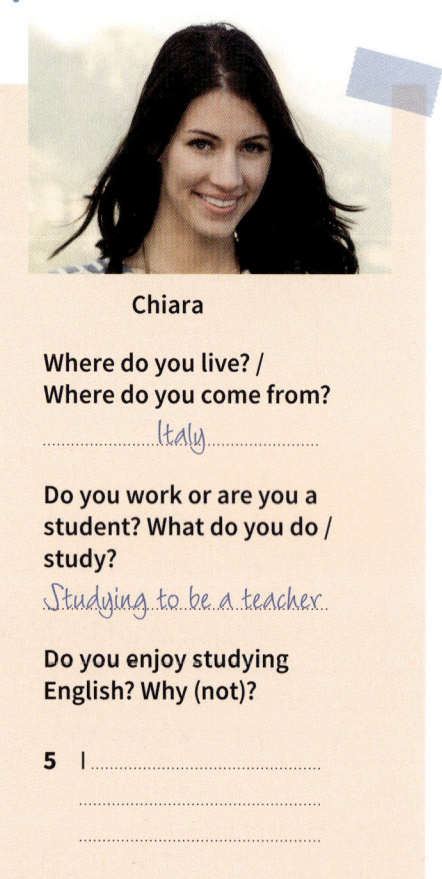

### Chiara

**Where do you live? / Where do you come from?**
Italy

**Do you work or are you a student? What do you do / study?**
Studying to be a teacher

**Do you enjoy studying English? Why (not)?**

**5** I …………………………………

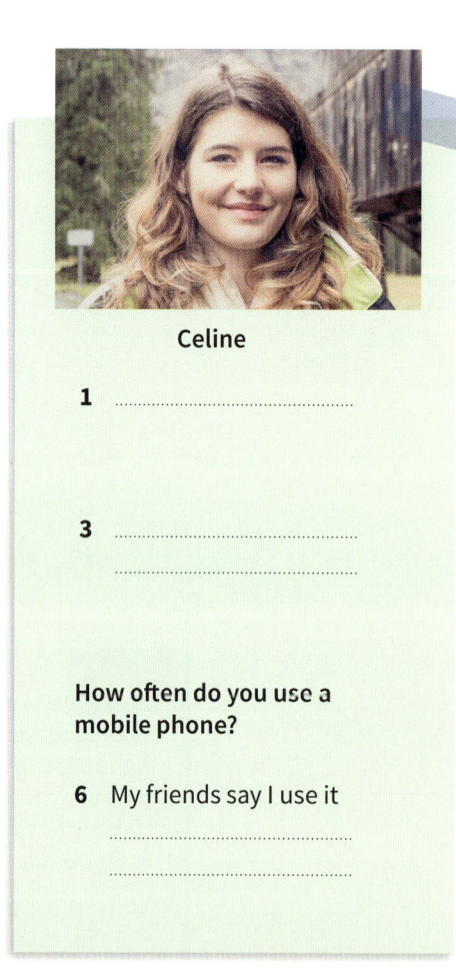

### Celine

**1** …………………………………

**3** …………………………………

**How often do you use a mobile phone?**

**6** My friends say I use it …………………………………

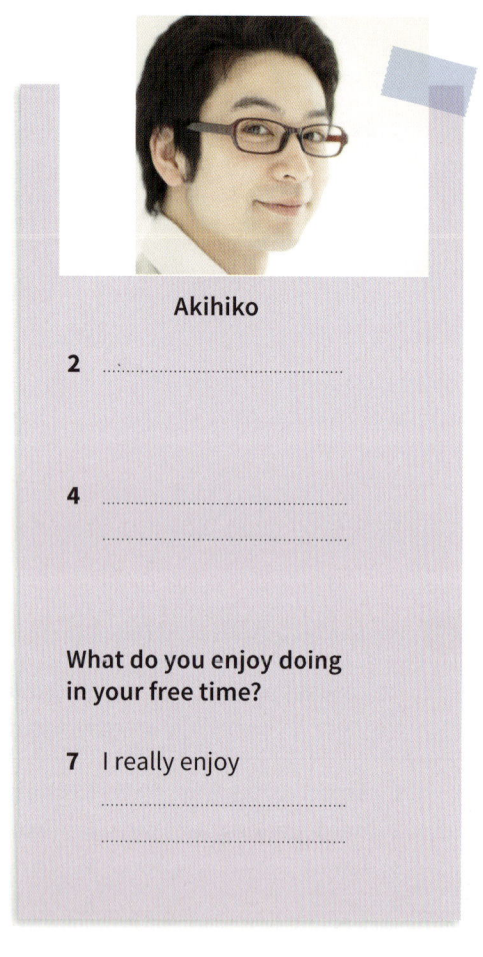

### Akihiko

**2** …………………………………

**4** …………………………………

**What do you enjoy doing in your free time?**

**7** I really enjoy …………………………………

---

**2** Listen again and answer the questions.

🎧 43

1. Do you think the candidates answer their last questions well? Why / Why not?
2. What does Celine say when she doesn't understand the examiner's question?
3. Does the examiner repeat the same question to Celine?

> • The examiner will ask you general questions about where you live, your daily routine, things you like, etc.
> • Always try to give more than a one-word answer.
> • Don't try to repeat sentences you have already prepared.
>
> **Exam advice**

**3** Read this part of a Speaking Part 1 test. How could you improve Enrico's answers?

**Examiner:** What's your name?
**Enrico:** Enrico.
**Examiner:** Where do you live, Enrico?
**Enrico:** Porto, Portugal.
**Examiner:** Do you work or are you a student?
**Enrico:** Work.
**Examiner:** What do you do?
**Enrico:** Journalist.

**4** Work in groups of three. Take turns to be the examiner. Ask and answer the first three questions from the table in Exercise 1, and one extra question.

76

## Writing Part 2

▶ Page 148 Writing bank
An article

**1** Work in groups. Look at the information from the *Cambridge Learner's Dictionary* about punctuation on page 162. Which of the uses are the same in your language?

**2** Exam candidates often make mistakes with punctuation. There is no punctuation in sentences 1–6. Correct the mistakes.

1 dear sam i had a great time with my friends last weekend too
2 what about you who is your best friend
3 on saturday i took my cousins dog to the beach
4 after that we ate salad chicken and ice cream
5 he loves english he thinks that its easy
6 im looking forward to seeing you soon

**3** Read this Writing Part 2 exam task and underline the important words.

---

You see this notice in an international English-language magazine.

### Articles wanted!
#### The person who I admire

*Who is it? Is it a member of your family, a friend or perhaps someone famous?
What does he or she look like?
What is he or she like?
Why do you admire him or her?*

Write an article answering these questions and we will publish the most interesting articles in our magazine.

Write your **article** in about **100** words.

---

**4** Read Zahra's answer. Do you think her teacher gave her full marks? Why / Why not?

If i had to choose one person, it would be my cousin Hasan. He was born in Istanbul but he grew up in London. Hes medium height with curly dark hair an brown eyes. Everybody gets on well whit him becouse he's easygoing honest and reliable. Apart from being such a nice person, Hasan is hardworking and generous to. He's always been keen on drawing. When he was just 19 years old, he set up his own online company wich sells his T-shirt designs. He gives some of the money he earns to help an international children's charity

**5** Answer the questions and check your ideas in Exercise 4.

1 Does the article include all the information for the task?
2 Does the article use adjectives to describe the person?
3 Does the article give reasons and examples? (e.g. *Why is Hasan generous?*)
4 Is the punctuation and spelling correct?
5 Is the article about 100 words?

**6** Read Zahra's article again. Underline and correct her five spelling mistakes and her four punctuation mistakes.

> **Exam advice**
> - If you are asked to describe someone or something, don't write long lists of adjectives. Give reasons and examples instead.
> - Always check your work, in particular your punctuation and spelling.

**7** Now write your own answer to the task from Exercise 3.

**8** Use the writing checklist in Exercise 5 to check your work.

Influencers

# 7 Vocabulary and grammar review

## Grammar

**1** Complete sentences 1–8 using *too* or *enough* and the adjectives from the box.

> big  cold  dark  expensive  old
> sleepy  thick  ~~warm~~

1 Put the heating on, please. It's not *warm enough* in this room.
2 I'd like to wear those shoes but they aren't ................. for me. I'm size 44.
3 It was nearly midnight and it was ................. to see anything.
4 You can't skate on the lake. The ice isn't ................. to be safe.
5 I must go to bed. I'm ................. to stay awake any longer.
6 My sister's only 16, so she's not ................. to drive a car yet.
7 Put a jumper on. It's ................. to go outside in just a T-shirt and jeans.
8 I really liked that laptop but it was ................. for me to buy.

**2** Choose the correct option in *italics*.

1 **A:** How's Andrea these days?
   **B:** She *'ll / ('s going to)* have a baby.

2 **A:** Have you got any plans for tonight?
   **B:** Yes, I *meet / 'm meeting* Ryan at 9 o'clock.

3 **A:** You look tired.
   **B:** Yes, I think I *'m going / 'll go* to bed early.

4 **A:** When's the last bus?
   **B:** The timetable says it *leaves / is leaving* at midnight.

5 **A:** My computer has just crashed!
   **B:** Don't worry. I *'m going to / 'll* repair it.

6 **A:** The score's now England 0, Brazil 5!
   **B:** Brazil *will / are going* to win.

## Vocabulary

**3** Match the beginnings of the sentences with the endings.

1 It's much healthier to go by      *d*
2 We left the terminal and got onto   ......
3 The driver and passenger got into   ......
4 In big cities, many people go by    ......
5 You should let other people get off ......
6 The police told the thief to get out of ......

a the car and drove to the airport.
b bus instead of taking the car.
c the train before you get on.
d bike than to sit in a car or a bus.
e the car and put his hands up.
f the plane, after a six-hour delay.

**4** Complete the crossword with words from Unit 7.

**Across**
1 below a temperature of 0°C
4 the opposite of 'hot'
6 a place where two roads meet
7 a bag you carry when you travel somewhere
8 a word which means the same as 'very much'
9 a bright light you see in a thunderstorm

**Down**
2 something you read before or when you travel to a new place on holiday
3 visiting interesting places
5 a type of weather when you can't see things very well

# Vocabulary and grammar review 8

## Vocabulary

**1** Choose the correct word for each gap.

### ANGELIQUE KIDJO

Angelique, also **(1)** *known* as The Queen of African Music, is one of the greatest female singers **(2)** ................. the world. She was born in Cotonou, Benin, West Africa, and she **(3)** ................. in Cotonou with eight brothers and sisters. Her uncles, aunts and grandparents come from Ouidah, a small village. She was **(4)** ................. in a family of performers. Angelique took **(5)** ................. singing when she was six years old. Angelique is good **(6)** ................. languages and sings in French, English and two African languages: Fon and Yoruba.

By the 1980s, the political situation in Benin was difficult. Angelique said to herself, 'Unless I **(7)** ................. Benin, I'll have problems.' In 1983 she left for Paris, France, where she studied both Jazz and Law. She couldn't decide between being a lawyer or a musician but thought, 'I will make a bigger difference to the world **(8)** ................. I become a musician' and so she developed her music career. She first **(9)** ................. her future husband, who is musician Jean Hebrail, at Le CIM, a jazz school in Paris. Now they both live in New York. She has also been a Goodwill Ambassador for UNICEF **(10)** ................. 2002, helping to bring education to children all over the world, in particular in Africa.

| 1 | A told | B called | C named | D known |
| --- | --- | --- | --- | --- |
| 2 | A of | B in | C on | D at |
| 3 | A grew up | B got on with | C grew | D born |
| 4 | A set up | B made up | C brought up | D grown up |
| 5 | A on | B off | C out | D up |
| 6 | A in | B at | C on | D of |
| 7 | A leave | B don't leave | C will leave | D won't leave |
| 8 | A when | B unless | C if | D so |
| 9 | A knew | B found out | C made up | D met |
| 10 | A for | B in | C since | D ago |

**2** Exam candidates often make mistakes with punctuation and spelling. Correct one mistake in each of the following sentences.

1 I only go shopping if I have to becouse most of the shops are expensive.
2 I've just received your email. You ask me wich film stars I like.
3 Since than we have been very good friends.
4 You asked me if i had fun last weekend.
5 On friday, my family and I got on a boat to the island.
6 I think you now him. He is called Patrick.

## Grammar

**3** Complete these conditional sentences, using your own ideas.

1 If I didn't have to work, … *I'd spend more time with my friends.*
2 If I stay up late, …
3 If I found a wallet on the floor, …
4 I won't go out if …
5 When I stop learning English, …
6 I'd be annoyed if …
7 Unless the weather is awful, …
8 If I could live in another country, …

**4** Read this text about Jane's favourite cousin, Axel, and think of the word which best fits each gap. Use only one word in each gap.

If I had to choose a favourite member of my family, I **(1)** *would* choose my cousin Axel. He's rather short, **(2)** ................. curly blond hair and green eyes. He's **(3)** ................. very easy-going person who never gets angry. Now he's studying at university in Germany but he grew **(4)** ................. in Innsbruck in Austria. We haven't seen each other **(5)** ................. about two years. He'll come and visit me this summer, unless he has **(6)** ................. work in his dad's café.

Vocabulary and grammar review 79

# 9 Stay fit and healthy

## how FIT AND ACTIVE ARE you?

Take this short and simple test to find out …

1. **How do you usually go to work?**
   - A I go by car.
   - B I use public transport.
   - C I walk or cycle.

2. **What's your perfect way to spend a free afternoon?**
   - A shopping with friends
   - B relaxing at home
   - C going for a run, playing football or doing another sport

3. **How many times a week do you actually exercise? (You can include things like dancing or doing housework.)**
   - A never
   - B 3–4 times
   - C most days

4. **You're bored and want to find something to do. What's your first choice?**
   - A Go for a bike ride, or go out for a walk.
   - B Chat online with your friends.
   - C Meet up with your friends.

5. **If you have to run to catch a bus or train, how do you feel afterwards?**
   - A I'm exhausted.
   - B I'm fit, so I feel fine.
   - C I'm a bit out of breath.

6. **How much time do you usually spend watching TV or online entertainment?**
   - A more than two hours a day
   - B 1–2 hours a day
   - C less than an hour a day

## Starting off

1. Work in pairs. Look at the photos. Discuss what the people are doing and how often you do these kinds of activities.

2. Work in pairs. Do the quiz.

3. Check your score on page 162. Should you make any changes to the way you live? Why? / Why not?

80

## Listening Part 2

**1** Look at the first two lines of questions 1–6 in Exercise 2. Answer the questions.
- What's the situation in each question?
- Who will you hear?
- What do you have to listen for?

> **Exam advice**
> - Make sure you always know which question and which situation you are listening to.
> - After you hear each situation and write your answer, forget about that question and move on to the next one.

**2** Listen to people talking in six different situations. For each question, choose the correct answer. Then listen again and check.

1. You will hear a woman telling her friend about running in a 20-kilometre race. Why did she decide to run in the race?
    - A  A friend intended to take part.
    - B  She wanted to win a prize.
    - C  It would improve her level of fitness.

2. You will hear two friends talking about a film they have just watched. They agree that
    - A  there was a surprising ending.
    - B  it was better than the previous film they saw.
    - C  everyone else in the cinema seemed to like it.

3. You will hear a student telling his friend about his bicycle. Why does he want to sell it?
    - A  He rarely uses it.
    - B  He needs the money.
    - C  He would like to buy a better bike.

4. You will hear a young man telling his friend about a concert he went to. He thought it was
    - A  rather boring.
    - B  too short.
    - C  very expensive.

5. You will hear a man telling his friend about his illness. How does he feel now?
    - A  He has a high temperature.
    - B  His stomach still hurts.
    - C  He gets tired very quickly.

6. You will hear two friends talking about their local sports centre. They agree that
    - A  it offers a good range of activities.
    - B  it is an easy place to get to.
    - C  it charges too much for some sports.

## Vocabulary
### Illnesses and accidents

**1** Listen and read the sentence. Then answer the questions.

*I had a nasty cough, a sore throat and a stomach ache.*
1. How do we say the underlined words?
2. What do they mean?

**2** A *cough*, *sore throat* and *stomach ache* are types of illness. Work in pairs. Decide if the words in the box are types of illness, accidents or treatments.

> aspirin   bandage   bruise   cut   earache   fever   flu
> fracture   high temperature   injury   medicine
> operation   pill   plaster   plaster cast
> sprain   test   wound   X-ray

*injury – accident*

**3** Write the verb forms of the nouns.
1. injury  *injure*
2. cut
3. bruise
4. cough
5. sprain

**4** Look at the examples. Complete the rules with *illnesses*, *treatments* or *parts of the body*.

*I've cut my thumb.*
*She injured her leg.*
*He's got the flu.*
*I've had an operation.*
*Joe took a pill for his headache.*
*A nurse put a bandage on my arm.*

> **Rules**
> 1 We normally use *me, your, their,* etc. with ...................
> 2 We use *have* or *have got* with ...................
> 3 We use *take, have* or *put* with ...................

**5** Work in groups. Find someone who has done the things in the box. Ask them what happened, how they felt and how they got better.

> sprained their ankle   had the flu   taken an aspirin
> broken a bone   had a bandage put on   had a sore throat
> taken medicine   had a stomach ache   put a plaster on

Have you ever sprained your ankle?

Yes I have, when I was running.

How did you feel?

Stay fit and healthy   81

# 9

## Grammar
### Relative clauses

▶ Page 134 Grammar reference
Defining and non-defining relative clauses

**1** Read this text about sports injuries and choose the correct relative pronoun in *italics*.

Most people **(1)** *which / that* do regular sport are healthier, and often feel happier, than those **(2)** *who / whose* do little or no exercise. Care must be taken, though, to avoid the injuries **(3)** *when / which* sport can sometimes cause. People who run or do the long jump, for instance, often injure themselves **(4)** *when / which* they don't warm up properly. Training **(5)** *where / that* involves doing the same exercise again and again can cause serious damage, particularly to athletes in their teens, **(6)** *whose / which* bodies are still developing. It is important not to do too much too soon. Everyone should 'warm up' before they begin – if possible in the place **(7)** *who / where* they are going to exercise. It is important, too, for people to follow any safety advice **(8)** *when / that* they receive.

**2** Complete the rules with the correct words from Exercise 1.

### Rules

**Defining relative clauses**

We use **defining** relative clauses to give **essential information** about someone or something we are talking about.

We use:
- (1) ...*that*... and (2) .................. for people
- (3) .................. and (4) .................. for things
- (5) .................. for times
- (6) .................. for places
- (7) .................. for possessions.

**3** Complete the sentences with *where*, *which*, *when*, *who*, *whose* or *that*. Sometimes there may be more than one possible answer.

1. The TV series ...*which/that*... starts tonight is about doctors.
2. People .................. swim a lot are usually quite fit.
3. This is the park .................. I fell over and injured myself when I was younger.
4. I had a horrible cough .................. took about two weeks to go away.
5. Elena has a brother .................. name is Ryan.
6. Winter is the time .................. many people get the flu.

**4** Work in pairs. Complete the sentences in as many ways as you can.

1. Going shopping is something which … *I really enjoy! / I do once a month.*
2. The living room is the place where …
3. Watching sport is something that …
4. Summer holidays are the time when …
5. A good friend is someone who …
6. I know somebody whose …

### Rules

**Non-defining relative clauses**

- We use **non-defining** relative clauses to add **extra information** about someone or something.
- **Commas** separate this clause from the rest of the sentence.
- We **cannot** use *that* to begin a non-defining relative clause.

**5** Look at the rules. Then answer the questions.

1. What is the relative pronoun in the sentence below?

*Cycling to school, **which is very healthy**, is getting more and more common.*

2. What is the relative clause?
3. Does the sentence make sense without the relative clause?
4. Can we leave out the relative pronoun from the non-defining relative clause?

82

**6** Rewrite the pairs of sentences 1–6 as one sentence. Use non-defining relative clauses.

1 My arm is better now. I hurt it last week.
My arm, which ...... I hurt last week, is better now. ......

2 My cousin Sally works in the hospital. You met her.
My cousin, who ......................................................

3 We went to the lake in the next valley. We hired a boat there. The lake, where ......................................................

4 Ricky is my best friend. His sister is a teacher.
Ricky, whose ......................................................

5 In 2018 the sports centre opened. I was 19 then.
The sports centre opened in 2018, when ......................................................

6 Surfing is popular in my country. It is a new Olympic sport. Surfing, which is a new Olympic sport, ......................................................

**7** Exam candidates often make mistakes with relative clauses. Underline the mistakes in the sentences and correct them.

1 I want to know who sport is your favourite.
2 I can play my favourite sport, that is tennis.
3 They filmed students which were playing football.
4 This is the book who my best friend Joey gave me.
5 One sport who I think is good is swimming.
6 I want to learn more about tennis, that is my hobby.

## Vocabulary
### Sports

**1** Match comments 1–3 with pictures A–C. Do you like or watch any of these sports? Why / Why not?

1 'Doing Taekwondo is great exercise and I'm going to get my black belt soon!'
2 'I really enjoy playing volleyball – it's so fast-moving.'
3 'I always look forward to going surfing in the summer.'

**2** Look at comments 1–3 from Exercise 1 again. Which verb (*do*, *go* or *play*) do we use with each sport?

**3** Do we use *do*, *go* or *play* with these nouns?

athletics   baseball   basketball   climbing
cycling   football   golf   gymnastics
ice hockey   jogging   mountain biking
rollerblading   running   skateboarding
skiing   swimming   tennis   volleyball

**4** Choose the correct option in *italics*.

We usually use …
1 *go / play* with sports that use balls.
2 *do / go* with outdoor sports.
3 *do / play* with the word *sports* and activities which we do alone.

**5** Exam candidates often make mistakes with verbs and nouns. Underline and correct the mistakes.

1 I practise horse riding twice a week.
2 You can make a lot of sports and activities.
3 In winter you can make snowboarding.
4 We have done table tennis.
5 At first, we made aerobics.
6 We played windsurfing.

**6** Work in groups. Write down sports that are played in these places. How many do you know?

- on a court
- in a gym
- on a pitch
- in a stadium
- on a track

**7** Which of these clothes and equipment are used in each sport?

bat   boots   gloves   helmet
net   racket   trainers

**8** Complete the sentences with the verbs from the box.

~~beat~~   draw   lose   score   win

1 You ......beat...... a player or team.
2 You ........................ a goal.
3 You ........................ , ........................ or ........................ a match or game.

**9** Work in groups. Discuss which sports you like or dislike. Which is the most popular sport?

Stay fit and healthy   83

# 9

**Reading Part 3**

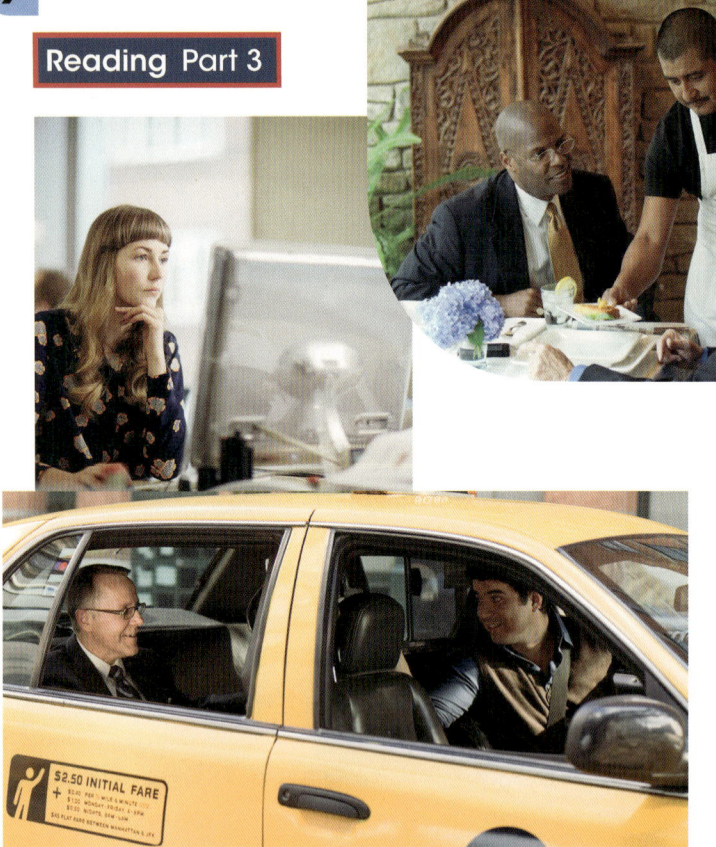

# EXERCISE AT WORK

How many hours a day do you spend sitting down? According to research from AXA PPP Healthcare, nearly three-quarters of workers spend 4 to 8 hours sitting during office hours. In addition, 27% sit for 30–60 minutes travelling to and from work, and 81% spend between 2 and 6 hours of their leisure time sitting down. Worryingly, 73% have had health problems such as back, neck and shoulder pain, which may all be caused by long periods without moving.

Evie Scott experienced just that after she had changed job. 'I used to work in a department store, where I was on my feet talking to customers all day,' she says, 'but I needed a higher salary so I got an office job instead. That meant many hours sitting at a desk and I soon found I had less energy and also various aches and pains. Although the challenge of the new job was quite exciting and I quickly made friends there, for a while I wondered whether I'd made a big mistake.'

So Evie, who travels into town by rail every day, decided to do something about her fitness level. She explains: 'I didn't want to move house and it took far too long by bike, but what's really helped is getting off several stations before the city centre and then walking. I'm also thinking of going to the gym opposite work, and I might also take up squash after work, too. Some of my workmates say it's made them much fitter.'

She's made some small changes at work, too. 'I avoid sitting still for too long, for instance by making phone calls standing up, walking over to colleagues' desks rather than emailing them and simply standing up every ten minutes. I've even moved things like my printer so that I have to get up to use it. I get some funny looks but I really don't care. Actually, it helps if others are involved because then you can have short meetings standing up, or walking around the office. Over a working day all this adds up to a fair amount of extra exercise, which I'm convinced helps me work more efficiently – and happily.'

**1** Work in pairs. Look at the photos and discuss the questions.

- Do any of the people in the pictures have a job that is good for their health? Why? / Why not?
- How many hours a day do you spend sitting down while you are:
  working or studying / travelling to work or college / at home?
- Do you think you spend too much time sitting down? If so, how could you reduce this?

**2** Read the exam instructions and follow these steps.

1 Look at the title of the text and the first line of each question. Decide which questions ask you to understand the whole text, and which only part of the text.
2 For each of the questions where you only have to read part of the text, find the paragraph you need.
3 Write the question number next to that paragraph.
4 Read what the text says about that question and decide on your answer.

**Exam advice**

- Most of these questions focus on opinion and attitude, not fact.
- The last question may ask about the general meaning of the text.

**3** For each question, choose the correct answer.

1. What is the writer doing in the first paragraph?
   A advising people what to do if they have back pain
   B warning people against taking office jobs
   C suggesting ways office workers can get more exercise
   D explaining why most people are spending more time sitting down

2. At first, how did Evie feel about working in the office?
   A She found her job rather boring.
   B She missed chatting with other shop assistants.
   C She felt she wasn't paid enough there.
   D She began to feel less healthy.

3. Evie believes that she feels better as a result of
   A doing sports with colleagues.
   B training in a gym near her office.
   C doing shorter train journeys.
   D cycling to and from work.

4. What does Evie say about getting exercise in the office?
   A Don't listen to any colleagues who start laughing at you.
   B You may find that it reduces the amount of work you can do.
   C Doing a lot of little things can make a big difference.
   D It's best for each person to exercise on their own.

5. Which message might Evie send to a friend?
   A 'I'd like to do more exercise at work but I worry about what my colleagues might think.'
   B 'I'm enjoying this job a lot more now that I'm keeping myself more active during the day.'
   C 'I really regret leaving my job at the store and one day I would like to go back there.'
   D 'I would rather live near the office so that I could spend less time travelling to and from work.'

**4** Work in pairs. Look at these tips for getting more daily exercise. Discuss which you think might be useful. Say why.

HOME    POST    **TIPS**    PHOTOS    CONTACT

1 Don't take a seat on the bus or train. Always stand.
2 Stand up to read paper documents or textbooks.
3 Go for walks to local parks in your lunch break with colleagues.
4 Use the stairs instead of taking the lift. Try to climb them two at a time!
5 Move while you're working. For instance, stand up to take phone calls and slowly turn your upper body from side to side.
6 Walk faster to work or college, going up hills if possible. Get a phone app or special watch to record the number of steps you take. Try to increase the number each day.

Stay fit and healthy

# 9

## Grammar
### Past perfect

▶ Page 135 Grammar reference
Past perfect

**1** We use the past perfect when we are already talking about the past and we want to say something happened earlier. Look at the sentences. Then answer the questions.

*Evie Scott experienced just that after she had changed job.*

*For a while I wondered whether I'd made a big mistake.*

1 How do we form the past perfect? What is the negative form?
2 Does the past perfect describe the first action or the second action?

**2** We often use the past perfect to form longer sentences when we want to give more information about the past. Join the sentences using the past perfect.

1 I sprained my ankle. I didn't go to fitness training.
   I didn't go to fitness training *because I'd sprained my ankle.*
2 I walked all the way home. I felt tired.
   I felt tired because ...............................
3 The match started. I arrived at the stadium.
   By the time I ...............................
4 I left my trainers at home. I couldn't run in the race.
   Because I ...............................

**3** Work in pairs. Complete the sentences by saying what happened next. Use the ideas in the box.

> go to hospital
> leave their trainers there
> the film started    ~~win the race~~

1 I'd run faster than everyone else, so I
  *won the race.*
2 I'd hurt myself, so
  ...............................
3 When I went into the gym, I noticed someone ...............................
4 The bus was late and by the time I got to the cinema
  ...............................

## Writing Part 2

▶ Page 150 Writing bank
A story

**1** Look at the exam instructions and answer the questions.

> • Your English teacher has asked you to write a story.
> • Your story must begin with the following sentence:
>   *It was the most frightening experience of my life.*

1 Do the instructions give you a title or the first line?
2 Should you write in the first person (I) or the third person (he/she/it)?
3 Which are the key words?

**2** Read the story and decide in which paragraph the things happened.

a  describes the main events  *2*
b  sets the scene for the action
c  describes the writer's feelings afterwards
d  tells us about the final event
e  explains what really happened
f  introduces the story, saying who did what, where and when

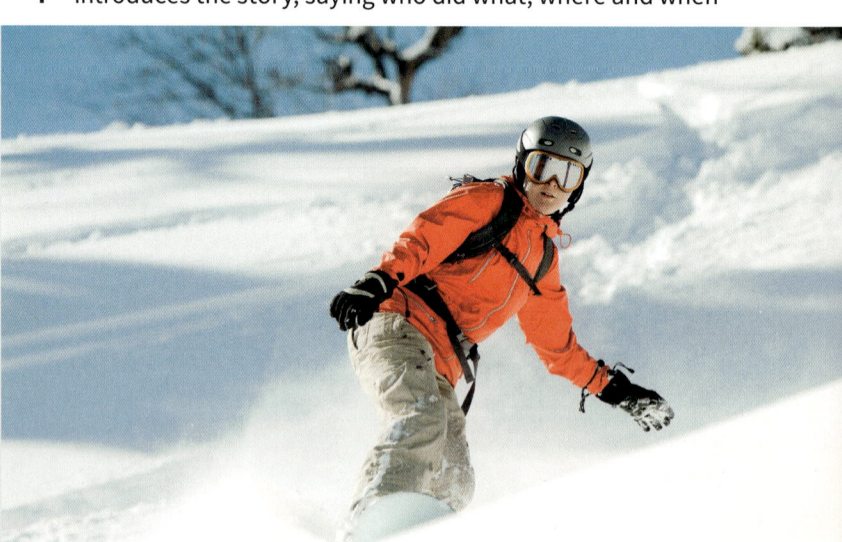

> 1 Last month I went snowboarding in Canada with my friend Lucy, who is a champion snowboarder. I was feeling nervous when we reached the top of the mountain because it had started to snow heavily and I couldn't see much.
>
> 2 Lucy went first, but by the time I started snowboarding, she had disappeared. I went down faster and faster and I thought I saw her go off to the right, so I turned right, too. But soon I came to some cliffs and had to stop. I was terrified. Had she gone over the edge?
>
> 3 I waited and shouted, and suddenly, Lucy was there. I'd gone the wrong way but she'd heard me calling and then she'd found me. I felt safe at last.

86

**3** Underline examples of 1–3 in the story.
1 a verb used with a sport
2 a non-defining relative clause
3 six examples of the past perfect

**4** Look at the Writing Part 2 task. Answer the questions from Exercise 1.

- Your English teacher has asked you to write a story.
- Your story must begin with this sentence:
  *I felt nervous when the game began.*

**Exam advice**
- Use a range of past tenses in your story (the past simple and past perfect for events, and the past continuous for background information).

**4** Listen and repeat. Stress the same words.

**5** Work in pairs. Discuss the questions for at least four minutes. Give reasons for your answers.

Which sports do you think are …
- the most popular in your country?
- the most/least exciting to play?
- the most/least exciting to watch?
- the best for people's fitness and health?
- on TV too often / not often enough?

**Exam advice**
- You can talk about your own experiences, but you must not change the topic.
- When your partner is speaking, show you're listening to them.
- Remember there are no right or wrong answers. Say what you think!

**5** Write your story in about 100 words. Write three or four paragraphs and include points a–f from Exercise 2.

## Speaking Part 4

▶ Page 161 Speaking bank

**1** Listen and complete the expressions.
1 You may be ....*right*...., but …
2 I'm not really ........................ about that.
3 Yes, I ........................ agree with you.
4 I don't think ........................ because …
5 That's not the ........................ I see it.
6 I don't agree at ........................ .
7 That's ........................ .
8 I think so ........................ .

**2** Match the expressions from Exercise 1 to the uses (a–c).
a agreeing  3
b disagreeing strongly
c disagreeing politely

**3** /P/ Word stress: agreeing and disagreeing
Listen again. Underline the stressed word(s) in each expression from Exercise 1.

You may be right, but …

Stay fit and healthy

# 10 Looks amazing!

A

B

C

D

E

## Reading Part 2

1. Work in pairs. Look at the title of the guide, the names of the stalls and the pictures. What do you think you will have to do in this Reading Part 2 task?

2. The following five groups of people would like to have lunch at the street food market. Read the descriptions and underline the important information.

1. Caroline and Hailey have tried most of the stalls, so want to try something new on Tuesday. Both of them really like fish and they want a hot drink with their meal.

2. Jack and his university classmates have read that some of the stalls have won prizes and they want to try one of those. They would like a vegetarian main meal, but they are short of money.

3. Sara and her friends fancy having a light lunch together on Saturday, but they are not willing to pay very much. They would like to sit down to eat at the stall.

4. Samuel's grandmother would like to take him for a meal on Sunday but she doesn't want to walk too far around the market. Samuel would like a proper meal, but she just wants a dessert.

5. Tania and her dad feel like trying a spicy vegetable dish before the cinema on Sunday. They won't have much time before the film so they'll need to take away their dessert.

## Starting off

1. Work in groups. Look at the photos. What food groups can you see? Add at least two more examples of food or drink to each group.

2. Work in pairs. Discuss the questions.
   1. What are your favourite things to eat and drink?
   2. Are there any types of food you don't eat? Which ones? Why not?
   3. How often do you eat out? Where? Who with?

**3** Answer questions 1–5, without reading the text.
1. Caroline and Hailey want a hot drink with their meal. *What type of drink could they have?*
2. Jack and his friends fancy a vegetarian meal. *What sort of food do they not want to eat?*
3. Sara and her friends aren't willing to pay very much. *What words do you expect to read in the description of their most suitable restaurant?*
4. Samuel's grandma doesn't want to walk too far around the market. *What sort of words do you need to look for in the descriptions?*
5. Jack and his classmates would like a main meal while Sara and her friends fancy having a light lunch. *What words do you expect to read in the descriptions?*

> **Exam advice**
> - To match the people with an answer, look for a text that says the same things, but in different words.
> - For each person or group of people, only one option is correct. Three of these options are not needed.

**4** Read the street food market guide and decide which food stall (A–H) would be the most suitable for each group of people (1–5).

**5** Work in pairs. Talk together about which street food stall you would (and wouldn't) like to eat at.

## OUR TOP PICKS AT THE street food market

**A** *Amazing Food by Jason*
If you're looking for a main meal, try the delicious curry from Mauritius here. Don't miss the Creole Chicken, which is spicy fried chicken cooked in tomatoes and served with rice and salad. Not cheap but visit the stall on Tuesdays for a free glass of hot tea.

**B** *Scandinavian Kitchen*
Looking for a light lunch? Order the picnic box at this stall, which opens this week, and you won't be disappointed. We recommend the top-quality turkey with bread and cheese. Or why not try the salmon special, which comes with free coffee and cake? Perfect for those who feel like a change but don't have much time!

**C** *Just Right Burgers*
All reviews recommend these reasonably priced beef or tuna burgers. The vegetarian burger is grilled vegetables with just the right amount of mushrooms with or without cheese. Something new for those who fancy a light lunchtime meal. Order a homemade soft drink with your meal.

**D** *Aladdin's Cave*
Expect to queue for a light Middle Eastern meal from this stall. Their lunchbox contains fresh salad, spicy potato chips, garlic sauce and bread. Even meat eaters will consider becoming vegetarians here. Not cheap, but their homemade desserts are amazing!

**E** *Barbecue Hut*
If you fancy a main meal, sit down here and for less than €10, the prize-winning chefs will barbecue a juicy steak and serve it with fries. Try their range of sauces from hot pepper to yoghurt. Finish with their famous apple pie and a hot drink! Right next to the market entrance.

**F** *Blue Dog*
You must try a piadina (an Italian flatbread) from the newly opened Blue Dog. Vegetarians should order the spinach and mushroom piadina which is very reasonably priced. Perfect for those who don't want a heavy meal. Ask for a piadina with hot chocolate sauce for dessert – not suitable for takeaway. Near the clock tower at the back of the market. Seating available.

**G** *Fred Gonzalez*
Fred Gonzalez has been voted chef of the month many times since he set up his Mexican food stall. His customers are happy to wait while his team prepares freshly cooked burritos filled with fish, beef or vegetables and rice, beans, lettuce and hot peppers. Half-price meals for students, but expect queues.

**H** *Food Planet*
If you think vegan curry is boring, think again. Their potato and pea curry is hot but it is one of the most delicious dishes in the market. Ask for a slice of their carrot cake in a bag and save it for later. Higher-than-average prices but worth it. Very short waiting time. Comfortable seating area.

Looks amazing!

# 10

## Vocabulary
*course*, *dish*, *food*, *meal* and *plate*

**1** Exam candidates often make mistakes with the words *course*, *dish*, *food*, *meal* and *plate*. Match the words (1–5) with their definitions from the *Cambridge Learner's Dictionary* (a–e).

1 **course** *noun* [C]
2 **dish** *noun* [C]
3 **food** *noun* [C, U]
4 **meal** *noun* [C]
5 **plate** *noun* [C]

a food that is prepared in a particular way as part of a meal, e.g. *fish and chips* or *lasagne*
b a flat, round object which is used for putting food on
c when you eat, or the food that you eat at that time, e.g. *breakfast, lunch and dinner*
d a part of a meal, e.g. *starters and desserts*
e something that people and animals eat to keep them alive

**2** Which of the words in Exercise 1 are countable and which are uncountable nouns? How do you know?

**3** Complete Elsa's email to Lee about the food in her country using *courses*, *dish*, *food*, *meals* and *plate*.

---

Hi Lee,

I'm from Quito, Ecuador. In my country we eat simple but tasty **(1)** ......*food*...... – like meat, fish and rice. We eat three **(2)** .................. a day: breakfast, lunch and dinner. In the morning, my mum often leaves different cakes or bread on a **(3)** .................. on the table. Lunch and dinner are usually a little heavier than breakfast. Lunch is three **(4)** ..................: a starter, which is often soup, a main course and a dessert. My favourite **(5)** .................. is fanesca, which is a fish soup, often made with cod.

Write back soon,
Elsa

---

## Grammar
Commands and instructions

▶ **Page 136 Grammar reference**
Commands and instructions

**1** Work in pairs. Look at these photos of three dishes from around the world and answer the questions.

1 Where do you think the dishes are from?
2 What ingredients do you think you need to make these dishes?

**2** Listen to three short recordings about the dishes from Exercise 1 and check your ideas. 🎧 47

**3** Listen again. Complete instructions 1–6 with a verb. 🎧 47

1 First of all, ......*mix*...... the chicken together with salt, pepper and chilli.
2 .................. it on a high heat, or the burrito will be rather dry.
3 .................. one and a half cups of sushi rice.
4 .................. cucumber, carrot and tuna for your first sushi rolls and then .................. other things.
5 .................. the dosa from an Indian supermarket.
6 .................. to serve your dosa with lassi, an Indian yoghurt drink.

**4** What words do we use in the instructions (1–6) to tell people what to do? What words do we use to tell people what <u>not</u> to do?

**5** Choose one of your own favourite dishes and write some instructions on how to make it. Don't forget to say what <u>not</u> to do.

**6** Work in groups. Take turns to read your instructions from Exercise 5 without saying the name of the dish. Guess what each other's favourite dish is.

90

## Listening Part 1

**1** Look at the first question from Listening Part 1 and the three pictures. Complete the sentences.

1  What will Natalie buy for the picnic?

A    B    C

- We know that the woman will get a **(1)** loaf of bread and a **(2)** ............................ (Pictures A, B and C).
- We don't know if the woman will take a **(3)** ............................ (Picture A) or some **(4)** ............................ (Picture B) or some **(5)** ............................ (Picture C).

**2** Listen to the first part of the recording. What do you think the answer is?

**3** Listen to the last part of the recording. Choose the correct answer.

**4** Read questions 2–7 from Listening Part 1. Underline the key words in the questions. Then look at the pictures and think about the information you need to listen for.

2  What did the woman take to the party?

A    B    C

3  What food will the man try?

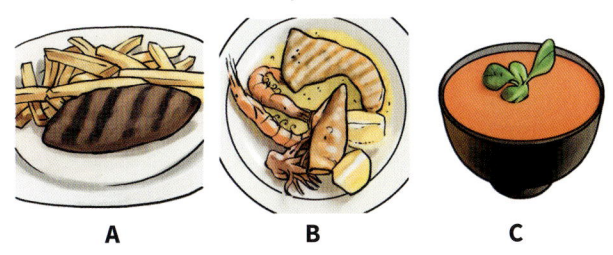

A    B    C

4  Where did the woman go yesterday?

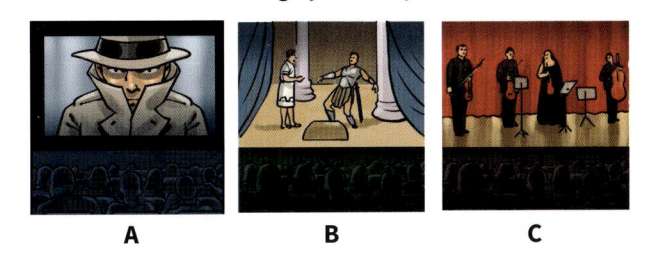

A    B    C

5  What do they need to bring for training tomorrow?

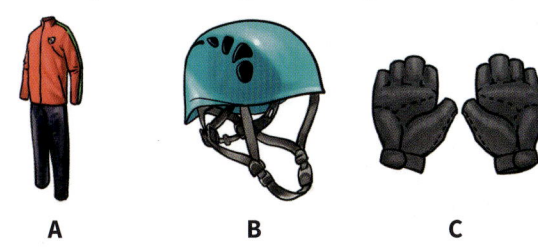

A    B    C

6  What activity did the man do for the first time on holiday?

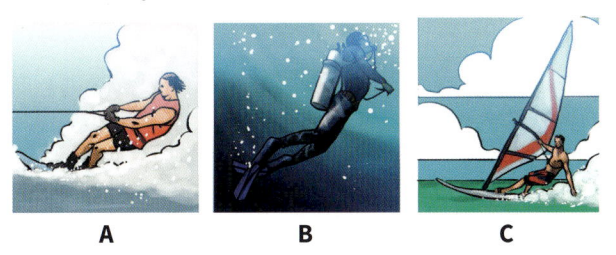

A    B    C

7  Where has the woman been?

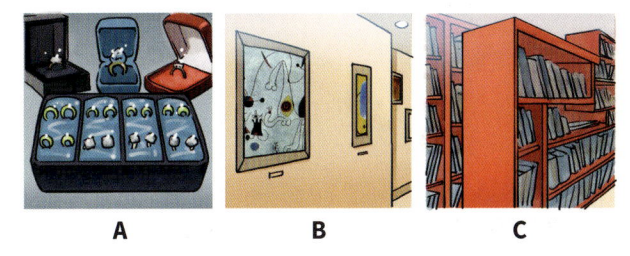

A    B    C

> **Exam advice**
> - Listen carefully to the beginning, middle and end of each recording. The information you need may come anywhere.

**5** Listen and choose the correct answer. Then listen again and check.

**6** /P/ Connected speech: linking sounds
Listen to this sentence. What do the linking lines mean? Read the information in the box and check.

*I'm going tomorrow to get her some ⌣earrings⌣or⌣a necklace from that new jewellery shop⌣on the corner.*

If a word ends with a consonant sound and the next word begins with a vowel sound, it often sounds like these words are connected.

**7** Read the sentences and draw linking lines between the connected words. Then listen and practise saying the sentences.

1  I baked a cake instead.
2  This is a plate of mixed fried fish.

**8** Work in small groups. Do you enjoy shopping? What are your favourite kinds of shops?

Looks amazing!   91

# 10

## Vocabulary
### Shops and services

**1** Look at these photos of shopping streets from around the world. What can you see in each one?

**2** Match the types of shop in the box with the things you can do there (1–6).

> bakery   bookshop   butcher's   chemist   dentist
> dry cleaner's   garage   hairdresser's
> library   supermarket   travel agent's

1 make an appointment
2 buy or pay for something
3 borrow something
4 book a holiday
5 have something repaired
6 complain and ask for your money back

**3** Listen to three short conversations. Match speakers 1–3 to the correct place from Exercise 2.

1 ................................
2 ................................
3 ................................

**4** Listen again. Discuss what you think Layla, Lewis and Charlie should do next.

## Grammar
### Have something done

▶ Page 136 Grammar reference
Have something done

**1** Look at the sentences. Choose the correct options in *italics* in the rules.

**Layla:** I normally have my hair cut at Gabrielle's.
**Lewis:** I'm having the scooter repaired.
**Vicki:** I had this dress cleaned last week.

**Rules**

When we talk about an action **(1)** *we do for ourselves / somebody does for us*, we can use *have something done*. For example:

Layla does not cut her own hair, she **has** her hair **cut**.

*Get something done* (e.g. *She **gets** her hair **cut***) is also possible, but usually in **(2)** *formal / informal* situations.

**2** Look at the pictures. Complete the sentences with *Polly* or *Ginny*.

My flatmate Polly

My flatmate Ginny

1 ................................ rarely has her hair cut.
2 ................................ gets her hair cut every three weeks.
3 ................................ tries to clean her own nails.
4 ................................ has her nails done.
5 ................................ always cleans her bedroom.
6 ................................ had her bedroom cleaned last year.
7 ................................ got her car washed two years ago.
8 ................................ washed her scooter this morning.

92

**3** Complete the table.

|  | I do it myself | someone does it for me |
|---|---|---|
| present simple | I cook my own meals | (1) I *have my meals cooked* |
| present continuous | I'm cleaning my flat | (2) I'm ............................................. |
| past simple | I cut my hair | (3) I ............................................. |

**4** Complete the conversations with *have* or *get*. If both verbs are possible, write *have* and *get*.

**Receptionist:** Good morning! Linda's Hair Salon. How can I help you?
**Ginny:** I'd like to book an appointment to **(1)** ........................... my hair done.
**Friend:** Polly, can't you do something with your hair? It looks awful!
**Polly:** Don't worry! I'll **(2)** ........................... it cut when I'm ready.

**5** Write a sentence about each situation using the words given.
Use the correct form and tense of the verb *have*.
1  I / hair / cut / three times a year.
*I have my hair cut three times a year.*
2  I can't finish this report because I / laptop / mend / at the moment.
3  My bike is broken again and I / it / repair / a week ago.
4  Jack isn't at work. He / teeth / check today by the dentist.
5  Keith and Pete are going to a New Year's Eve party. They / suits / clean last week.

**6** Work in groups. Ask and answer questions about the things people do for you.

| How often do you / When did you last | have | your hair cut? / your photo taken? / your teeth checked? / your computer mended? / your bedroom painted? / your eyes tested? |

How often do you have your hair cut?

I have it cut every six weeks.

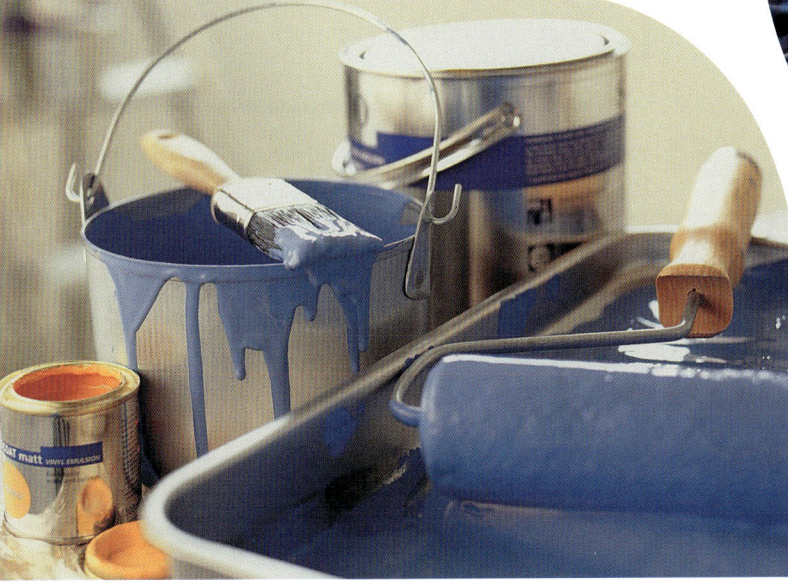

Looks amazing!

# 10

## Speaking Part 2

▶ Page 154 Speaking bank

A

B

C

1. Listen to Luna describing one of the three photos. Which photo is she describing? Which things does she talk about?

   1. the place
   2. the weather
   3. what the people are doing
   4. what the people are wearing
   5. everyday objects

2. Listen to Luna again. Complete the sentences with the phrases she uses to describe the objects she doesn't know.

   1. One of them is carrying something. I can't remember the word for this object. ............................ the rain … we open it when it rains.
   2. On her back, she's got … a … ............................ a bag.

3. Work in pairs. Take turns to describe some of the objects in the pictures using phrases from the table. Guess what your partner is describing.

| What is it? | What is it made of? | What is it used for? |
|---|---|---|
| It's a kind of … It's something like a … | It's made of … (metal/plastic/ wood/glass, etc.) | It's used for … |

**Exam advice**
- Imagine you're talking to somebody who can't see the photo.
- If you don't know the word for an object, use another expression to describe it.

4. Work in different pairs. Take turns to describe one of the photos for a minute. Listen to your partner and put a tick (✓) against the things in Exercise 1 your partner describes.

94

# Writing Part 2

▶ Page 148 Writing bank
An article

**1** Read the Writing Part 2 exam task and underline the key words.

> You see this notice in an international English-language magazine.
>
> ### Articles wanted!
> ### Going Shopping
>
> Where do you and your friends go shopping nowadays?
> Do you prefer going to indoor shopping centres or to town centres?
> Or perhaps you'd rather do all your shopping online?
> Tell us what you think!
> Answer these questions and we will publish the best articles in our next magazine.
>
> Write your **article** in about **100** words.

**2** Work in groups. Discuss the questions from the Writing Part 2 task. Make a note of your answers.

**3** Now discuss the questions in this Writing Part 2 task. Make a note of your answers. Then decide which exam task your group has more to talk about.

> You see this notice in an international English-language magazine.
>
> We're looking for new writers for our magazine!
> ### A good meal
> What makes a good meal?
> Is it the place, the people, the food – or all of these things?
> How important is it to eat out and try different kinds of food from different countries?
> Tell us what you think!
> We will publish the most interesting articles in our next magazine.
>
> Write your **article**.

### Exam advice

- In the exam, you can choose between an article and a story. Choose the one which you are more interested in and which you can write more about.
- If you choose the article, check it includes all the points in the question.
- Check your work for mistakes. Make sure you have written about 100 words.

**4** Choose <u>one</u> of the Writing Part 2 exam tasks and write your answer in about 100 words. Use your notes from Exercise 2 or 3 to help you.

**5** Check your work. Answer the questions below.
1. Have you written an interesting article?
2. Have you included all the information?
3. Are your ideas connected with words like *because*, *and*, etc.?
4. Have you checked the article for mistakes, in particular with spelling and punctuation?
5. Have you written about 100 words?

Looks amazing! 95

# 9 Vocabulary and grammar review

## Grammar

**1** Match the sentence beginnings with the endings. Then add relative pronouns in the box to form complete sentences.

> when (x2)   where   which   who   whose

| 1 | Sunday is the day | a | cut his hand. |
| 2 | All the races | b | people play tennis. |
| 3 | Winter is the time | c | I relax at home. |
| 4 | James is the boy | d | took place were exciting. |
| 5 | A court is a place | e | husband is very ill. |
| 6 | That's the woman | f | people catch the flu. |

1 c — Sunday is the day when I relax at home.
2 
3 
4 
5 
6 

**2** Put the words in the correct order. Add commas to form non-defining relative clauses.

1 a snowboarding champion / is / Zara / only 19 / is / who
   Zara, who is only 19, is a snowboarding champion.

2 we play tennis / the weather / good / in summer / when / is

3 won / the best player of all / was / whose / Stevie / team

4 we live / a lot of pollution / is / where / in the city centre / there

5 better now / who / my brother / an accident / is feeling / had

6 a team sport / on a court / which / is / volleyball / is played

**3** Complete the story using the past simple or the past perfect form of the verbs in brackets.

## My first match

At ten o'clock last Saturday morning, I **(1)** ......was...... (be) ready to play my first real match at the tennis club. I **(2)** ................ (practise) all the previous week and I really **(3)** ................ (feel) good, especially as I **(4)** ................ (bring) my lucky trainers.

When I **(5)** ................ (put) them on, I walked onto the court. I noticed that the grass **(6)** ................ (be) very wet, as it **(7)** ................ (rain) a lot the night before, but that **(8)** ................ (not seem) important.

Jack, the other player, **(9)** ................ (be) a little late because he **(10)** ................ (leave) his racket at home, but as soon as he arrived we **(11)** ................ (start) the match. I quickly **(12)** ................ (realise) that in the past I **(13)** ................ (play) against stronger players than him, and I **(14)** ................ (be) sure that I could win.

Suddenly, I **(15)** ................ (slip) on the wet grass and **(16)** ................ (fall). I **(17)** ................ (know) immediately that I **(18)** ................ (injure) my ankle badly, so that was the end of the game. I **(19)** ................ (go) to hospital, and fortunately I **(20)** ................ (not broke) it. But after that I never **(21)** ................ (wear) my 'lucky' trainers again!

## Vocabulary

**4** Choose the correct option in *italics*.

1 Skiers have to wear good *(gloves)* / *boots* / *trainers* to keep their hands warm.
2 Last week I was coughing and I had a really *hurt* / *sore* / *injured* throat.
3 In last night's football match, Brazil *won* / *beat* / *drew* the United States 6–0.
4 I was practising hitting the ball with a baseball *racket* / *bat* / *net*.
5 Sophia is good at *jogging* / *gymnastics* / *athletics*, especially the long jump and 100 metres.
6 If I have a headache, I usually take a *medicine* / *pill* / *test* with a glass of water.
7 After I fell off my bike, I had a big purple *bruise* / *flu* / *disease* on my leg.

96

# Vocabulary and grammar review 10

## Vocabulary

**1** Complete sentences 1–5 with a suitable verb.

1 If you have toothache, you should ...*make/book*... an appointment to see the dentist.
2 If you are not happy with something in a shop, you should always ............................ and ask for your money back.
3 If you want to go on a trip, it's better to ............................ it through a travel agent than online.
4 You don't need to buy books, you can ............................ them from the library.
5 You can save time and money if you learn how to ............................ broken things yourself.

**2** Read the email below from Shane and choose the correct answer.

> Dear Ryan,
>
> Let me tell you something about myself. I **(1)** ......*was*...... born in Hong Kong but now I live in Singapore. One of the most amazing things about Singapore is the variety of **(2)** ............................ and other places to eat out. You can eat in expensive restaurants or **(3)** ............................ street food markets where the cooks prepare your food in front of you. My favourite **(4)** ............................ is 'Chicken Rice'. This is boiled chicken **(5)** ............................ is served on top of rice with cucumber. And if you prefer to eat at home, there are plenty of **(6)** ............................ for you to buy your own meat, fish, fruit and vegetables.
>
> Shane

| | A | B | C | D |
|---|---|---|---|---|
| 1 | am | be | was | have |
| 2 | plates | food | courses | restaurants |
| 3 | cheap | cheaper | more expensive | richer |
| 4 | drink | plate | course | dish |
| 5 | which | who | whose | what |
| 6 | dry cleaners | butchers | bakers | markets |

## Grammar

**3** Complete these sentences using the correct form of *have something done*. Use the correct tense and an object pronoun.

1 My uncle didn't have time to wash his car before my cousin's wedding, so he ...*had his car washed*... at the garage.
2 My sister tried to cut her own hair but it looked terrible so she went to the hairdresser to ............................ .
3 We wanted to have a photo of the whole class so we ............................ by a professional photographer.
4 We live on the ninth floor and we can't clean the windows ourselves because it's dangerous. Once a month, we ............................ by a professional.
5 When I had problems with my bike, I tried to repair it with a friend but we couldn't. In the end I ............................ at a bike shop.

**4** Read about a wedding and think of a word which best fits each gap. Use only one word in each gap.

> My cousin Max **(1)** ......*met*...... his girlfriend when they were at university and they decided to get married last year. I went to their wedding two weeks **(2)** ............................ . Before the wedding, I went to the hairdresser with my mum and we **(3)** ............................ our hair cut. We also went to the dry cleaner to **(4)** ............................ our dresses cleaned. It was a fantastic day and we all **(5)** ............................ a really good time there. As Max and his new wife **(6)** ............................ leaving on their honeymoon, I shouted 'Don't forget to send me a postcard!' They haven't written to me yet!

# 11 The natural world

## Starting off
### The environment

**1** Work in pairs.

1 Which environmental issue does each photo 1–5 show?

1: *plastic waste, polluting the water and harming sea creatures*

2 Photos A–E show some things you can do to help. Match them with 1–5.

*1 — D, carry your own water bottle, fill it each time you go out*

3 Choose two problems and think of more ways you can help.

*1 — recycle plastic bottles, pick up rubbish on the beach*

**2** Work in pairs. Discuss the questions.

Apart from the issues in 1–5 above, which other environmental problems are there in your country? What can people do about them?

## Listening Part 4

**1** Work in pairs. Discuss the questions.
1 Which of the world's creatures are becoming less common? Why?
2 What effects does that have on the environment, and on people?
3 How can we protect the animals that are in danger?

> **Exam advice**
> - For each question or statement, underline the key word(s). Then do the same for options A, B and C.
> - Listen for words with similar or opposite meanings to the ones you underlined.

**2** For each question, choose the correct answer. You will hear a young woman called Ellie talking about a trip to southern Spain to see the Iberian lynx.

1 Why did Ellie and Marta decide to go to the stream?
  A Both of them had been there before.
  B A lynx had been seen there recently.
  C There were very few rabbits in the area.

2 As they walked to the stream, they felt
  A glad because they could see where they were going.
  B very tired because of the steep hills they had to climb.
  C uncomfortable because the weather was so hot.

3 Ellie and Marta hid
  A among the trees.
  B behind the rocks.
  C in a small building.

4 When they saw the first animal they were
  A surprised that it was a little cat.
  B delighted that it was a young lynx.
  C disappointed that it was a rabbit.

5 What did the young lynx do after it came out of the bushes?
  A It waited for its mother.
  B It caught a rabbit.
  C It saw Ellie and Marta.

6 They started walking back to the village
  A as soon as the sun went down.
  B when it was completely dark.
  C very early the next morning.

**3** Work in pairs. Which animals are becoming less common in your country? Which human activities are causing this?

## Vocabulary
### Noun suffixes

**1** Look at the underlined nouns and answer the questions.

*... which location did you choose, and why?*
*... I can imagine your excitement!*
*... we kept going in the right direction.*

1 What is the verb form of each noun?
2 Which suffix does each noun have?
3 Which noun drops the letter 'e' from the verb form? Why?

**2** Complete the table with the noun form of the verbs from the box. Be careful with any spelling changes.

> ~~admire~~  announce  attract  celebrate  collect
> complete  confirm  connect  create  develop
> disappoint  discuss  educate  enjoy  entertain
> examine  explore  improve  inform  invent
> invite  move  pollute  prevent  protect
> relax  replace  reserve  translate

| -ment | -ation | -ion |
|---|---|---|
|  | admiration |  |

The natural world

# 11

**3** Complete the news article with the noun form of the verbs from the box.

> disappoint   explore   improve   inform   ~~invent~~   move

## Scientists use robot chick to study penguins

Scientists in Antarctica have used a new (1) _invention_ to help them study penguins close up: a tiny robot on wheels that looks like a baby penguin. The robot, similar to those used in the (2) _____ of the moon and Mars, provided lots of exciting new (3) _____ about the birds. Scientists, working some distance away, controlled every (4) _____ the robot made and it was immediately accepted by penguin families as one of them. The adults even sang to it, though to the penguins' great (5) _____ the 'baby' didn't reply. The scientists are now working on a new model with one important (6) _____ – it will be able to play penguin songs.

**4** Listen and check your answers to Exercise 3.
🎧 57

**5** **/P/ Word stress in longer nouns**
🎧 57
Listen again and <u>underline</u> the stressed syllable in nouns 1–6 in Exercise 3. Then answer the questions.

- Which syllable is stressed in each word?   in<u>ven</u>tion
- Which word in the first column of the table in Exercise 2 does not follow this pattern?

**6** Practise saying the words in Exercise 2 with the correct stress.

## Grammar
### The passive

▶ **Page 137 Grammar reference**
The passive: present simple and past simple

**1** Look at sentences A–D and answer the questions.

A   This new technology <u>reduces</u> air pollution.
B   Air pollution <u>is reduced</u> by this new technology.
C   The guides <u>allowed</u> the tourists to take photos.
D   The tourists <u>were allowed</u> to take photos.

1   Which sentences are active? Which are passive?
2   Which two sentences describe an event in the past?
3   Which two sentences use a form of *be* and the past participle of the verb?
4   What is the subject and what is the object in A? How is B different?
5   What is the subject and what is the object in C? How is D different?
6   What information is in sentence C, but not D?

**2** Complete the rules with *active*, *passive* and *by*.

### Rules

1 We often find the _passive_ in formal texts (e.g. news reports, textbooks, etc.).

2 In _____ sentences, we always use the past participle form of the verb.

3 We often use the _____ when we are speaking, or writing informal letters, etc.

4 We use the _____ when we focus on who or what did an action.

5 We use the _____ when we focus on the *action* rather than who or what did it.

6 We can add _____ + noun if it is important to say who or what did it. In the passive, we often leave this out.

## 3 Complete the sentences with the present or past passive form of the words in brackets.

1 The mountain road ........is not used........ (not use) in winter.
2 When ...was the island discovered... (the island / discover)?
3 I wanted to go to the natural history museum, but it ............................... (close).
4 The view down the valley ............................... (spoil) when they built the motorway.
5 Climate change ............................... (blame) for the lack of rain this year.
6 The rocks in the water ............................... (not notice) until the boat was near the cliffs.

## 4 Write passive sentences. Begin with the underlined words and only use *by* where necessary.

1 Those machines waste a lot of electricity.
   *A lot of electricity is wasted by those machines.*
2 People saw two giraffes near the trees.
3 One small cloud hid the moon.
4 They don't allow cars in the national park.
5 They grow rice in the east of the country.
6 Someone wrote a poem about this waterfall.
7 Fire partly destroyed the forest.

## 5 Underline nine more passive forms in the article. What is the infinitive form of each main verb?

In the past, bears and wolves were considered a danger to both people and farm animals so their numbers were reduced, often to zero. Nowadays, however, a lot more is understood about how they form an essential part of nature, and some years ago international agreements were made to bring back these magnificent creatures. A lot of money was spent, large areas where they could move freely across borders were created, and they are now protected by law. In Europe, bears and wolves are once again found in many countries, from Spain to Scandinavia, where they are allowed to live in places with few people. They are sometimes seen in mountain areas or forests, but usually they prefer to keep away from humans. So if we keep well away from them, we are not in any danger.

## 6 /P/ Word stress in passive forms

Listen to this sentence. Which part of the underlined passive form is stressed? How do you say the other part?

...bears and wolves were considered a danger to both people and farm animals.

## 7
Work in pairs. Try to say the sentences in Exercise 4 with the correct stress. Listen and check.

The natural world

# 11

## Reading Part 5

**1** Work in pairs. Look at the photos and complete the sentences with the words in the box.

> Ecuador  ~~Galápagos~~  hard  Pacific
> South  tail  unique  weight
> west  wings

The (1) *Galápagos* Islands lie approximately 1000 kilometres (2) .................... of the coast of (3) .................... America in the (4) .................... Ocean. They belong to (5) .................... and consist of 13 main islands plus 6 smaller ones. They are most famous for their (6) .................... wildlife: creatures that are not found anywhere else in the world. The Galápagos giant tortoise, which has a (7) .................... shell of up to 150 centimetres, may reach a (8) .................... of over 400 kilos and can live for more than 100 years. The marine iguana is the only lizard that lives both on land and in water: it has a long flat (9) .................... that helps it swim quickly. The flightless cormorant is also an excellent swimmer, although it cannot fly because its (10) .................... are too small.

**2** Quickly read the text in Exercise 4 and answer these questions.

1. What kind of text is it?
2. Where have the people gone?
3. What kind of work will they do there?
4. What is special about the islands?
5. What could they do on their days off?

**3** Read the text again. Try to fill in gaps 1–6 without looking at options A–D. Use these questions to help you.

1. Which noun means 'a group of people working together to achieve something'?
2. Which verb do we use to talk about just some of a larger group of things?
3. Which verb that means 'stop' goes with the preposition *from*?
4. Which noun forms a phrase that means 'join others in an activity'?
5. Which verb means 'look around a place for the first time'?
6. Which verb, with 'by', means 'have on all sides'?

## WORKING ON THE GALÁPAGOS ISLANDS

Six students from the University have today flown from Quito to the wonderful Galápagos Islands to spend a month doing volunteer work on San Cristóbal Island. They will join a (1) .................... of young adults already working on a range of vital environmental projects there. These (2) .................... planting trees on national park lands, picking up rubbish and improving paths next to farm land to (3) .................... crops from being damaged by humans or animals. The volunteers will also take (4) .................... in a new project that aims to help tourists understand the importance of protecting the islands' unique environment. At weekends they will have plenty of free time to (5) .................... the magnificent landscape and study the amazing wildlife, such as the famous giant tortoises. Or they can sail to the other islands and go diving in clear blue water, (6) .................... by beautiful fish of all colours, shapes and sizes.

**4** Read the text and choose the correct word for each space.

| | A | B | C | D |
|---|---|---|---|---|
| 1 | club | crowd | band | team |
| 2 | include | employ | contain | consist |
| 3 | direct | prevent | control | manage |
| 4 | place | care | advantage | part |
| 5 | join | follow | explore | guide |
| 6 | surrounded | supported | covered | attached |

102

# 11

**5** Work in groups. Which of the projects in the text could help protect the environment in your country? What other projects can you think of? Use these ideas or your own.
- clean up rivers and lakes
- help to prevent forest fires
- look after sick or injured wild animals
- plant fruit trees to provide food for wild animals

## Grammar
### Comparative and superlative adverbs

▶ Page 137 Grammar reference
Comparative and superlative adverbs

**1** Look at examples A–D. Then answer questions 1–5.

A *The number of lions is increasing more quickly than in the wild.*
B *We should speak more quietly.*
C *In a check on local water pollution, the lake did even worse than the river.*
D *It's hard to decide which birds sing the most beautifully.*

1 Underline three examples of comparative adverbs and one example of a superlative adverb.
2 How do we usually form comparative adverbs?
3 Which adverb in A–D doesn't follow this rule?
4 When we compare two actions, which word normally follows the adverb?
5 How do we usually form superlative adverbs?

**2** Complete the table.

| adverb | comparative | superlative |
|---|---|---|
| quietly | more quietly | |
| | | (the) most carefully |
| slowly | | |
| | | (the) most easily |
| | faster | |
| badly | | |
| | | (the) hardest |
| | better | |
| | earlier | |

**3** Complete the sentences with the comparative or superlative form of the adverbs in brackets.

1 Which cities in the world do you think are growing ..(the).fastest. (fast)?
2 Should we try ........................ (hard) to protect the countryside?
3 Why do the stars shine ........................ (bright) in the countryside than in the city?
4 Which kind of animal do you see or hear ........................ (frequent) where you live?
5 In which season does it rain ........................ (heavy) in your country?
6 Is eating meat ........................ (bad) for the environment than being vegetarian?

**4** In pairs, discuss the questions in Exercise 3.

> I think cities in Asia, such as Shanghai and Delhi, are growing fastest.

> I'm not sure. I recently read that Lagos in Nigeria is growing the fastest in the world.

The natural world 103

# 11

## Speaking Part 4

▶ Page 161 Speaking bank

**1** Work in pairs. Discuss the questions.

1. How are the people in the pictures wasting water?
2. How do you think they could reduce this waste?

**2** Listen to Ethan and Lily. What three suggestions do they make for saving water?

**3** Listen again and complete the expressions Ethan and Lily use to give examples.

1. At home, ......for instance......, you can have …
2. … when you're brushing your teeth, ........................., you should …
3. … when you're doing other things, ......................... washing your hair.
4. … especially in places ......................... our college.
5. … a tap which loses one drop a second, ........................., wastes 20 litres a day!

**4** Work in groups. In what other ways can you save water? Use phrases from Exercise 3 to discuss your ideas.

### Exam advice

- Give reasons and examples to support what you say and feel.
- Help your partner to talk by asking them for their opinions.

**5** Work in different pairs. Discuss the questions. Give examples and stress important words.

- What do you think are the best ways to save electricity at home?
- Which do you think is better for the environment – travelling by car or by bus? Why?
- Which do you think is the most interesting kind of animal in your country? Why?
- Do you like watching TV programmes about animals? Why / Why not?
- Do you think we are doing enough to protect wild animals? Why / Why not?

# Writing Part 1

▶ Page 145 Writing bank
An email

**1** Look at the exam task and answer the questions.

1. How do you know that Chloe has received a message from you?
2. What have you already told Chloe you are going to do?
3. Which four things must you put in your reply?

---

Read this email from your English-speaking friend Chloe, and the notes you have made.

**To:**

**From:** Chloe

Hi,

It was great to hear from you and I'm really glad you're coming to visit. Shall we go to the countryside while you're here? — *Good idea!*

We could take a bus and then walk, or cycle there. It's not far and I've got a spare bike. — *Tell Chloe.*

There's lots of wildlife in that area, too. What would you most like to see? — *Suggest ...*

My family have a little cottage there, so we can take a day trip or go all day Saturday and Sunday. Which would you rather do? — *Say which and why.*

All the best,

Chloe

Write your **email** to Chloe in about **100** words, using **all** the **notes**.

---

**2** Work in groups. Read Leo's reply and answer the questions.

1. Which paragraph deals with each of the four notes on Chloe's message?
2. Leo has written a good email but has made one mistake in each paragraph. Can you find and correct each one? Mark the mistakes *G* for grammar, *V* for vocabulary, *WO* for word order, or *Sp* for spelling.
3. Which words and phrases does Leo use to avoid using these parts of Chloe's message?

- go to the countryside — *getting out of the city*
- walk
- Saturday and Sunday
- wildlife
- rather

---

Dear Chloe,

Yes, getting out of the city sounds like a really good idea. Besides, there's far too much noise and polluteion there.

I'd love to stay overnight in the country so I think I'd prefer to spend the weekend whole there. I really like cottages!

Let's drive there by bike. We can get around much more quickly than on foot, and go to more places.

The animals I'd most like to see are deer, but I don't know if they find there. I like watching birds too, especially really big ones.

Looking forward to seeing you,

Leo

---

**Exam advice**

- Try to use your own words instead of copying words from the email you received.
- Check you have included all the points in the email you received.
- Write clearly and make sure you haven't made any mistakes.

**3** Look again at the exam task. Then plan and write your own email. Try to include comparative/superlative adverb forms.

**4** Work in pairs. Check your partner's email. Where you think there are mistakes, write *G, V, WO* or *Sp* in pencil. Then discuss your corrections.

The natural world

# 12 Express yourself!

## Starting off
### Collocations: using your phone

**1** Work in pairs. What do you and your friends use your phones for? Talk about the things from the box and your own ideas.

> call friends   check the time and weather   listen to music
> play games   read the news headlines   set an alarm
> share photos and videos   take selfies

**2** Work in groups. Look at this information about smartphone use and answer the questions.

- Is the information true for you and the people you know?
- How do you think it is different for older and younger generations?

**66%** Over 66% of the world's adult population owns a smartphone (94% in the Netherlands).

The average person looks at their phone **27** times a day.

**90%** of 18–29 year-olds sleep with their mobile phone.

But they don't use their phones to make calls. They prefer to text or send emails.

## Reading Part 4

**1** Look at the title of the article and the photo on page 107. Then read the first sentence in bold and answer the questions.
1. What is the 'challenge'?
2. Would you agree to take up the challenge?
3. Would you find it easy?

**2** Read the complete article but do not complete the gaps for now. Did Becky find the challenge easy?

**3** Read the second paragraph of the article again. Is sentence A or B the correct answer for gap 1? How do you know?

106

**4** Read the article again. Five sentences have been removed from the text below. For each question, choose the correct answer. There are three extra sentences which you do not need to use.

**Exam advice**
- Before you choose a sentence, check that the verb and noun forms (singular or plural) in the main text all match.
- After you choose a sentence, cross it out so you don't have to keep reading all of A–H.
- After you have chosen your answers, read the text to make sure it all makes sense.

# Can you live without your smartphone for a week?

Becky Barnes, a university student, takes up the challenge.

**Day 1**
Most mornings, I check my phone for messages, have a look at Instagram and read the headlines. Not this morning! And surprisingly, I was ready for class much earlier than usual.
On the train, I couldn't look at my phone so I was bored.
I counted the number of people on theirs – the woman sitting opposite me, some young kids, a couple. **(1)** _____ This was going to be a long week.

**Day 2**
As I couldn't use my phone, I borrowed an alarm clock. I set it for later than usual but I was still out of the house before my flatmates. At university, my classmates told me about some news that had been posted the night before. **(2)** _____ This conversation was unexpected. We don't usually talk to each other first thing in the morning because we normally spend the previous evening sending each other messages.

**Day 3**
I woke up feeling positive until I remembered that there was a lecture on the other side of town and I didn't have a lift. Normally, I can arrange this quickly by posting a message.
**(3)** _____ It was stressful but I learnt that I needed to plan if I wanted to live without my phone.

**Day 4**
I felt more prepared today. My friends and I had arranged to have dinner at Anna's house and I managed to get a lift there.
The evening started well with Anna telling us jokes. **(4)** _____ Everyone was checking their phone.

**Day 5**
On Friday evening, I was at home. I'd just seen my favourite series and I wanted to talk about it. **(5)** _____ I wanted my phone back.

- **A** I wanted to use my phone, I wanted to be like her.
- **B** I felt jealous of them, I was missing mine.
- **C** I could imagine the messages my friends would post about the show.
- **D** I enjoyed having a real conversation about them.
- **E** I spent an hour organising transport.
- **F** However, fifteen minutes later, we were sitting in silence.
- **G** I enjoyed hearing all about it.
- **H** Everyone had left their phones at home.

**5** Work in pairs. Read the sentence and write down three reasons for and three reasons against the following opinion.

*We should all turn off our smartphones for at least three days every week.*

**6** Work in groups. Discuss the opinion in Exercise 5. Remember to give reasons for and reasons against. Then decide together whether you agree or disagree with the opinion.

> People don't know how to talk to each other.

> We need our phones to stay in touch with our friends.

Express yourself!

# 12

## Vocabulary
*ask, ask for, speak, talk, say* and *tell*

**1** Choose the correct words in *italics* to complete the rules.

### Rules

**ask** or **ask for**
We use **(1)** *ask / ask for* if we want someone to do something.
*I asked my friends to bring some food to the party.*
We can use **(2)** *ask / ask for* when we want someone to give us something.
*I asked my English teacher for the answers to the homework I missed.*

**speak** or **talk**
We **(3)** *speak / talk* a language. We do not **(4)** *speak / talk* a language.
*She speaks French.* ~~She talks French.~~

**say** or **tell**
We can use *say* or *tell* with direct or indirect speech, but **(5)** *say / tell* is always followed by the person.
**(6)** *Say / Tell* is never followed by the person.
*She said me she was unhappy.*
*He told me he lived in Rome.*
We also use **(7)** *say / tell* to report instructions.
*The football coach told the team to sleep well before the match.*

**Note:**
- We use **(8)** *say / tell* with greetings: *hello, goodbye, goodnight,* etc.
- We use **(9)** *say / tell* with the following nouns: *the truth, a lie, a joke, a story,* etc.

**2** Exam candidates often make mistakes with these verbs. Choose the correct option in *italics*.
1. Olga knows how to *speak / talk* English well.
2. He *said / told* me to go to 6th Avenue.
3. I'll *ask / ask for* more information about the new pool.
4. At first we were bored but then we started to *say / tell* jokes.
5. When we are together, we *say / talk* about lots of different things.
6. A waiter came and *told / asked* us what we wanted.

**3** Complete the mind map with *ask*, *ask for*, *say*, *speak*, *talk* and *tell*. Add at least one more phrase to each verb.

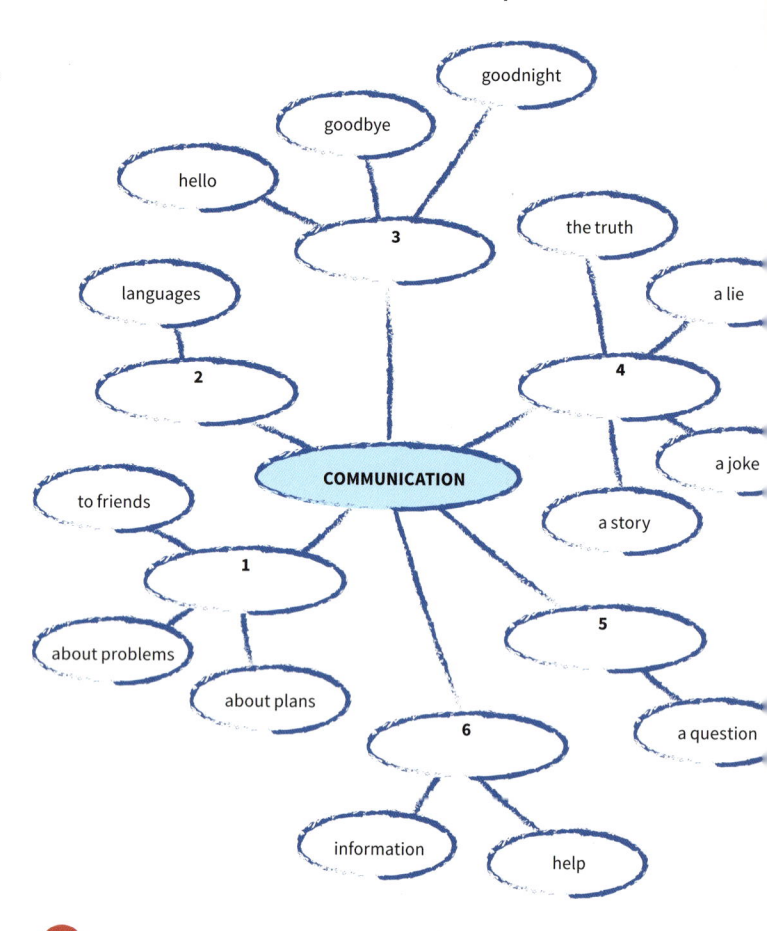

- goodnight
- goodbye
- hello
- **3**
- the truth
- languages
- a lie
- **2**
- **4**
- a joke
- to friends
- **COMMUNICATION**
- a story
- **1**
- **5**
- about problems
- about plans
- **6**
- a question
- information
- help

**4** Complete the questions with a noun from the mind map.
1. When you're doing your homework, how often do you ask for .................... ?
2. Do you say .................... when you enter a classroom?
3. Has someone told you a .................... recently? What was it?
4. Can you speak two .................... ?
5. Who do you go to when you want to talk about your .................... ?
6. Is it easy or difficult for you to tell a .................... ?

**5** Work in pairs. Ask and answer your questions.

**6** Answer the questions using the verb + noun combinations from the mind map. Work in pairs and compare your answers.

What makes …
- a great friend?
- a great parent?
- a great teacher?
- a good sports trainer?

> I think someone who always tells the truth makes a great friend.

## Grammar
### Reported speech

▶ Page 138 Grammar reference
Reported speech

**1** Listen to a group of friends talking about how they can raise money during a charity weekend. What events do Adam, John and Nina suggest?

**2** Rewrite Adam, John and Nina's words in reported speech.

1 **Adam:** <u>Last year</u> we organised a street party to collect money.
Adam said that they _____ the year before.

2 **Adam:** <u>We</u> can organise a similar event again.
Adam said <u>they</u> _____ .

3 **Adam:** <u>We</u> don't have to hold it outside.
Adam said <u>they</u> _____ .

4 **John:** I've thought about organising a football match.
John said <u>he</u> _____ .

5 **John:** In <u>my</u> sister's town, groups of friends are going to play against each other.
John said in <u>his</u> sister's town, groups of friends _____ .

6 **Nina:** <u>We're</u> all using our phones <u>right now</u>.
Nina said <u>they</u> _____ then.

7 **Nina:** <u>We'll</u> hold some traditional events instead.
Nina said <u>they</u> _____ some traditional events instead.

**3** Listen to Sonia telling Lisa about the meeting. Check your answers from Exercise 2.

**4** Use your answers from Exercise 2 to complete this table.

| direct speech | reported speech |
|---|---|
| present simple | (1) *past simple* |
| present continuous | (2) |
| present perfect | (3) |
| past simple | (4) |
| will + infinitive | (5) |
| is/are going to | (6) |
| can | (7) |

**5** Use the <u>underlined</u> words from Exercise 2 to complete the table.

| direct speech | reported speech |
|---|---|
| today | (1) *that day* |
| last year | (2) |
| my | (3) |
| we | (4) |
| right now | (5) |

**6** Work in pairs. Decide what to say in situations 1–3. Complete the sentences.

1 Mark says: 'I can't play tennis; I've hurt my arm.' Later you see him playing basketball.
'You said *you couldn't play tennis because you had hurt your arm* .'

2 Ruth says: 'Someone left their phone in the kitchen at the party.' Later your cousin says she has lost her phone.
'Ruth said _____ .'

3 Your brother is studying abroad. He phones you and says: 'I'm having a great time here.' Later one of his friends asks you if you've spoken to him.
'My brother said _____ .'

**7** Choose a situation from Exercise 6 and write a story in reported speech.

*Last week I wanted to play tennis with Mark, but he told me he couldn't play because …*

### Reported commands

▶ Page 138 Grammar reference
Reported commands

**8** In the meeting about the charity weekend, Helen told her friends to do four things. Complete the reported commands.

1 'Be quiet!'
Helen told them *to be quiet* .

2 'Close the door, Paul!'
Helen told Paul _____ .

3 'Think about the suggestions.'
Helen told them _____ .

4 'Don't forget the meeting.'
Helen told them not _____ .

Express yourself! 109

# 12

**9** Rewrite each instruction 1–4 as a reported command.

'Keep in touch.'
1 Lisa's family told her ........................................... .

'Don't be late.'
2 She told her brother ........................................... .

'Don't bring more pizza.'
3 Dave told his friend ........................................... .

'Don't forget to download Season 3 for me.'
4 Charlie's mum told him ........................................... for her.

## Listening Part 3

**1** You will hear a woman called Catherine Bryant talking about a competition on the radio. Read the notes. What do you learn about the competition?

### APP Competition

**Design an app and win fantastic prizes!**

You should apply online before
(1) ........................................... June.
The subject of this year's challenges is
(2) ........................................... .
The judge is Fran Maddison, author of *Apps*
(3) ........................................... .
The prize for the winner of the final is a
(4) ........................................... to California.
Food and drink will be provided but bring your own
(5) ........................................... .
The next competition will be held in Prague at the
(6) ........................................... .

**2** Read the notes again carefully. What kind of information is missing in each gap?

**3** Look at gap 4. Is the answer a singular or plural noun? Why?

> **Exam advice**
> - Write clearly, so that you can read your answers later.
> - Make sure your answers are grammatically correct.

**4** Listen, and for each question, write the correct answer in the gap. Write one or two words or a number or a date or a time.

**5** Listen again and check.

**6** Work in groups. Discuss the questions.
1 How many apps have you got on your phone?
2 What's your favourite app? Why?
3 What app would you like that you don't have at the moment? (If it doesn't exist yet, what would you like it to do?)

110

# 12

## Grammar
### Reported questions

▶ Page 139 Grammar reference
Reported questions

**1** Listen. Write the questions that people ask Catherine about the app competition.
1. Can I choose the members of my team?
2. ............................................................
3. ............................................................
4. ............................................................
5. ............................................................

**2** Listen again. Complete the questions with the callers' names: *Connor, Charlotte, Emily, Samir* or *Peter*.
1. *Emily* asked if she could choose the members of her team.
2. ............... asked if they needed to pay anything to take part.
3. ............... asked how they registered for the competition.
4. ............... asked what they did if they had technical problems.
5. ............... asked what the prizes were.

**3** Look at the reported questions from Exercise 2. Choose the correct option in *italics* for a–e, to complete the rules about reported questions.

#### Rules
In reported questions …
a the normal question order *stays the same / changes*.
b the tense *stays the same / changes*.
c we *always / never* use an auxiliary verb (e.g. *do, does* or *did*).
d we use *if* when there *is / isn't* a question word (*what, when*, etc.).
e we *use / don't use* a question mark at the end.

**4** Emily's team wins the competition. Listen to her friends asking about the winning app. What does the app do? Do you think it's a good idea? Why / Why not?

**5** Write her friends' questions in reported speech.
1. Cindy asked Emily ............................................................ .
2. Harry asked her ............................................................ .
3. Phil asked her ............................................................ .
4. Diana asked her ............................................................ .
5. Lily asked her ............................................................ .

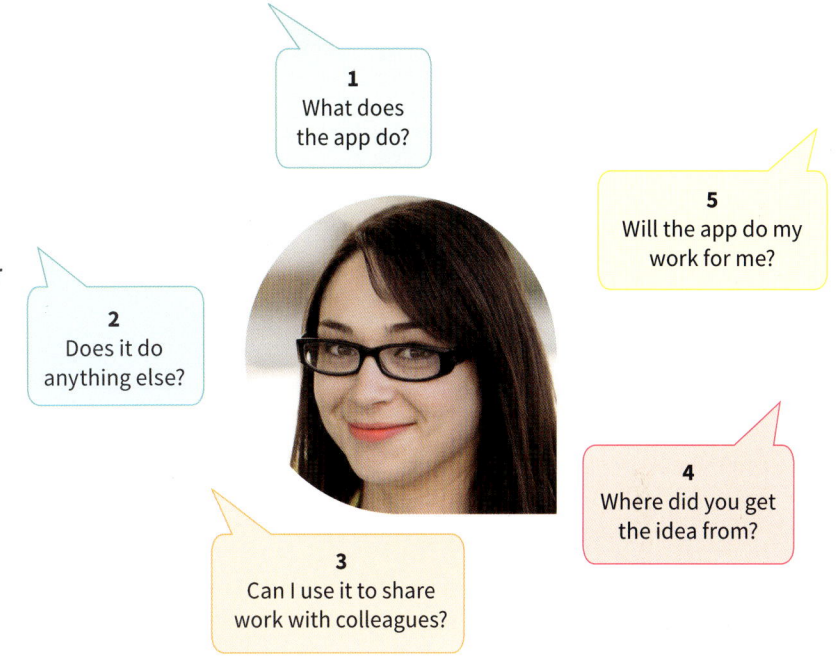

1 What does the app do?
2 Does it do anything else?
3 Can I use it to share work with colleagues?
4 Where did you get the idea from?
5 Will the app do my work for me?

## Vocabulary
### Negative prefixes

**1** Emily said that an app which did our work for us would be *unfair*. Make these adjectives negative by writing *im-*, *in-* or *un-*.
1. ......... friendly, comfortable, believable
2. ......... correct, expensive, complete
3. ......... possible, polite, patient

**2** Add *im-*, *in-* or *un-* to form negative adjectives.
1. Would you like to have an app that does your work for you? Or would it be *un*fair?
2. Some people use the internet for more than four hours a day. Is this ......... healthy?
3. How often do you get ......... patient when you're using new technology?
4. Do you ever feel ......... sociable and stay at home watching films?
5. Do you need to spend a lot of money on a phone? Or is an ......... expensive one just as good?
6. Will we ever be able to communicate without speaking or writing, just thinking? Or will it be ......... possible?

**3** Work in pairs. Ask and answer the questions.

Express yourself! 111

# 12

## Speaking Part 1

▶ Page 152 Speaking bank

**1** Listen to three students answering questions for the Speaking Part 1 exam. Complete the table with a tick (✓) or a cross (✗). Who do you think gives the best answer and why?

|   | Anton | Eleni | Victoria |
|---|---|---|---|
| 1 Does he/she give a suitable answer? | ✗ |   |   |
| 2 Does he/she answer in full sentences? |   |   |   |
| 3 Does he/she use a range of grammar and vocabulary? |   |   |   |

**2** How could you improve Anton and Eleni's answers?

**Examiner:** Do you walk to work every day?
**Anton:** Bus.
**Examiner:** Eleni, tell us about a good friend.
**Eleni:** Her name is Maria. She's tall. Her hair is long and straight. She is very nice. I like her.

**3** Listen to Eleni and Victoria doing the complete Speaking Part 1 exam. Complete the questions.

1 What's .................... .................... ?
2 Where .................... .................... ?
(or Where .................... .................... .................... from?)
3 Do .................... .................... or are you a student?
4 .................... .................... study?
(or .................... .................... do?)
5 .................... .................... .................... use the internet?
6 .................... .................... .................... a good friend.

- Listen carefully to the examiner's questions. You can ask the examiner to repeat the question.
- Answer the questions in full sentences, using a range of grammar and vocabulary.
- Look at the examiner when you're answering the questions.

**Exam advice**

**4** Work in groups of three. Take turns to ask a question from Exercise 3 and another question below.

- Who uses the internet the most in your house? What for?
- Do you use the internet mainly for fun or mainly for study or work? Why?
- Do you often buy things online? Describe the last thing you bought online.
- Do you usually write by hand or on a computer? Which do you prefer?

## Grammar
### Indirect questions

▶ Page 140 Grammar reference
Indirect questions

**1** Work in groups. Discuss the questions.
1 How many kinds of social media do you use and what do you use them for?
2 What are some dangers of using social media?

**2** Listen to a TV journalist talking to Bradley. What are his answers to the questions from Exercise 1?

**3** Listen again and complete the indirect questions.

| direct questions | indirect questions |
|---|---|
| Could I ask you some questions? | (1) I was wondering if I *could ask you* some questions. |
| What's your name, please? | (2) Could you tell me what ...................., please? |
| How many different kinds of social media do you use? | (3) I'd like to know how many different kinds of social media ..................... |
| What do you use each one for? | (4) Could I ask you .................... each one for? |
| Are your social media accounts safe? | (5) Do you have any idea if .................... safe? |

**4** Answer the questions.
1 Can we use question words in indirect questions?
2 Do we change the tense in indirect questions?
3 Do we change the word order in indirect questions?
4 Are indirect questions more polite than direct questions?
5 Do we always use a question mark at the end of an indirect question?

**5** /P/ **Intonation in direct and indirect questions**
Listen to the direct questions in Exercise 3. Does the speaker's voice go up or go down at the end?

**6** Listen to the indirect questions again. Does the speaker's voice go up or down?

**7** Work in pairs. Choose <u>one</u> of the topics below and write indirect questions about it.

following celebrities online    keeping in touch
keeping up-to-date with the news
making plans    playing games

**8** Work in groups. Ask and answer your questions.

# Writing Part 2

▶ Page 150 Writing bank
A story

**1** Work in groups. Look at the pictures and sentences. What do you think happened next?

**1** The message began, 'Congratulations! You've won first prize!'

**2** I was in class when my phone rang.

**2** Read the Writing Part 2 tasks and answer the questions.

**1**
- Your English teacher has asked you to write a story.
- Your story must begin with this sentence:
The message began, 'Congratulations! You've won first prize!'

**2**
- Your English teacher has asked you to write a story.
- Your story must begin with this sentence:
I was in class when my phone rang.

1 What do you have to write for each question?
2 Who do you have to write it for?

**3** Now read this story, and answer the questions.

> I was in my English class when my phone rang. I couldn't believe it. I had forgotten to switch it off. I didn't know what to do, because it was still ringing. Should I answer it? The teacher stopped talking and looked directly at me. She asked all the students what the noise was, and we said that it was a phone. Suddenly, she looked embarrassed. She told us that she had to leave the classroom for a minute. She picked up her bag and left the room. As soon as the teacher closed the door, the ringing noise stopped.

1 Which task does it answer?
2 Why did the phone stop ringing when the teacher closed the door?

**4** Work in pairs. Decide if these sentences are true or false.
1 The story is about 100 words.
2 It is well organised.
3 The story has a clear ending.
4 The ideas are connected using *and*, *because*, etc.
5 There are different tenses.
6 There are some reported questions and some reported speech.

**5** Write a story in about 100 words using one of the tasks from Exercise 1.

> **Exam advice**
> - Make sure you write a proper ending for the story. Try to surprise your readers.
> - Check there are no mistakes in your story and it is the correct length.
> - In the exam, you will need to choose between **a story** and **an article**. You <u>won't</u> be able to choose between two different stories.

Express yourself!

# 11 Vocabulary and grammar review

## Grammar

**1** Choose the correct option in *italics*.

My partner and I **(1)** *are lived* / *live* in an old house on the coast. When it **(2)** *built* / *was built* in the 19th century, it was over 500 metres from the sea, but now the water **(3)** *seems* / *is seemed* to be getting closer all the time. The sea level **(4)** *is risen* / *is rising* every year, and the waves **(5)** *are washing* / *are washed* away the beach. Sometimes, when there is a storm, the water **(6)** *is reached* / *reaches* the house. Last February, for instance, the ground floor **(7)** *completely flooded* / *was completely flooded* by sea water, and a small building near our house **(8)** *disappeared* / *was disappeared* overnight. Unless something **(9)** *does* / *is done* immediately, we **(10)** *are known* / *know* that our home will be next. Some other houses along the coast **(11)** *saved* / *were saved* when a strong wall **(12)** *put up* / *was put up* in front of them, and we want the same here.

**2** Complete sentences 1–8 with the comparative or superlative adverb form of the words in the box.

> bad   careful   ~~early~~   frequent   good
> hard   heavy   quick

1. You should get up ……*earlier*…… in the morning.
2. The ice melted …………………… as soon as the temperature increased.
3. Of all the people at the meeting, Lauren spoke …………………… . She made a great speech.
4. Buses stop here …………………… now – every ten minutes.
5. We must try …………………… to find solutions to environmental problems.
6. They're all bad musicians in that band, and the guitarist plays …………………… of all.
7. It began to rain …………………… when the storm approached.
8. If we all use energy ……………………, we can reduce the amount of pollution we cause.

## Vocabulary

**3** Complete the text with the noun form of the verbs in brackets.

A few years after I finished my secondary **(1)** ……*education*…… (educate) at Canal Street Secondary, I received an **(2)** …………………… (invite) to return there. It was for a **(3)** …………………… (celebrate) organised by the school for ex-pupils following the **(4)** …………………… (complete) of several new buildings. When I arrived I was very impressed. The new gym was a great **(5)** …………………… (improve) on the old one where we used to take all our **(6)** …………………… (examine). The **(7)** …………………… (develop) of some land next to the school also meant it now had far more classrooms. My only **(8)** …………………… (disappoint) was that none of my old classmates was there, but I still enjoyed my day back at school!

**4** Complete the crossword with words from Unit 11.

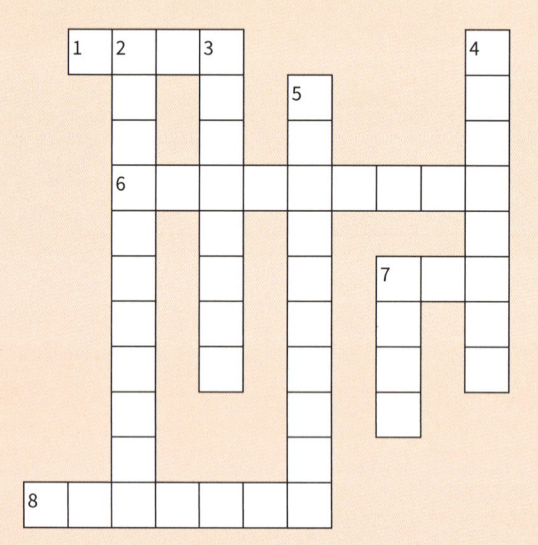

**Across**
1. a group of people working together
6. the appearance of an area of land
7. a yellow and black flying insect
8. a bird which cannot fly and lives in a cold place

**Down**
2. the noun of the verb 'explore'
3. a very high place
4. the noun of the verb 'move'
5. the noun of the verb 'discuss'
7. a large animal that lives in forests or mountains

114

# Vocabulary and grammar review 12

## Vocabulary

**1** Complete these sentences with the verbs in the box in the correct form. You will need to use some verbs more than once.

> ask   ask for   say   ~~speak~~   talk   tell

1 Most of my friends can ....*speak*.... two or three languages really well.
2 Ben .................... 'thank you' to everyone for his presents.
3 My friend .................... me if I wanted to go to the cinema that night.
4 One of my friends likes .................... jokes all the time.
5 In your email you .................... me about my plans for the summer holidays.
6 I'm going to .................... some help because I can't install this program on my laptop.
7 I became very nervous and decided to .................... my flatmates the truth.
8 When I get together with Matt, we love .................... about food and cooking.
9 Can you .................... a little more slowly, please? I don't understand.
10 In class today, we .................... in groups about how to prepare for an English exam.

**2** Add *im-*, *in-* or *un-* to these words to complete the sentences.

> expensive   fair   healthy   patient   polite   ~~possible~~

1 I can't live without my mobile phone. It's ....*impossible*.... .
2 I got a tablet online for €40. It was .................... .
3 It's .................... to charge students the same price as working adults.
4 My neighbour spends all day playing video games. That must be .................... .
5 Wait for the app to download completely. Stop being so .................... .
6 Don't eat with your mouth open. It's .................... .

## Grammar

**3** Underline and correct the mistake in each sentence.

1 In my English class, the teacher asked me what <u>was my name</u>.  *my name was*
2 A friend asked me what was my dog called.
3 Marta asked me why didn't I go to the party.
4 My sister asked me why was I crying.
5 Nicky asked me what was I going to do.
6 Danny asked me what new sport should he take up.
7 I imagine you are wondering when am I going to visit.

**4** Evie is talking about how she spends her free time. Rewrite her sentences in reported speech.

1 'I like hanging out with my friends and watching films with them.'
   She said ....*she liked hanging out*.... with her friends and watching films with them.
2 'We're looking forward to seeing the new film.'
   She said .................... to seeing the new film.
3 'I've just bought a new laptop to watch my favourite series online.'
   She said .................... a new laptop to watch her favourite series online.
4 'I'm going to invite my friends round to my house tonight.'
   She said .................... her friends round to her house that night.
5 'We won the hockey match yesterday.'
   She said .................... the hockey match the day before.
6 'I'm sure we'll have a lot of fun.'
   She said .................... a lot of fun.

**5** Complete the text with the words which best fit each gap. Use only one word in each gap.

> I was in the library when my mobile phone rang. I **(1)** ....*said*.... sorry to everyone and switched it off. A friend asked me **(2)** .................... I knew who had called and I said that I didn't know. She **(3)** .................... me that her phone had rung while she was in the library **(4)** .................... day before and somebody had started shouting at her. She thought it **(5)** .................... very unfair. At that moment, a security guard told us **(6)** .................... be quiet or go outside.

Vocabulary and grammar review   115

# Grammar reference

## 1

### PREPOSITIONS OF TIME

We use *at*:
- for times of the day: **at** 7 o'clock, **at** breakfast time
- in expressions like: **at** the weekend, **at** night, **at** New Year

We use *on* for:
- days: **on** Tuesday
- dates: **on** May 17th

We use *in* for:
- years: **in** 2017
- seasons: **in** summer
- months: **in** August
- parts of the day: **in** the morning

#### PRACTICE

**1** Complete the conversation with *at*, *in* or *on*.

A: Are you busy (1) ............... Saturday?
B: Yes, I'm with my grandmother (2) ............... the morning. I have to be there (3) ............... 11 o'clock. It's her birthday party. Her birthday is (4) ............... August 28th – that's Monday, but everyone's busy then.
A: Do you want to meet (5) ............... the evening (6) ............... Saturday?
B: OK!

### FREQUENCY ADVERBS

- always (100%)
- usually
- often
- sometimes
- occasionally
- hardly ever
- never (0%)

- We usually put frequency adverbs before the main verb.
  I **usually/sometimes/never** go to work in the evening.
  I don't **often** go to work at the weekend.

- We don't use *never*, *hardly ever* and *always* at the beginning or end of sentences.

- We put frequency adverbs after the verb *be*.
  I am **often** ill in the winter.
  She is **usually** at university at 8 o'clock.

There are other expressions that we can use to talk about frequency. These expressions are used at the beginning or end of sentences, not in the middle.

- every day, every week, every month, every year …
- once a day, twice a week, three times a month …
- on Fridays, at weekends …
- most days, most nights, most weeks …

**On Fridays**, I go to the office by bike.
I go running **twice a week**.

#### PRACTICE

**1** Put the words in order to make sentences.

1 a / go / gym / I / the / to / twice / week.
..................................................................
2 an / hour / I / more / hardly ever / spend / than / there.
..................................................................
3 an / for / half / hour. / I / run / sometimes
..................................................................
4 I / I'm / listen / music / running. / to / usually / while
..................................................................
5 always / exhausted. / get / home, / I / I'm / When
..................................................................
6 every / Friday. / friends / go / I / my / out / with
..................................................................

116

# PRESENT SIMPLE AND PRESENT CONTINUOUS

## Present simple

### Positive/Negative forms

| I/You/We/They | take | photos. |
|---|---|---|
| | don't take | |
| He/She/It | takes | |
| | doesn't take | |

### Question forms

| Do | I/you/we/they | take | photos? |
|---|---|---|---|
| Does | he/she/it | | |

### Short answers

| Yes, | I/you/we/they | do. |
|---|---|---|
| | he/she/it | does. |
| No, | I/you/we/they | don't. |
| | he/she/it | doesn't. |

We can use the present simple to talk about something that:
- happens regularly (and routines):
  I **play** tennis every Tuesday.
- is generally true and permanent at the present time:
  My brother **lives** in France.
- is a fact or always true:
  The sun **rises** in the east.

## Present continuous

### Positive/Negative forms

| I | am/'m<br>am/'m not | working at the moment. |
|---|---|---|
| You/We/They | are/'re<br>are not / aren't / 're not | |
| He/She/It | is/'s<br>is not / isn't / 's not | |

### Question forms and short answers

| Am | I | working at the moment? |
|---|---|---|
| Are | you/we/they | |
| Is | he/she/it | |
| Yes, | I | am. |
| | you/we/they | are. |
| | he/she/it | is. |
| No, | I | am / 'm not. |
| | you/we/they | aren't. |
| | he/she/it | isn't. |

We can use the present continuous to talk about
- something happening now:
  They**'re living** with friends while their house **is being decorated**.
- a temporary situation which is true now:
  He**'s cooking** in the kitchen.
- something happening in the present but not necessarily at the moment:
  My sister**'s studying** art.

### PRACTICE

**1** Choose the correct option in *italics*.

Many people (1) *take up / are taking up* cycling these days. Cycling is great because it (2) *helps / is helping* our general fitness. When we cycle, we (3) *use up / are using up* more energy than when we (4) *walk / are walking*. (5) I *go / am going* cycling regularly, but only on small roads where there aren't many cars. At the moment, (6) I *train / I'm training* for a race so (7) I *spend / I'm spending* a lot of time on my bike.

Grammar reference 117

## STATE VERBS

State verbs refer to a state or a condition, rather than an action. They are not normally used with continuous verbs.

✓ I **prefer** apples to oranges.

✗ I'm preferring apples to oranges.

- This is a list of common state verbs.

> agree   appear   believe   depend   hear   hope
> know   like   look   love   need   own   possess
> prefer   see   seem   smell   suppose   taste
> think   understand   want   weigh   wish

- There are verbs which can be both state verbs and action verbs, but have a different meaning.
  She **looks** tired. (look = appear)
  She**'s looking** for her phone. (look = search)
  He **has** an apartment. (have = own)
  He**'s having** breakfast. (have = eat)

### PRACTICE

**1** Complete the sentences with the present simple or present continuous form of the verbs in the box.

> cost   have   help   own   prefer
> smell   think   want   weigh

1 **A:** How much ............................ you ............................ , Ben?

   **B:** I don't know. About 60 kilos, maybe? I ............................ not to know actually.

2 Paul is a computer expert. He ............................ people with their IT problems.

3 The flowers in our garden ............................ beautiful.

4 My flatmate ............................ a lot of problems with his car at the moment.

5 A cinema ticket ............................ €15! I ............................ that's a lot of money!

6 Lucas ............................ a new bike, but he ............................ to sell it.

## COUNTABLE AND UNCOUNTABLE NOUNS

**Countable nouns**

Countable nouns refer to nouns which can be counted. They have singular and plural forms: **tree – trees; knife – knives; child – children; man – men**.

- Singular countable nouns can be used with *a/an*:
  a **book**, an **elephant**.
- Plural countable nouns can be used with numbers, *some* and *any*:
  Our family has some **animals** – a dog and three **cats**.

**Uncountable nouns**

Uncountable nouns refer to nouns which cannot be counted. They have no plural form: **advice** advices, **furniture** furnitures, **information** informations, **homework** homeworks, etc.

**Both countable and uncountable**

Some nouns can be countable and uncountable.

I love **lambs** but I don't eat **lamb**.

lamb (countable) = animal

lamb (uncountable) = meat from a lamb

- To make uncountable nouns countable, use countable nouns like *piece, slice, spoonful, box*, etc.
  a **piece of advice**
  three **slices of bread**
  two **spoonfuls of sugar**
  a **bowl of rice**

### PRACTICE

**1** Underline the countable nouns and circle the uncountable nouns in this short text.

> As well as giving us energy, sugar in our diet makes our food taste better. Sometimes we add sugar to our breakfast cereals. Sugar is also used in biscuits, ice cream, chocolate and many other things we eat. It is also in fruit and vegetables and even in a glass of milk!

## A FEW, A BIT OF, MANY, MUCH, A LOT OF AND LOTS OF

These words and phrases are quantifiers. They tell us how much or how little of something there is.

- For small quantities, use *a few* with plural countable nouns:
  **A few** people in my office speak English.
- Use *a bit of* with uncountable nouns:
  I'd like **a bit of** advice about going to university, please.
- For large quantities, use *many* with plural countable nouns:
  There aren't **many** trains at night.
  How **many** times have you been to London?

- Use *much* with uncountable nouns in questions and negative sentences.
  How **much** money do you need?
  We don't have **much** time.
- Use *a lot of* or *lots of* with plural countable nouns or uncountable nouns.
  **A lot of / Lots of** students ride bikes to college.
  You can save **a lot of / lots of** money if you cycle or walk.

### PRACTICE

**2** <u>Underline</u> and correct the mistakes in these sentences.

1 We haven't got many time.
2 I drink a few water when I wake up.
3 There are lot of things we need to talk about.
4 Can you help? I need some informations about train times.
5 How much friends do you have online?
6 We have a lot of furnitures in our house.

## PREPOSITIONS OF PLACE

We use prepositions of place to say where something is.

- We use *at* with points: **at** the bus stop, **at** the station, **at** home, **at** university

- We use *in* with spaces or to say something is inside another thing: **in** the kitchen, **in** the sea, **in** the car, **in** France

- We use *on* with surfaces: **on** the wall, **on** the floor, **on** the ceiling, **on** the table

### PRACTICE

**1** Complete the sentences with *at*, *in* or *on*.

1 My computer is .................... the desk .................... my living room.
2 I live .................... the end of the road.
3 Your shoes are .................... a box .................... the shelf.
4 There's someone .................... the door.

Grammar reference 119

# 2

## PAST SIMPLE

**be**

| Positive/Negative forms | | |
|---|---|---|
| I/He/She/It | was / wasn't | here yesterday. |
| You/We/They | were / weren't | |

| Question forms and short answers | | |
|---|---|---|
| **Was** | I/he/she/it | here yesterday? |
| **Were** | you/we/they | |
| Yes, | I/he/she/it | was. |
| | you/we/they | were. |
| No, | I/he/she/it | wasn't. |
| | you/we/they | weren't. |

**Other verbs**

*play* (regular)
*go* (irregular)

| Positive/Negative forms | | |
|---|---|---|
| I/You/We/They/He/She/It | played / didn't play | tennis yesterday. |
| | went / didn't go | to work yesterday. |

| Question forms and short answers | | |
|---|---|---|
| **Did** | I/you/we/they/he/she/it | play | tennis yesterday? |
| | | go | to work yesterday? |
| Yes, | I/you/we/they/he/she/it | | did. |
| No, | I/you/we/they/he/she/it | | didn't. |

**Spelling of regular past simple verbs**

For regular verbs, we add *-ed* to the base form of the verb, or *-d* if the verb already ends in *e*.

| for verbs: | present simple | past simple |
|---|---|---|
| • ending in a consonant + *-y*, add *-ied* | study<br>carry | stud**ied**<br>carr**ied** |
| • ending in a vowel + a consonant (with stress on last syllable), double the final consonant and add *-ed* | plan<br>prefer<br>drop | plan**ned**<br>prefe**rred**<br>dro**pped** |
| • ending in a vowel + *-l*, double the *l* and add *-ed* | travel<br>control | trave**lled**<br>contro**lled** |
| • ending in a vowel + consonant (with no stress on the last syllable) | happen<br>visit | happen**ed**<br>visit**ed** |

We use the past simple to talk about
- past actions/events/states which have finished:
  Jenny **was** tired after she **went** ice skating.
- repeated past actions:
  I **cycled** to university every day when I was a student.
- a sequence of past actions:
  We **left** home, **walked** to the station and **caught** the train.

## PAST CONTINUOUS

| Positive/Negative forms | | |
|---|---|---|
| I/He/She/It | was / wasn't | studying all evening. |
| You/We/They | were / weren't | |

| Question forms and short answers | | |
|---|---|---|
| **Was** | I/he/she/it | studying all evening? |
| **Were** | you/we/they | |
| Yes, | I/he/she/it | was. |
| | you/we/they | were. |
| No, | I/he/she/it | wasn't. |
| | you/we/they | weren't. |

We use the past continuous to talk about
- a particular moment in the past:
  Emily **was walking** the dog at 5 pm.
- temporary actions which give extra (less important) information:
  It **was raining**, so I decided not to go out.
- two or more actions happening at the same time:
  While I **was studying**, he **was playing** the guitar.
- an action happening when another action happened:
  He **was cleaning** his bike when he hurt his hand.

### *when, while* and *as*

We can use these words with the past continuous to introduce an action happening at the same time as another.
**When** Joe was walking home, it started to rain.
The phone rang **while** I was having breakfast.
They arrived **as** we were leaving.

120

## PRACTICE

**1** Choose the correct option in *italics*.

1 While I *watched / was watching* TV, my flatmate was studying.
2 My friends *often phoned / were often phoning* me when I was at work.
3 While I was talking to my friend, I *realised / was realising* that something was wrong.
4 It was a lovely day. The sun *shone / was shining* and the birds *sang / were singing*.
5 Lionel Messi *won / was winning* a gold medal for Argentina in the Beijing Olympics.

**2** Complete the sentences with the past simple or past continuous form of the verbs in brackets.

1 While I ................... (tidy) my living room, I ................... (find) some old photographs.
2 As I ................... (leave) the cinema, I ................... (realise) that I'd left my phone behind.
3 While Simon ................... (watch) television, his brother ................... (cook) dinner.
4 When we ................... (hear) the fire alarm, we all ................... (stop) what we ................... (do) and ................... (walk) out of the building.
5 My computer ................... (crash) while I ................... (update) my web page.

## USED TO

**Positive/Negative forms**

| I/You/He/She/It/We/They | used to | enjoy watching football. |
|---|---|---|
| | didn't use to | |

**Question forms and short answers**

| Did | I/you/he/she/it/we/they | use to | play football? |
|---|---|---|---|
| Yes, | I/you/he/she/it/we/they | did. | |
| No, | | didn't. | |

We use *used to* to talk about the past. There is no present form of *used to*.
**Note:**
In negative and question forms, the spelling is *use* not *used*.
We use *used to* + an infinitive form to talk about:
- things that happened regularly in the past but don't now.
  I **used to** drink milk for breakfast, but now I always drink orange juice.
- actions that didn't happen in the past, but happen now.
  I **didn't use to** drink orange juice, but now I love it.
- past states or conditions that are different from the past.
  I **used to** have long, dark hair. (= I don't any more)

## PRACTICE

**1** Rewrite the sentences so that they mean the same as the original sentence. Use the correct form of *used to*.

1 I like hot weather now, but I didn't in the past.
..................................................................
2 My brother played football until he broke his leg.
..................................................................
3 My hair was blond, now it's brown.
..................................................................
4 Did you go on holiday with friends when you were a child?
..................................................................
5 When I was younger, I didn't get up late.
..................................................................

## SO (DO) I AND NOR/NEITHER (DO) I

We can use *so (do) I* and *nor/neither (do) I* to show that you think the same as another person.

- We use *so* in positive sentences when we have the same feelings or experiences.
  A: *I love chocolate.* B: *So do I.*
  A: *I ate a lot of chocolate yesterday.* B: *So did I.*
- We use the same auxiliary verbs or modal verbs in the reply.
  A: *I am hungry.* B: *So am I.*
  A: *I will have lunch at one o'clock.* B: *So will I.*
- We use *nor* or *neither* in negative sentences. We use the same auxiliary verbs or modal verbs in the reply.
  A: *I don't like chocolate.* B: *Nor/Neither do I.*
  A: *I haven't had coffee for ages.* B: *Nor/Neither have I.*

**Note:** We use *don't* to respond to positive statements. We use *do* to respond to negative statements.
  A: *I love chocolate.* B: *I don't!*
  A: *I don't like chocolate.* B: *I do!*

## PRACTICE

**1** Write replies to these sentences using *so* or *nor/neither*.

1 I spent a long time at the office yesterday.
..................................................................
2 I didn't understand the question.
..................................................................
3 I like ice cream.
..................................................................
4 I don't like hot weather.
..................................................................
5 I have two brothers.
..................................................................

Grammar reference 121

# 3

## VERBS FOLLOWED BY *TO* OR *-ING*

- Some verbs are always followed by an infinitive (*to* + verb):
  When I was 15, I **decided to become** a professional musician.
- Others are always followed by the *-ing* form of the verb:
  Mike **kept falling** asleep at his desk.
- There are some verbs which can be followed by either an infinitive or the *-ing* form. Unfortunately, there are no rules to help you work out whether verbs are followed by the infinitive or the *-ing* form, or either, so you will need to learn them.

**Verbs followed by the infinitive**

> afford   agree   arrange   attempt   choose   decide   expect
> help   hope   intend   learn   manage   offer   plan
> promise   refuse   seem   want   would like

**Verbs followed by *-ing***

> admit   avoid   can't stand*   consider   dislike*   don't mind*
> enjoy*   fancy*   feel like   finish   give up   imagine   mind
> miss   postpone   practise   prevent   put off   suggest

**Note:** The verbs marked * all express likes or dislikes.

**Verbs followed by the infinitive or *-ing* with no difference in meaning**

> begin   continue   intend   start

**Verbs followed by the infinitive or *-ing* with little difference in meaning**

> hate   like   love   prefer

There is a small difference in meaning between the two forms.

- *-ing* form: the action or experience is more important.
  He likes **baking** cakes.
- infinitive form: result of the action is more important, or to describe a habit / something we prefer.
  He likes **to bake** cakes for special occasions.
- The *-ing* form is more common after *hate* and *love*:
  I hate **playing** ball sports. I love **doing** gymnastics.

**Verbs followed by the infinitive or *-ing* where there is a clear difference in meaning**

|        | infinitive | -ing |
|--------|------------|------|
| forget | I **forgot to say** thank you. (= I didn't say thank you.) | I **forgot saying** that. (= I have no memory of this.) |
| go on  | He **went on to talk** about his childhood. (= This was the next thing he talked about.) | He **went on talking**. (= He continued talking.) |
| remember | I **remembered to lock** the door. (= I did something I had to do.) | I **remember locking** the door. (= I have a memory of this.) |
| stop   | Let's **stop to buy** flowers. (= in order to do something) | Let's **stop buying** flowers. (= not continue) |
| try    | I **tried to learn** Japanese, but it was too difficult, so I stopped. (= try something, and not succeed) | I **tried eating** spinach, but I didn't like it. (= try something and find out what it's like) |

- In negative sentences, we put *not* after the first verb.
  He's **decided not to go** to university next year.
  She **considered not going** away for the weekend. (= but now she is going)
- In sentences which include an object, we put the object after the first verb.
  I **helped my friend to fix** his car.
  We should **stop people using** their phones or eating while they're driving.

### PRACTICE

**1** Complete the conversation with the correct form of the verbs in brackets.

A: It's really hot here, isn't it? Do you fancy
   (1) ............................ (go) for a swim?
B: Yes, I'd love (2) ............................ (have) a swim.
A: Can I suggest (3) ............................ (go) this afternoon?
B: I'd planned (4) ............................ (go) to the cinema this afternoon, but I don't mind (5) ............................ (do) that tomorrow instead.
A: I can't imagine (6) ............................ (live) in a hot country all the time.
B: I'm sure you'd manage (7) ............................ (have) a nice time.
A: Maybe I'd get used to it. I certainly enjoy
   (8) ............................ (spend) my holidays here.

**2** Tick (✓) the pairs of sentences which have the same meanings.

1. **A** My boss continued talking even though it was time to go home.
   **B** My boss continued to talk even though it was time to go home. ☐
2. **A** I began to learn German two years ago.
   **B** I began learning German two years ago. ☐
3. **A** Ben stopped to phone his parents.
   **B** Ben stopped phoning his parents. ☐
4. **A** I prefer to watch football than to play it.
   **B** I prefer watching football to playing it. ☐
5. **A** I like to watch the sunrise.
   **B** I like watching the sunrise. ☐
6. **A** They went on to tell us about their holiday.
   **B** They went on telling us about their holiday. ☐

## PHRASAL VERBS

A phrasal verb is a verb with two or three parts. The meaning of the verb is sometimes different from the meaning of its separate parts. Phrasal verbs can combine verbs with prepositions or adverbs. For example: *to take off, to put on, to catch up with, to look forward to*

There are two main types of phrasal verbs
- verbs which need an object:
  She **took off** her hat.
  He **put on** his shoes.
  We're **looking forward to** our holiday.
- verbs which do not need an object:
  They **set off** early.
  We **got up** late.
- Sometimes, it is possible to put the object in between the verb and the preposition/adverb. Sometimes, it is not.
  ✓ He **took** his hat **off**.
  ✓ He **took** it **off**.
  ✗ He **took off** it.

  ✓ We're **looking forward** to the weekend.
  ✗ We're **looking** the weekend **forward to**.

### PRACTICE

**1** Underline the phrasal verbs in questions 1–6. Then match them with answers a–f.

1. What should you do if your TV breaks down?
2. Which of your parents do you take after?
3. Do you like to dress up when you go to a party?
4. Who do you really look up to?
5. Do you ever have to look after anyone?
6. What do you think about people who show off?

a. No, I prefer to wear my normal clothes.
b. I don't like them.
c. Ask someone to repair it.
d. I'm like my mother.
e. My father. He's my hero.
f. I sometimes babysit my little brother.

**2** Rewrite the underlined words with a phrasal verb from the box. Make any other necessary changes.

> get on with   give up   look forward to   sign up for   take up

1. I have a good relationship with everyone in my family.
   ....................................................................
2. I've put my name down for an English course.
   ....................................................................
3. I can't wait to see my friend again.
   ....................................................................
4. My father has stopped eating sugar.
   ....................................................................
5. My brother has just started playing basketball.
   ....................................................................

Grammar reference 123

# 4

## COMPARATIVE AND SUPERLATIVE ADJECTIVES

We use comparative adjectives (e.g. *bigger than*) to compare two people or things and to say if one has more of a quality (e.g. size, height, etc.) than the other. Comparative adjectives are usually followed by *than*.

We use superlative adjectives (e.g. *the fastest, the most important*) to say that in a particular group, something has the most of a quality.

### Regular adjectives

|  | comparative | superlative |
|---|---|---|
| • For most adjectives, add *-er* or *-est*. | **small** → **small**er<br>Italy is **smaller** than Spain. | → the **small**est<br>Vatican City is **the smallest** country in the world. |
| • For short adjectives ending in *-e*, add *-r* or *-st*. | **large** → **large**r<br>Canada is **larger** than China. | → the **large**st<br>Russia is **the largest** country in the world. |
| • For short adjectives with a vowel + a consonant, double the consonant and add *-er* or *-est*. | **hot** → **hott**er<br>Algeria is **hotter** than Mexico. | → the **hott**est<br>Libya is the **hottest** country in the world. |
| • For two-syllable adjectives ending in *-y*, change the *y* to *i* and add *-er* or *-est*. | **heavy** → **heav**ier<br>Elephants are **heavier** than crocodiles. | → the **heav**iest<br>Blue whales are **the heaviest** animals in the world. |
| • For some two-syllable adjectives, we can either add *-er, -est* or use *more, the most*. These are adjectives ending in *-ow, -le, -er* and *polite, quiet, common* and *stupid*. | Mia is **more polite** than me. (= Mia is **politer** than me.) | Mia is **the most polite** student in the class.<br>(= Mia is **the politest** student in the class.) |
| • For longer adjectives, or two-syllable adjectives ending in *-ful*, put *more/less* or *the most/least* in front of the adjective. | **difficult** → **more/less difficult**<br>Some people think it's **more difficult** to make friends when you are older. | → **the most/least difficult**<br>Is it true that Japanese is **the most difficult** language for English speakers to learn? |

### Irregular adjectives

There are three irregular adjectives: *good, bad, far*.

bad → worse → the worst
good → better → the best
far → farther/further* → the farthest/furthest*

*There is no difference in meaning, but *further / the furthest* is more common.

### PRACTICE

**1** Complete the comparative and superlative adjectives.

| 1 | thin | thinner than |  |
|---|---|---|---|
| 2 | nice | than | the nicest |
| 3 |  | lazier than | the laziest |
| 4 | comfortable | than | the most comfortable |
| 5 | good | better than |  |
| 6 | bad | than | the worst |
| 7 |  | farther/further than | the farthest/furthest |

**2** Complete the sentences with the comparative or superlative form of the adjectives in brackets.

1 It rained every day in December 2015 in Portland, USA. It was ........................... December for 75 years. (wet)

2 Some people think that the Sydney Opera House is ........................... modern building in the world. (beautiful)

3 A blue whale is ........................... than an elephant. (heavy)

4 I felt ill all weekend, but I'm much ........................... now. (good)

5 This writer's new book is ........................... than her others. (bad)

6 We've moved house. Now, we live ........................... from my office than we used to. (far)

124

### *a bit, a little, slightly, (not) much, far, (not) a lot*

We can use these words with comparative adjectives.

- We use *a bit, a little, slightly, not much* or *not a lot* to describe a small difference:
  My brother is **a little** younger than me.
  I'm **a bit** older than him.

- We use *much, a lot* or *far* to describe a large difference:
  I'm **much** fitter than my brother, but he's **a lot** faster than me.
  He's **much** more polite than his cousin.

### *(not) as … as*

- We use *as* + adjective/adverb + *as* to say that two things are the same.
  Hannah is **as tall as** Jess.
  Today is **as warm as** yesterday.

- We use *not as* + adjective/adverb + *as* to say that one thing is less than another.
  My brother is**n't as fit as** me. = I am fitter than my brother.
  I'm **not as fast as** my brother. = My brother is faster than me.

### PRACTICE

**3** Rewrite the sentences so that they mean the same thing as the original sentence. Use the words in brackets.

1. Roman is taller than Josh.
   Josh ........................... (not as)
2. My old phone was cheap. My new phone is very expensive.
   My new phone ........................... (much)
3. Burgers aren't as healthy as fruit.
   Fruit is ........................... (a lot)
4. Spain is a big country in Europe. It's 505,370 km². France is a little bigger, at 643,801 km².
   Spain is ........................... (a bit)
5. The old shopping centre was good, but the new one is much nicer.
   The new shopping centre is ........................... (far)

## GRADABLE AND NON-GRADABLE ADJECTIVES

- Most adjectives are gradable. This means we can make them stronger or weaker by using words like *very*. We cannot use words like *completely* or *absolutely* with these adjectives.
  ✗ *I'm completely cold.*
  ✓ I'm **very cold**.
  ✓ Our English exam was **fairly difficult**.
  ✓ Harry's new car is **quite big**, isn't it?
  ✓ Ben was **pretty tired** after a long day's work.

- Non-gradable or extreme adjectives are adjectives which we cannot make stronger or weaker by using words like *very*. We can use these words with non-gradable adjectives: *completely, absolutely, totally, really*.
  ✗ *I'm very freezing.*
  ✓ I'm **absolutely freezing**.
  ✓ Our English exam was **absolutely impossible**.
  ✓ Harry's new car is **really enormous**, isn't it?
  ✓ Ben was **totally exhausted** after a long day's work.

### PRACTICE

**1** Match gradable adjectives 1–7 with non-gradable adjectives a–g.

| 1 | bad       | a | amazed    |
|---|-----------|---|-----------|
| 2 | big       | b | delighted |
| 3 | cold      | c | excellent |
| 4 | good      | d | exhausted |
| 5 | pleased   | e | freezing  |
| 6 | surprised | f | terrible  |
| 7 | tired     | g | huge      |

**2** Choose the correct options in *italics*.

1. My friend was absolutely *pleased / delighted* when she heard she'd passed her exam. Her parents were quite *surprised / amazed*, too. They thought she might fail.
2. The office heating system broke down, so we felt very *cold / freezing* all day.
3. I was totally *tired / exhausted* after running 10 kilometres.
4. I had a very *bad / terrible* night's sleep. That's why I'm pretty *tired / exhausted* now.
5. I really enjoyed the film last night. I thought it was absolutely *good / excellent*.
6. The audience for the concert was absolutely *big / huge*. I think there were thousands of people there.

Grammar reference 125

# 5

## MODAL VERBS: *CAN, COULD, MIGHT* AND *MAY* (ABILITY AND POSSIBILITY)

**Talking about ability and inability**

- We use *can/can't* and *could/couldn't* to talk about ability or inability. They are followed by the infinitive without *to*.
  Anna **can speak** French, but she **can't speak** Chinese.
  Max **could walk** when he was a year old, but he **couldn't talk** until he was two.

  | | |
  |---|---|
  | **Can** Anna speak French? | Yes, she **can**. |
  | **Can** she speak Chinese? | No, she **can't**. |
  | **Could** Max walk when he was one? | Yes, he **could**. |
  | **Could** he talk when he was one? | No, he **couldn't**. |

**Talking about possibility**

- We use *might*, *may* and *could* to talk about possibilities in the present or the future.
  We use *can* to talk about possibilities in the present but not the future. These modal verbs are followed by the infinitive without *to*.
  It **might be** very hot tomorrow.
  We **may go** swimming this afternoon.
  There **could be** a storm later this evening.
  It **can snow** here in April, but it doesn't often happen.

- To talk about negative possibilities we can use *may not* or *might not*, but not *can not* or *could not*.
  Laura is not feeling well, so she **may not go** to work today.
  You have to accept that you **might not win** the lottery this week.

- The form of these verbs never changes. For example, we cannot say ~~He cans~~ / ~~They mighted~~.

- We can use *May I …?* or *Could I …?* to ask for permission.
  **May I** sit here?

- We rarely use the short form *mightn't*. We don't use *mayn't*.

### PRACTICE

**1** Complete the sentences with *can, can't, could, couldn't, may* or *might*. Sometimes more than one answer is possible.

1 I've looked for my phone, but I .................. find it.
2 My brother .................. swim when he was four years old.
3 I'm not sure what to do tomorrow. I .................. go to Jo's party.
4 She isn't looking very well. I think she .................. have flu.
5 I .................. play the piano but I don't play very often.
6 Kieran .................. drive a car until he was nearly 30.

**2** Match the sentence beginnings (1–5) with the endings (a–e). Then choose the best modal verb in *italics*.

1 I don't know where Luis is. He *may / can*
2 I have some free time, so I *can / might*
3 There's someone at the door. It *may / can*
4 We need to tidy up. Our friends *can / could*
5 Working too hard *can / could*

a be one of my friends.
b make you stressed.
c see her.
d still be at university.
e arrive at any minute.

## MODAL VERBS: *SHOULD, SHOULDN'T, OUGHT TO, MUST, MUSTN'T, HAVE TO, DON'T HAVE TO* (OBLIGATION AND PROHIBITION)

**should/shouldn't**

- We use *should/shouldn't* to give or ask for advice. *Should/shouldn't* are followed by the infinitive without *to*.
  You **should join** a gym if you want to keep fit.
  You **shouldn't eat** too much chocolate.
  What **should I do**?

- An alternative to *should* is *ought to* + infinitive. This is more formal.

**must, have to**

- We use *must* and *have to* to express obligation.
  You **must take** your passport with you when you travel abroad.
  We **have to show** our passports when we cross the border.

- We often use *must* to talk about rules or laws which we agree with or believe in.
  We **must wear** a seat belt in the car, even for short journeys.

- We often use *have to* to talk about rules or laws which were made by someone else or which we may not agree with.
  My teacher says that I **have to finish** the homework tonight or I'll be in trouble.

**don't have to**

- Use *don't have to* or *needn't* (but not *mustn't*) when it's not necessary to do something.
  We **didn't have to show** our passports when we went to Scotland.
  We **don't need to** wear smart clothes to the office.

**can/can't**

- We can also use *can/can't* to express permission or lack of permission.
  You **can leave** any time you like.
  You **can't bring** animals in here.
  **Can I use** your phone, please?

*mustn't*

- Use *mustn't* to express prohibition, to say that something is not allowed.
  You **mustn't use** your phone in the cinema.
- We can also use *can't* instead of *mustn't*.
  You **can't talk** during the exam.
- There is no past tense form of *mustn't*. Use *not allowed to*.
  We **weren't allowed to go** into the concert without a ticket.

## PRACTICE

**1** Complete the sentences with *can/can't, must* or *mustn't*. Sometimes there may be more than one possible answer.

1 We ............... bring a dog in here.

2 We ............... pay in cash. We ............... pay by credit card.

3 We ............... use wifi here.

4 We ............... sit at this table. It's reserved.

5 We ............... use our phones here.

**2** Choose the correct verbs in *italics*.

When my grandfather was young, children (1) *must not / didn't have to* stay at school until the age 18 or even 16. They (2) *could / couldn't* leave when they were 14. My grandfather had no choice. He (3) *had to / didn't have to* go out and earn money for his family. At the end of every week he (4) *could / had to* give his wages to his mother. She gave him a small amount of money which he (5) *had to / could* spend as he liked. When he was 18, he wanted to join the army, but he failed the medical examination so he (6) *had to / couldn't* do military service. This meant he couldn't fight for his country. Instead of being a soldier, he drove an ambulance.

## ADJECTIVES WITH *-ED* AND *-ING* ENDINGS

Many English adjectives which end in *-ing* or *-ed* are formed from verbs.

| verb | adjectives |
| --- | --- |
| relax | relaxed/relaxing |
| surprise | surprised/surprising |

- Adjectives which end in *-ed* tell us how a person feels.
  I'm going to bed because I'm **tired**.
- Adjectives which end in *-ing* describe the effect of something.
  I'm going to bed. I've had a **tiring** day at work.

## PRACTICE

**1** Choose the correct adjectives in *italics*.

1 **A:** Did you see that *interested / interesting* programme about the moon on TV last night?
   **B:** No, I'm not really *interested / interesting* in space.

2 **A:** You look very *relaxed / relaxing*. Did you have a good holiday?
   **B:** No, it wasn't *relaxed / relaxing* at all! I was ill.

3 **A:** What do you find most *annoyed / annoying* about your older brother?
   **B:** Everything he does makes me *annoyed / annoying*.

4 **A:** What's happened? You look really *excited / exciting*.
   **B:** Yes, I've just heard that I've won first prize in a competition. It's so *excited / exciting*!

Grammar reference 127

# 6 PRESENT PERFECT

We use the present perfect to connect the present with the past.

| Positive/Negative forms | | |
|---|---|---|
| I/You/We/They | have/'ve<br>have not / haven't | finished work. |
| He/She/It | has/'s<br>has not / hasn't | |

| Question forms and short answers | | |
|---|---|---|
| Have<br>Has | I/you/we/they<br>he/she/it | finished work? |
| Yes, | I/you/we/they<br>he/she/it | have.<br>has. |
| No, | I/you/we/they<br>he/she/it | haven't.<br>hasn't. |

- The present perfect is formed with the correct form of *have* in the present and the past participle of the main verb. The past participle of regular verbs and some irregular verbs is the same as the past simple. The past participle is underlined in the examples below.

| past simple | present perfect |
|---|---|
| I **finished** work. | I have **finished** work. |
| He **bought** a sandwich. | He has **bought** a sandwich. |

- Some irregular verbs have past participles which are not the same as the past simple form.

| past simple | present perfect |
|---|---|
| She **ate** her lunch. | She has **eaten** her lunch. |
| She **wrote** a letter. | She has **written** a letter. |

We use the present perfect to talk about:
- something which started in the past and is connected with the present:
  *Ed has broken his leg, so he can't play football this weekend.*
- something which started in the past and is still true:
  *Ben and Karen have lived in London for seven years.*
- past experiences which refer to an unstated time in the past, often with *ever* and *never*:
  *Anna has been to Brazil, but she has never been to Canada.*
- recent past actions:
  *Have you done your English homework?*

### *just*, *already* and *yet*

- *just* = *very recently*, a short time ago:
  *I've just emailed Marcus and told him the good news.*
- *already* = *before now*, often sooner than expected:
  *He's already eaten his dinner, so he can go out with his friends.*
- *Just* and *already* are placed between *have/has* and the past participle.
- *yet* = *until now* is used in negative sentences and questions to talk about things we plan to do in the future, but which are not done. *Yet* is placed at the end of a sentence:
  *I haven't finished my project yet.*
  *Have you finished your project yet?*

### PRACTICE

**1** Complete the sentences with *already*, *just* or *yet*.

1 I've ........................ arrived home. I got here five minutes ago.
2 **A:** Let's tell our friends the news.
   **B:** I've ........................ told them. I told them last week.
3 I'm not hungry because I've ........................ had lunch. I ate earlier.
4 Have you met Benoit ........................?
5 I haven't got dressed ........................ because I've just woken up.

### *since* and *for*

We can use *since* and *for* with the present perfect to talk about a time that started in the past and continues to the present.

- *since* is followed by the beginning of a period of time:
  *We've lived here since December 2017.*
  *for* is followed by a period of time:
  *She's lived there for six and a half years.*

### PRACTICE

**2** Complete the sentences with *for* or *since*.

1 My father has worked for the same company ........................ 20 years.
2 Megan has played football ........................ she was six years old.
3 I haven't eaten anything ........................ 7 o'clock this morning.
4 Sofia can't still be tired. She's slept ........................ 11 hours!
5 I've made lots of new friends ........................ I've been in this job.

## The present perfect or the past simple?

- We use the present perfect to talk about a past experience without saying when it happened.
  I **'ve been** to the top of the Eiffel Tower.
- To say when something happened, use the past simple.
  I **went** to the top of the Eiffel Tower last summer.
- We use the present perfect to talk about the continuing effect of a past event or action on the present.
  There **has been** an accident on the motorway. Now there are long queues of traffic into the city centre.
- We use the present perfect to talk about the time period up to the present.
  I **'ve been** to town this morning. (= It is still the morning.)
  My brother **has written** a short story. (= He may write more stories.)
- If the time period is now over, we use the past simple.
  I **went** into town this morning. (= It is now afternoon or evening.)
  Prince **wrote** over 150 songs. (= He died in 2016, so can't write any more.)

### PRACTICE

**3** **Underline** and correct the mistakes in the conversation. Some lines are correct.

A: Have you heard? My oldest sister's getting married.
B: Who to?
A: A guy called Elliot.
B: Really! How long did she know him?
A: Only six months. Apparently they've met at work.
B: Have you met Elliot already?
A: No, not yet, but my sister's told me a lot about him.
B: When have you seen her?
A: I've seen her last week. She drove me to work one day.

**4** Complete the conversations with the past simple or present perfect form of the verbs in brackets. Make any other changes necessary.

1 **A:** You look terrible. Are you OK?
  **B:** I'm alright. I ……………… (go) to bed late last night and I ……………… (just wake up).

2 **A:** Where's Chloe?
  **B:** I don't know. Her train ……………… (arrive) half an hour ago, but I ……………… (not see her yet).

3 **A:** Shall we go and see the new Star Wars film tonight?
  **B:** No, I ……………… it. (already see)
  **A:** Really?
  **B:** Yes, I ……………… it last week. (see)

4 **A:** What's the most expensive thing that you ……………… (ever buy)?
  **B:** My racing bike. It ……………… 500 euros. (cost)
  **A:** I ……………… as much money as that on anything! (never spend)

5 **A:** ……………… gymnastics? (you ever do)
  **B:** Yes, but I ……………… karate. (never do)

6 **A:** Where ……………… on holiday last year? (go)
  **B:** We ……………… to Florida. (go)
  **A:** Really? I've got relatives there, but I ……………… them. (never visit)

Grammar reference 129

# 7
## ADVERBS OF DEGREE

*extremely, fairly, quite, rather, really* and *very*

- We can use *extremely, really* and *very* to make adjectives and adverbs stronger.
  We've had an **extremely busy** day.
  I'm going to stay inside today. It's going to be **really hot**.
  It was so warm, they were walking **very slowly**.

- We can use *fairly* and *rather* to make adjectives and adverbs weaker (they mean 'not very').
  I think you'll pass the exam **fairly easily**.
  I'm **rather disappointed** that I failed the exam, but I'm not surprised.

- *Quite* has two opposite meanings: *completely* (with non-gradable adjectives) and *not very* (with gradable adjectives).
  I've been working hard, so I'm **quite tired**. (*quite* = a bit tired)
  I'm **quite exhausted** after running a marathon yesterday.
  (*quite* = completely)

### PRACTICE

**1** Put the words in order to make correct sentences.

1 because / coat / cold / forgotten / had / I / I / my / really / was
   ...........................................................................

2 exam / fairly / her / is / Mia / pass / she / sure / will
   ...........................................................................

3 is / moving / slowly / The / traffic / very
   ...........................................................................

4 Be / busy / careful / cross / extremely / roads / when / you
   ...........................................................................

5 a / difficult / question / rather / That / was
   ...........................................................................

*too* and *enough*

We use *too* to say something is more than is needed, wanted or allowed.

- *too* + adjective/adverb
  Anna's **too young** to drive.
  Hurry up! You're walking **too slowly**.

- *too* + adjective/adverb + *for someone* + infinitive
  This exercise is **too difficult for me to do**.
  They were talking **too quickly for me to understand**.

- *too* + *much* + uncountable noun
  You've made **too much food**.

- *too* + *many* + plural countable noun
  We've got **too many books**. I'm going to give some away.

- *too* + *much/many* + noun + *for someone* + infinitive
  There are **too many books for me to read**.

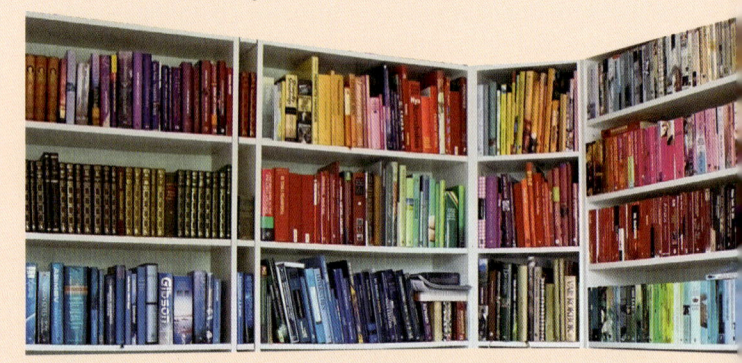

We use *enough* to say that there is (or isn't) as much as is needed.

- adjective/adverb + *(not) enough* (+ infinitive)
  Anna's **old enough to drive**.
  We're not running **fast enough to win** the race.

- adjective/adverb + *enough* + *for someone* + infinitive
  That car isn't **big enough for us all to get** in.

- *enough* + noun
  There are **enough chairs** for everyone to sit down.

### PRACTICE

**2** Complete the sentences with *enough* or *too* and a word from the box.

| big   good   hours   ill   money   rich |

1 Jane's staying at home today. She's ................... to go to work.

2 I couldn't believe I'd won the lottery. It was ................... to be true.

3 Ben's grown so quickly – his shoes aren't ................... for him now.

4 I'm really busy. There aren't ................... in the day.

5 I wish I had ................... for that car. But I know I'll never be ................... to buy one.

# FUTURE FORMS

*will*

| Positive/Negative forms | | |
|---|---|---|
| I/You/He/She/It/We/They | **will/'ll** | be late home. |
| | **will not / won't** | |

| Question forms and short answers | | |
|---|---|---|
| **Will** | I/you/he/she/it/we/they | be late home? |
| Yes, | I/you/he/she/it/we/they | **will**. |
| No, | I/you/he/she/it/we/they | **won't**. |

We use *will* to talk about:
- things we expect to happen or predict will happen:
  More people **will** buy electric cars in the future.
- things which are not certain:
  It probably **won't** be cold tomorrow.
- future facts:
  My app says that the sun **will** rise at 5 o'clock tomorrow.
- quick decisions about what to do next:
  There's someone at the door. I**'ll** get it.
- an offer or a promise:
  Don't worry. I **won't** be late.

*be going to*

| Positive/Negative forms | | |
|---|---|---|
| I | am/'m<br>am not / 'm not | |
| You/We/They | are/'re<br>are not / aren't | **going to** study tonight. |
| He/She | is/'s<br>is not / isn't | |

| Question forms and short answers | | |
|---|---|---|
| **Am** | I | |
| **Are** | you/we/they | **going to** study hard? |
| **Is** | he/she | |
| Yes, | I | **am**. |
| | you/we/they | **are**. |
| | he/she | **is**. |
| No, | I | **am/'m not**. |
| | you/we/they | **aren't**. |
| | he/she | **isn't**. |

We use *going to* to talk about:
- things we predict based on what we can see, or something that we think is certain to happen:
  I**'m going to** sneeze.
- future plans and things we intend to do:
  I**'m going to** watch the match on TV.

**Present continuous forms for the future**

We use the present continuous to talk about:
- arrangements or plans which have already been made.
  I**'m starting** a new course tomorrow.

**Present simple forms for the future**

We use the present simple to talk about:
- events in the future that are certain because they are facts.
  The film **starts** at 3.30 pm. Don't be late!
- fixed or planned events.
  The lesson **ends** at 7.30 this evening.

## PRACTICE

**1** Choose the most appropriate option in *italics*.

1 *We see / We're going to see* the new *Spider-Man* film tomorrow. I bought the tickets online.

2 I don't think *I'll be / I am* late home. The class usually finishes at 6 o'clock.

3 I've got an important exam tomorrow, so *I go / I'm going to go* to bed early this evening.

4 Our train *leaves / is leaving* at 10.45 am.

5 **A:** We've run out of bread.
  **B:** OK, *I'll go / I'm going to go* and get some more.

Grammar reference 131

## PREPOSITIONS OF MOVEMENT

**by**
- We use *by* to talk about ways of travelling.
  We went to Holland **by** boat.
  We go **by** car to the supermarket.
  I prefer to travel **by** train than **by** air.
  More goods travel **by** road than **by** rail.

**Note:** We say *on foot* (not ~~by foot~~)
I usually go to work **on foot**.

**in/into, out of**
- We use these prepositions to say how we move into or out of something like a car, taxi, etc.
  Ben got **out of** the car.
  The parents and their two children got **into** the taxi.

**on/onto/off**
- We use these prepositions to say how we start or stop using something like a bike, bus, plane or train.
  We got **on(to)** the bus near our home and got **off** at the station.
  I got **off** my bike and locked it.

### PRACTICE

**1** Complete the sentences.

1 The floods destroyed the roads so we travelled everywhere ..................... foot.

2 In some places it is cheaper to travel ..................... air than ..................... rail.

3 We got ..................... the plane just before it took off.

4 The taxi broke down, so we all got ..................... it and walked into town.

5 The quickest way to get to France from England is to go ..................... train.

6 We got ..................... the car when it started raining, so we didn't get wet.

# 8

## CONDITIONAL SENTENCES

We use conditional sentences to talk about possible situations and their results. Conditional sentences usually have a conditional (*if*) clause and a main clause (*usually a result*).

| possible situation or action (conditional clause) | main clause / result |
|---|---|
| If I see Matt, | I'll tell him to call you. |

There are three types of conditional sentences which can refer to the present or the future.

- We use the zero conditional about things which are true.

| conditional clause: *if* + present verb | main clause / result clause: present simple verb |
|---|---|
| If the sun is too hot, | it burns you. |

- We use the first conditional to talk about likely situations.

| conditional clause: *if* + present simple | main clause / result: *will\** + infinitive |
|---|---|
| If we go by bus, | we'll get there on time. |

*We can also use modal verbs with future meaning (*shall, can, might* etc.) in first conditional sentences.
*If we collect enough money, we can buy our colleague a present.*

- We use the second conditional to talk about unlikely situations. We can also use it to talk about the present or future.

| conditional clause: *if* + past simple | main clause / result: *would\** + infinitive |
|---|---|
| If I had a lot of money, | I'd buy a new smartphone. |

*We can also use other modal verbs (*should, might, could*).
*If I knew how to snowboard, I could enter the competition.*

- We can use *were* instead of *was* in the conditional clause.
*If I **were/was** you, I'd look for a new hobby.*

**Note:** Conditional (*if*) clauses can come before or after the main clause. When the conditional clause comes before the main clause, it is followed by a comma.

### PRACTICE

**1** Match the sentence beginnings (1–8) with the correct endings (a–h) to make zero, first and second conditional sentences.

1 If I have time,
2 If I had more time,
3 If you mix blue and yellow,
4 You wouldn't be hungry
5 She would be really angry
6 If he phones her,
7 If my computer breaks again,
8 If I had enough money,

a you get green.
b she refuses to speak.
c if she knew the truth.
d I'll phone you.
e I'll throw it in the bin.
f I'd buy a new computer.
g I'd cycle to work.
h if you ate more.

**2** Make second conditional sentences.

1 I'd like to do the high jump but I'm not very tall.
If ....*I were/was taller, I'd do the high jump.*....

2 She can't study in Canada because she doesn't speak English.
If ................................................................

3 I haven't got enough free time to learn to play a musical instrument.
If ................................................................

4 I'd like to buy a laptop, but I haven't got enough money.
If ................................................................

## CONJUNCTIONS: *WHEN, IF, UNLESS* + PRESENT, FUTURE

**when**
- Use *when* to talk about things that happen at a particular time in the future:
***When** I get home this evening, I'll have a shower.*

**if**
- Use *if* for things that may or may not happen, or to say what happens if something else happens:
***If** I finish work early, I'll go swimming.*

**unless**
- *unless* means the same as 'if not'.
***Unless** I get home early, I won't go swimming.*
(= If I do not get home early, I won't go swimming.)

### PRACTICE

**3** Complete these sentences with *if*, *when* or *unless*.

1 ................ you take me to the station, I'll have to walk there.
2 We'll fail the exam ................ we revise.
3 ................ we hurry, we'll get there in time.
4 Let's watch the late film ................ you are not too tired to watch anything.
5 In the UK, you can't drive ................ you're over 16.
6 ................ I'm sad, I usually talk to my friends.
7 ................ you're not feeling better tomorrow, you should go to the doctor.
8 I'll watch some TV ................ I get home tonight.

Grammar reference  133

# 9

## DEFINING AND NON-DEFINING RELATIVE CLAUSES WITH *WHICH, THAT, WHO, WHOSE, WHEN, WHERE*

Relative clauses are used to link different pieces of information in one sentence.
*The film Titanic,* **which made Leonardo DiCaprio famous**, *was made in 1997.*

We use relative clauses to avoid short, simple sentences like these ones.
*The film* Titanic *was made in 1997. It made Leonardo DiCaprio famous.*

**Defining relative clauses**

- These clauses give us essential information which tells us exactly which person or thing we are referring to.
  *The actor* **who plays Luke Skywalker** *is Mark Hamill.*

- Without the information in the relative clause, we would not know which actor we are talking about.
  ✗ *The actor is Mark Hamill.*

**Non-defining relative clauses**

- These clauses give us extra non-essential information. The sentence still makes sense without this relative clause.
  *The first Star Wars film,* **which was directed by George Lucas**, *came out in 1977.*
  ✓ *The first Star Wars film came out in 1977.*

**Relative pronouns**

Use these relative pronouns to introduce relative clauses:
- *who* refers to people
- *which* refers to things
- *that* can refer to people or things
- *whose* refers to possession or relationships:
  *The student* **whose** *brother was on TV is at my university.*
- *where* refers to places:
  *The village* **where** *I live is on the outskirts of the city.*
- *when* refers to times:
  *The time* **when** *I was my happiest was my years at school.*
- *why* refers to reasons or explanations:
  *The reason* **why** *I got up so early is that I couldn't sleep.*

| defining clauses | non-defining clauses |
| --- | --- |
| • Do not have commas. | • Have commas – they are like pauses in spoken English. |
| • Use these relative pronouns: *who, which, whose, where, when, why, that.* | • Use these relative pronouns: *who, which, whose, where, when, why.* |
| • *that* can be used instead of *who* or *which*. | • Don't use *that*. |
| • *who, which* or *that* can be left out if they are the object of the clause. | • Relative pronouns cannot be left out. |

### PRACTICE

**1** Complete the sentences with a relative pronoun. Sometimes there may be more than one possible answer.

- ☐ 1 Ben's the person ................................ bike was stolen last week.
- ☐ 2 That's the dog ................................ tried to bite me.
- ☐ 3 She doesn't like people ................................ are unfriendly.
- ☐ 4 That's the house ................................ they want to live in.
- ☐ 5 Where are the keys ................................ were on the kitchen table?
- ☐ 6 We're moving to a quiet place ................................ we can't hear the traffic.
- ☐ 7 The company ................................ David works for makes computers.
- ☐ 8 I read a lot of books ................................ I was ill at home.

**2** Tick (✓) the sentences in Exercise 1 where it is possible to leave out the relative pronoun.

**3** Rewrite these sentences into one sentence using relative clauses.

1 The music was by Mozart. Gisela was playing the music last night.
The music which ..................................................

2 The violin was not hers. Gisela was playing the violin in the concert.
The violin that ..................................................

3 James is also a musician. Gisela borrowed James's violin.
James, ..................................................

4 We've just listened to Gisela's latest recording. Gisela's recording is number 1 in the classical charts.
We've just listened ..................................................

5 Gisela's mother is very proud of her. Gisela's mother was in the audience tonight.
Gisela's mother, ..................................................

6 Tomorrow, Gisela is going back to Vienna. Gisela plays in an orchestra in Vienna.
Tomorrow, Gisela is ..................................................

## PAST PERFECT

| Positive/Negative forms | | |
|---|---|---|
| I/You/He/She/It/We/They | had/'d | **finished** work by 5 o'clock. |
| | had not / hadn't | |

| Question forms and short answers | | |
|---|---|---|
| Had | I/you/he/she/it/we/they | **finished** work by 5 o'clock? |
| Yes, | I/you/he/she/it/we/they | **had.** |
| No, | I/you/he/she/it/we/they | **hadn't.** |

We use the past perfect to:

- make clear the order of past events. The past perfect describes something that happened before an action/event in the past.
  *My flatmates **had left** when I arrived home.* (= My flatmates were not there when I arrived home.)

- say what was completed before a specific past time.
  *By 9 o'clock, I**'d phoned** three people and **had sent** five emails.*

- explain past events or situations or give background information.
  *He**'d drunk** nothing all day, so he was really thirsty.*
  *I**'d got** up at 5 o'clock, so by midday I was very tired.*

- talk about situations that have changed.
  *I**'d planned** to finish writing my essay this morning, but I've got a terrible headache.*

### PRACTICE

**1** Complete the sentences with the past simple or past perfect form of the verbs in brackets.

1 It .................... (rain) all night and, although it .................... (stop), the ground .................... (be) still very wet.

2 We .................... (plan) to have a picnic, but then it started raining, so we .................... (have to) think of something else to do.

3 It .................... (be) sunny every day for two weeks, but then it .................... (start) to snow.

4 We .................... (can not) go for a walk in the forest because the snow and ice .................... (make) the paths too dangerous.

5 Yesterday, we .................... (go) to the cinema because there was a new film that none of us .................... (see).

Grammar reference 135

# 10

## COMMANDS AND INSTRUCTIONS

We use the imperative form for giving commands.
**Stand** up!

The imperative form of verbs is the same as the infinitive without *to*. Imperative forms have no subject.

✓ **Wake** up!
✗ ~~You wake up!~~

✓ **Do not use** your mobile phone.
✗ ~~You do not use your mobile phone.~~

We can also use the imperative form for giving:
- instructions, for example in recipes:
  **Boil** for 10 minutes.
- advice:
  **Put** on a warm coat.
- encouragement:
  **Keep** trying.
- warnings:
  **Be** careful.

### PRACTICE

**1** Complete the meaning of the signs using the imperative form of verbs in the box.

| be | drink | eat | turn | use |

1 ............................ or ............................ here.

2 ............................ left.

3 ............................ cameras here.

4 ............................ quiet.

## HAVE SOMETHING DONE

- Use *have something done* to talk about things we ask other people to do for us, things that we do not want to, or cannot do ourselves.
  I'm **having my teeth checked** tomorrow.

- We can also use *get something done*. It has the same meaning but is more informal:
  I'm **getting my hair cut** tomorrow.

- Notice the order of words: *have* + object + past participle. A different word order changes the meaning.
  She **has her hair cut**. (= Someone does it for her.)
  She has cut her hair. (= She did it herself recently.)

- Use *have something done* in any tense.
  I **(don't) have my hair cut** every week.
  We're **(not) having our flat decorated**.
  We **had (didn't have) our computer repaired** yesterday.
  We'll **have our car washed** tomorrow.

### PRACTICE

**1** Put the words in order to make correct sentences.

1 you / your / had / cut / have / hair / ?
  Have ............................

2 bedroom / have / painted / I / might / my / blue
  I ............................

3 fixed / had / Michael / yet / bike / his / has / ?
  Has ............................

4 get / teeth / I / every / my / months / polished / six
  I ............................

5 checked / your / have / computer / viruses / should / you / for
  You ............................

**2** Make sentences with *have* something *done* using the words given and the tense in brackets.

1 he – hair cut – beard shave off (present perfect simple)
  ............................

2 she – car – wash – yesterday (past simple)
  ............................

3 he – shoes – clean (present perfect simple)
  ............................

4 they – house – paint (present continuous)
  ............................

5 he – tooth – take out – this morning (past simple)
  ............................

6 she – eyes – test – tomorrow (*will*)
  ............................

# 11

## THE PASSIVE: PRESENT SIMPLE AND PAST SIMPLE

We form the passive by using the correct form of *be* followed by the past participle.

| active | passive |
| --- | --- |
| We **feed** our cat twice a day. | Our cat **is fed** twice a day. |
| They **built** our school in 2012. | Our school **was built** in 2012. |

We use passive verbs rather than active verbs when:
- we are more interested in who or what is affected by the action of the verb than who or what does the action:
  *My car **was made** in France.* (The focus is on *my car* rather than the workers or the company that made it.)
  *We **were given** a lot of essays to do in the holidays.* (Here, *we* are the focus, not the essays or the lecturers who gave the essays.)
- we don't know who did the action:
  *My bike **was stolen** yesterday.* (I don't know who stole it.)
- when who or what did something is obvious:
  *The driver of the car **was arrested**.* (We know that the police arrest people so we don't need to mention them.)

To say who or what did the action we can add a *by* phrase.
*This opera **was composed by** Mozart.* (Mozart is the person who did the action.)

### PRACTICE

**1** Complete the sentences with the passive form of the verbs in brackets. Use the present simple or the past simple.

1 Last year's final, which ................... (play) in the new stadium, ................... (watch) by over 2 million people.
2 In the past most children walked to school, but now many ................... (take) by their parents. Most of them ................... (drive) by car.
3 I've just finished reading a science fiction novel that ................... (write) in 1980. Many of the things that ................... (predict) by the author have come true.

**2** Change the active sentences into passive ones. Mention who did the action, if necessary.

1 A vet sees our cat twice a year.
...................
2 The police closed the roads because of the storm.
...................
3 A famous author wrote the book.
...................
4 They play cricket in Australia.
...................
5 My father taught me how to sing.
...................

## COMPARATIVE AND SUPERLATIVE ADVERBS

| | comparative | superlative |
| --- | --- | --- |
| For adverbs with two or more syllables (e.g. *carefully*) | add *more* **more carefully** | add *most* **the most carefully** |
| For adverbs with one syllable (e.g. *fast, late*) | add *-er* **faster later** | add *-est* **the fastest the latest** |
| Irregular adverbs: *well, badly* | **better worse** | **the best the worst** |

- We often use *than* with comparative adverbs.
- Although *early* has two syllables, the comparative and superlative forms are *earlier* and *the earliest*.
- Use comparative adverbs to say how things are done or happen at different times.
  *Today it's raining **more heavily** than it did yesterday.*
- Use superlative adverbs to say how things are done by someone or something else.
  *Everyone in my class works hard, but Jon works **the hardest**.*

### PRACTICE

**1** Complete the sentences with the comparative or superlative form of the adverbs in brackets.

1 I can't read it. Please write ................... (clearly).
2 Our team played ................... (well) in our group.
3 Cars can travel much ................... (fast) than bicycles.
4 My brother works ................... (hard) than I do.
5 If you revised ................... (serious), you would do ................... (well) in your exam.
6 I run ................... (quickly) of all my friends.

**2** Underline the mistakes in the sentences and correct them.

1 Jan dances most beautifully than Lucy.
...................
2 We all write well, but Jon writes the better of all.
...................
3 Peter waited the more patiently to see the doctor.
...................
4 You need to work more hardly, especially at exam time.
...................
5 You must go to bed more earlier than you did last night.
...................
6 My sister runs more faster than me.
...................

Grammar reference  137

# 12 REPORTED SPEECH

Direct speech is what we call the words people actually say when they speak.
In the example below, the direct speech is underlined.
He said, '*I haven't seen you for a long time.*'
Indirect or reported speech is how we report (tell) what another person says.
He said he hadn't seen me for a long time.

- Verb tenses often change when we report what people said.

| direct speech | reported speech |
| --- | --- |
| present simple<br>'I **go** to university in the city centre.' | ➜ past simple<br>She said she **went** to university in the city centre. |
| present continuous<br>'I**'m waiting** for a bus.' | ➜ past continuous<br>He said he **was waiting** for a bus. |
| present perfect<br>'I **have** already **had** lunch.' | ➜ past perfect<br>He said he **had** already **had** lunch. |
| past simple<br>'I **enjoyed** my dinner.' | ➜ past perfect<br>She said she **had enjoyed** her dinner. |
| will future<br>'I**'ll** call you later.' | ➜ would<br>She said she **would** call me later. |
| can<br>'I **can** speak four languages.' | ➜ could<br>She said she **could** speak four languages. |

We also need to make other changes when we report what people said.

- Subject and object pronouns:
  '**I** have already told **you**.' ➜ She said **she** had already told **me**.
  '**We** live in Paris.' ➜ **They** said **they** lived in Paris.
- Possessive adjectives:
  'I've mended **my** bike.' ➜ He said **he**'d mended **his** bike.
  'We love **our** flat.' ➜ They said they loved **their** flat.
- Time references:
  'We're going on holiday **tomorrow**.' ➜ They said they were going on holiday **the next day**.
- Place references:
  'I want to stay **here**.' ➜ He said he wanted to stay **there**.

**Reported commands**
- We can use *tell* to report commands. We need to include the object (the person who needs to listen to the command) + infinitive after *tell*.

| direct commands | reported commands |
| --- | --- |
| 'Stop talking!'<br>'Don't be late!' | Their boss **told them to stop** talking.<br>The father **told his daughter not to be** late. |

## PRACTICE

**1** Write the reported speech as direct speech.

1 She said she was living in Moscow.
   *'I'm living in Moscow.'*

2 I said I was sorry, but I couldn't lend her any more money.
   ..........................................................

3 He says he still feels ill.
   ..........................................................

4 She says she's older than me.
   ..........................................................

5 They said they'd come and see me later.
   ..........................................................

6 Max said he'd left the day before.
   ..........................................................

7 She told him to stop worrying.
   ..........................................................

**2** Write the statements and commands as reported speech.

1 'I'm leaving university at the end of next year.'
   He said ..................................................

2 'I've got a surprise for you.'
   She said ..................................................

3 'Shut the door!'
   She told him .............................................

4 'We've all passed our English exam.'
   They said ................................................

5 'It's my birthday tomorrow.'
   He said ..................................................

6 'You're the only person I know who likes classical music.'
   She said .................................................

7 'Don't drink any more coffee!'
   He told Max ..............................................

8 'We went to Morocco for our holiday last year.'
   They said ................................................

138

# REPORTED QUESTIONS

The word order in reported questions is the same as for positive phrases.

| positive phrase | direct question | reported question |
|---|---|---|
| I **was smiling**. | 'Why are you smiling?' | He asked me why I **was smiling**. |

- We use *ask* when we report questions. We need to make changes to tenses, pronouns, times and places. We don't use question marks.

| direct question | reported question |
|---|---|
| '**Why** are you smiling?' | He **asked** me **why** I was smiling. |
| '**What** are you doing tomorrow?' | She **asked** us **what** we were doing the next day. |
| '**When** do you finish football practice?' | He asked me **when** I finished football practice. |
| '**Why** did you come here?' | She asked me **why** I had gone there. |

- With *yes/no* questions (questions that need either a *yes* or *no* answer), we need to use *if* or *whether* after *ask*.

| '**Are** you feeling OK?' | She **asked if/whether** I was feeling OK. |
|---|---|
| '**Do** you need a break?' | He **asked if/whether** I needed a break. |

## PRACTICE

**1** Rewrite the indirect sentences as direct questions.

1 They asked me why I went to Morocco on holiday.
  *'Why did you go to Morocco on holiday?'*

2 Helen asked me if I was enjoying my new course.

3 Alex asked if anyone had found his keys.

4 Sasha wanted to know what we'd done the day before.

5 I asked Veronika if she could come to my party that evening.

6 We asked a policeman if he could tell us where the station was.

7 Jan wanted to know who my favourite actor was.

8 I asked my brother if he had tried to phone me.

**2** Write the questions as reported questions.

1 'Why are you wearing your best clothes?'
  My colleague asked ........................................

2 'Where are you going?'
  My colleague asked ........................................

3 'What are you going to do there?'
  My colleague asked ........................................

4 'Are you going with anyone?'
  My boss asked ........................................

5 'Do I know who you're going with?'
  My colleague asked ........................................

6 'What time will you be back?'
  My boss asked ........................................

7 'How will you get back?'
  My colleague asked ........................................

8 'What will you do if you miss the last train?'
  My boss asked ........................................

Grammar reference

## INDIRECT QUESTIONS

Indirect questions are a polite way of asking for information. We use expressions like *Could you tell me …?* or *I was wondering …* to introduce the question.

| direct question | reported question |
|---|---|
| Are you busy later? | **Could you tell me if** you're busy later? |
| Do you know the time? | **I was wondering if** you know the time. |
| Where do you work? | **I'd like to know where** you work. |

- The word order in indirect questions is the same as for statements.
  'How long **have you lived** here?'
  'I would like to know how long **you have lived** here.'

- We do not use the auxiliary verbs *do*, *does* and *did* in indirect questions. However, we sometimes need to change the tense of the verb.
  'When **does** the train **leave**?'
  ✓ Could you tell me **when the train leaves**?
  ✗ Could you tell me when does the train leave?

  'When **did** you **get** home?'
  ✓ Could you tell me **when you got** home?
  ✗ Could you tell me when did you get home?

- If there is no question word (*what*, *when*, etc.), use *if* or *whether*.
  'Is the train late?'
  'Could you tell me **if** the train is late?'

### PRACTICE

**1** Write the questions as indirect questions.

1 'Where do you live?'
   Could you tell me ...................................................

2 'Are you doing anything at the weekend?'
   I was wondering ...................................................

3 'What did they do last weekend?'
   Can you tell me ...................................................

4 'What did you think of the film?'
   I'd like to know ...................................................

5 Is my seat number on this ticket?
   Could you tell me ...................................................

140

# Phrasal verb builder

A phrasal verb is a verb with two or three parts. The meaning of the verb is sometimes different from the meaning of its separate parts. Phrasal verbs can combine verbs with prepositions or adverbs.

This section focuses on phrasal verbs related to four topics: **relationships**, **travel**, **communication** and **daily routines**.

## RELATIONSHIPS

**1** Match the phrasal verbs to the definitions below.

> get together (with)   look after   bring (someone) up
> split up (with)   go out (with)   get on (with)

1 ........................... = look after children until they are adults
2 ........................... = have a friendly relationship with someone
3 ........................... = meet
4 ........................... = have a romantic relationship with someone
5 ........................... = take care of someone
6 ........................... = end a relationship

**2** Choose the correct option in *italics*.

1 I *get on* / *get together* with my friends every weekend to play football.
2 I *split up* / *get on* with everyone in my family. Everyone's very friendly.
3 My grandparents *brought up* / *went out* four children in a very small house.
4 I need to *look after* / *bring up* my flatmate's dog when she goes on holiday.
5 The band *got together* / *split up* because they didn't enjoy playing together any more.

**3** Write a sentence using each of the phrasal verbs.

## TRAVEL

**1** Match the phrasal verbs to the definitions below.

> check in   set off   break down
> get back   turn up   take off

1 ........................... = when something (e.g. a car or computer) stops working
2 ........................... = arrive at an airport as a passenger, or at a hotel as a guest
3 ........................... = return
4 ........................... = leave on a journey
5 ........................... = when a plane leaves the ground
6 ........................... = arrive, come

**2** Complete the sentences with the past simple form of the phrasal verbs from the box.

1 We ........................... ........................... for the airport at 7 o'clock in the morning.
2 After we had been driving for ten minutes, our car ........................... ..........................., so my friend called a garage. Five minutes later, a mechanic ........................... ........................... and fixed the problem.
3 When we got to the airport, we parked the car and ........................... ........................... at the departures desk.
4 Half an hour later, our plane ........................... ........................... and our holiday began!
5 When we ........................... ........................... home a week later, we felt very relaxed.

**3** Write a sentence using each of the phrasal verbs.

Phrasal verb builder  141

## COMMUNICATION

**1** Match the phrasal verbs to the definitions below.

> fill (something) in   switch (something) off
> ring (someone) up   hang up   call (someone) back

1 ........................... = return a phone call
2 ........................... = complete a form
3 ........................... = end a phone conversation
4 ........................... = make a phone call
5 ........................... = turn off something (e.g. a computer)

**2** Choose the correct option in *italics*.

> My internet stopped working yesterday, so I
> **(1)** *switched off / switched it off* and **(2)** *called back / rang up* a help line. But the line was busy so I **(3)** *filled in / hung up*. I waited ten minutes and then **(4)** *rang up / called back*. The person who answered the phone asked me to **(5)** *ring up / fill in* an online form, and gave me another number to call. In ten minutes, my internet was working again!

**3** Write a sentence using each of the phrasal verbs.

## DAILY ROUTINES

**1** Match the phrasal verbs to the definitions below.

> tidy up   get up   wake (someone) up
> put (something) on   pick (someone) up

1 ........................... = get out of bed
2 ........................... = collect someone in a car
3 ........................... = put clothes on your body
4 ........................... = make a place look clean
5 ........................... = stop (someone) sleeping

**2** Complete the sentences with the correct form of the phrasal verbs from the box. Add any other words you need.

> My flatmate and I have very different routines. Every morning, I **(1)** ........................... at 7 o'clock as I need to be at the office at eight and my colleague **(2)** ........................... in her car at 7.30. James works in a restaurant and usually doesn't **(3)** ........................... until 9 o'clock and sometimes doesn't **(4)** ........................... his clothes until midday! He likes the flat to be clean so he always **(5)** ........................... the living room and kitchen before he goes to work.

**3** Write a sentence using each of the phrasal verbs.

# Irregular verbs

| verb | past simple | past participle |
|---|---|---|
| be | was/were | been |
| beat | beat | beaten |
| become | became | become |
| begin | began | begun |
| bend | bent | bent |
| bite | bit | bitten |
| bleed | bled | bled |
| blow | blew | blown |
| break | broke | broken |
| bring | brought | brought |
| build | built | built |
| burn | burnt/burned | burnt/burned |
| buy | bought | bought |
| catch | caught | caught |
| choose | chose | chosen |
| come | came | come |
| cost | cost | cost |
| cut | cut | cut |
| deal | dealt | dealt |
| dig | dug | dug |
| do | did | done |
| draw | drew | drawn |
| dream | dreamt/dreamed | dreamt/dreamed |
| drink | drank | drunk |
| drive | drove | driven |
| eat | ate | eaten |
| fall | fell | fallen |
| feed | fed | fed |
| feel | felt | felt |
| fight | fought | fought |
| find | found | found |
| fly | flew | flown |
| forbid | forbade | forbidden |
| forget | forgot | forgotten |
| forgive | forgave | forgiven |
| freeze | froze | frozen |
| get | got | got |
| give | gave | given |
| go | went | gone |
| grow | grew | grown |
| hang | hung | hung |
| have | had | had |
| hear | heard | heard |
| hide | hid | hidden |
| hit | hit | hit |
| hold | held | held |
| hurt | hurt | hurt |
| keep | kept | kept |
| kneel | knelt | knelt |
| know | knew | known |
| lay | laid | laid |
| lead | led | led |
| learn | learnt/learned | learnt/learned |
| leave | left | left |
| lend | lent | lent |
| let | let | let |
| lie | lay | lain |
| light | lit | lit |
| lose | lost | lost |
| make | made | made |
| mean | meant | meant |
| meet | met | met |
| pay | paid | paid |
| put | put | put |
| read | read | read |
| ride | rode | ridden |
| ring | rang | rung |
| rise | rose | risen |
| run | ran | run |
| say | said | said |
| see | saw | seen |
| sell | sold | sold |
| send | sent | sent |
| set | set | set |
| sew | sewed | sewn |
| shake | shook | shaken |
| shine | shone | shone |
| shoot | shot | shot |
| show | showed | shown |
| shut | shut | shut |
| sing | sang | sung |
| sink | sank | sunk |
| sit | sat | sat |
| sleep | slept | slept |
| smell | smelt/smelled | smelt/smelled |
| speak | spoke | spoken |
| spell | spelt/spelled | spelt/spelled |
| spend | spent | spent |
| spill | spilt/spilled | spilt/spilled |
| spoil | spoilt/spoiled | spoilt/spoiled |
| stand | stood | stood |
| steal | stole | stolen |
| stick | stuck | stuck |
| strike | struck | struck |
| sweep | swept | swept |
| swim | swam | swum |
| swing | swung | swung |
| take | took | taken |
| teach | taught | taught |
| tear | tore | torn |
| tell | told | told |
| think | thought | thought |
| throw | threw | thrown |
| understand | understood | understood |
| wake | woke | woken |
| wear | wore | worn |
| win | won | won |
| write | wrote | written |

Irregular verbs  143

# Writing bank

## MAKING YOUR WRITING MORE INTERESTING

To make a sentence more interesting, we can add more details.

**1** Look at how the second sentence adds information. Match the new information (1–8) with the descriptions (a–h).

- I went to Spain.
  ¹Last year, I went to Spain, ²which is my favourite country.
- I like warm weather.
  I like warm weather, ³but I don't like cold weather.
- I've got an exam tomorrow.
  I've got an ⁴important exam tomorrow, ⁵so I have to wake up early.
- George was happy.
  George was ⁶really happy ⁷because it was his birthday.
- I read the letter.
  I read the letter ⁸slowly and carefully.

  a  adding a contrasting idea ......3......
  b  giving a reason ............
  c  saying when something happened ............
  d  giving the result of an action ............
  e  using a relative clause to give extra information ............
  f  using an adjective to describe something ............
  g  using an adverb to make an adjective stronger ............
  h  using adverbs to describe how something happens ............

**2** Complete the table with the words from the box.

> and  beautiful  because  but  completely  delicious
> easily  later that day  loudly  modern  quickly  so
> the next day  this morning  wonderful  yesterday

| adjectives | adverbs | linking words | time expressions |
|---|---|---|---|
|  |  |  |  |

**3** Make the sentences more interesting. Use the words from the box. Can you think of any other words to use?

> but   early   the next morning
> large   really   suddenly

1  It ..................... started to rain.
2  I called Max, ..................... he didn't answer his phone.
3  We set out for London ..................... .
4  I ordered a cup of coffee and a ..................... slice of cake.
5  The film was ..................... boring!

**4** Join the two parts of the sentences with *and*, *but*, *so* or *because*.

1  we didn't play tennis – the weather was bad

   *We didn't play tennis because the weather was bad.*

2  I was very tired – I went straight to bed

   .....................
   .....................

2  we all went to the party – everyone had a great time

   .....................
   .....................

4  Paul wanted to come with us – he couldn't

   .....................
   .....................

5  we all laughed – it was so funny

   .....................
   .....................

# WRITING PART 1: AN EMAIL

**1** Read the exam task. What information should you include in the email?

Read this email from your English-speaking friend Sam, and the notes you have made.

---

**To:**
**From:** Sam

Hi,

Guess what? Do you remember the sports competition I entered last month? They announced the results yesterday, and I've won two tickets to go and watch an international sports event! — *Amazing!*

Would you like to come to the event with me? We can choose to go in July or August. — *Yes — tell Sam when you can make it.*

We have to book which sport we want to see in advance. There are football and basketball matches. Which sport do you prefer to watch? — *Tell Sam.*

They sell lots of souvenirs at the stadium. What do you think we should buy? — *Suggest ...*

Bye for now,

Sam

---

Write your **email** to Sam, using **all** the **notes**.

## MODEL ANSWER

*Use an informal phrase to start the email.*

Hi Sam,

Thanks for your email. That's amazing news about the competition! Well done! — *Remember you are replying to Sam's email.*

Yes, I love sport, so it would be incredible to go to a big sports event with you. I can go with you in July, but I can't go in August because I'm on holiday then. — *This answers the question about when you can or can't make it, and gives a reason.*

I'm a big football fan, so I'd love to see an international football match. It would be brilliant to see some of my favourite heroes in action. — *This answers the question 'Which sport do you prefer to watch?'*

Why don't we buy football shirts as souvenirs? We can wear them at the match! — *This is a suggestion.*

See you soon,

Tom

*Use an informal phrase at the end.*

Writing bank  145

**KEY LANGUAGE AND IDEAS FOR EMAILS**

**Opening an email:**
Hi, Hi Tom, Hi there, Hello,

**Closing an email:**
Love, See you soon, Take care, Bye,

**Responding to an email:**
Thanks for your email. It's good to hear from you.

**Responding to good news:**
That's amazing news! I'm so happy for you! Wow! How exciting! Well done!

**Responding to bad news:**
I'm sorry to hear about …

**Making a suggestion:**
Why don't you/we …? You/We could … If I were you, I'd … Make sure you …

**Making an offer or promise:**
I could … if you like. Would you like me to …? I can … if you want.

**Making a request:**
Could you …? Can you …? Would you mind … -ing?

**Giving good or bad news:**
You'll be pleased to hear that … I'm afraid … Guess what …? I'm sorry, but …

**Linking words and phrases:**
and but so because also as well

**Informal language:**
- contractions: *I'm you're he's*
- informal words and phrases: *awesome great keep in touch take care I guess …*
- exclamation marks to show emotion: *That's great news! Wow!*

**2** Match the beginnings and endings of these sentences.
Then decide if each sentence is a suggestion (S), an offer (O), a promise (P) or a request (R).

1 Could you            a I'd definitely accept the job. ............
2 If I were you,       b some useful addresses if you want. ............
3 I can send you       c be there to help on the day. ............
4 Don't worry, I'll    d let me know what time you're arriving? ............

**3** Correct the underlined mistakes in the sentences giving good or bad news.
Use the Key language and ideas box to check your answers.

1 <u>I afraid</u> I won't be able to come to your party.
2 <u>Guess that where</u> I'm going next week?
3 <u>I'm sorry, and</u> Dan won't be here when you visit.
4 <u>You'll be pleased hear</u> that I've now finished all my exams!

**4** Choose the correct linking words in *italics*.

1 I finish work at six o'clock, *because / so* I can meet you at 6.30.
2 My sister Martha is *also / as well* coming home next weekend.
3 I'm not very good at singing, *because / but* I still enjoy it.
4 I'm a bit disappointed *because / so* my exam results weren't brilliant.
5 I'll find the document *also / and* send it to you in an email.

146

**5** Read the exam task. What information must you include in your email?

> **To:**
> **From:** Logan
>
> Hi,
>
> The weather forecast looks good next weekend, so my flatmates and I are having a barbecue to celebrate the beginning of summer. Would you like to come?
>
> I'd like to invite everyone in our English class. What kind of food do you think our classmates would like to eat at a barbecue?
>
> I'd also like everyone to play a sport after we eat. What sport do you think would be best for our classmates?
>
> See you soon,
>
> Logan

*Annotations:*
- Great idea!
- Yes — say which day.
- Tell Sam.
- Suggest …

**6** Before you write your reply to Logan, complete the table with ideas.

| | |
|---|---|
| **Paragraph 1** (respond to the invitation) | |
| **Paragraph 2** (suggest some food) | |
| **Paragraph 3** (explain your idea for a sport) | |
| **Useful phrases I can use** | |

**7** Write your email, using your notes from Exercise 6. Write about 100 words.

**8** Check your email and make changes if necessary.

☐ Have you answered all the questions and included all the necessary information?

☐ Have you used a suitable phrase to open and close your email?

☐ Have you tried to make your writing more interesting by adding details?

☐ Have you used informal language?

☐ Have you used linking words and phrases?

☐ Have you counted your words?

Writing bank 147

# WRITING PART 2: AN ARTICLE

## KEY LANGUAGE AND IDEAS FOR ARTICLES

**Use adjectives for describing people and things:**
*attractive brave calm cheerful convenient …*

**Use linking words and phrases:**
*and but so because although also as well …*

**Use an introductory sentence for each paragraph:**
*Paris is a city of variety. A good job should be creative. Photography is a great hobby.*

**Give your opinion:**
*I think … It seems to me that … I would say that …*

**2** Choose the best introductory sentence in *italics* for each opening paragraph.

1. *There are many benefits to keeping fit. / I don't really do enough exercise.* Doing regular exercise is good for your heart, and it helps you to lose weight. It can also improve your mood, especially if you are feeling tired or unhappy.

2. *Some older people are not used to the internet. / The internet has changed people's lives in many ways.* People can now go online to do their shopping and book restaurants and holidays. Students also have access to lots of information that was difficult to find before the internet.

3. *Teaching is a very difficult job. / I would like to become a teacher.* Students are not always interested in learning, and teachers have to work hard to encourage their students to study. Also, there are sometimes problems with bad behaviour from students.

**1** Read the exam task. What should your article be about? What information should it include?

> **Articles wanted!**
>
> **My favourite city**
>
> What's your favourite city?
>
> What's so special about this city?
>
> What city would you love to travel to in the future?
>
> Tell us what you think!
>
> **Write an article answering these questions and we will publish the most interesting ones on our website.**

### MODEL ANSWER

My favourite city is Paris because it is so lively and interesting. It is also full of surprises.

Paris is a city of variety. It has many beautiful old buildings, but it also feels modern. You can visit expensive designer shops or small, traditional markets. There are hundreds of restaurants which serve French food, or different food from around the world. You can meet all kinds of people, too. There is something for everyone.

I would love to travel to New York in the future because I've seen the city in so many films, and I would love to visit it in real life.

*The first paragraph answers the first question and gives a reason.*

*Adjectives make the article more interesting to read.*

*The second paragraph gives more details and answers the second question in the task.*

*The third paragraph is about a city the writer would like to go to in the future.*

**3** Complete the table with the adjectives from the box. Can you add any more adjectives?

> amusing   delicious   freezing   frightening   old-fashioned   peaceful   quiet   stormy   tasty   tight

| clothes | films | food | countryside | weather |
|---------|-------|------|-------------|---------|
|         |       |      |             |         |

**4** Read the exam task. What should your article be about? What should it include?

**5** Before you write your article, complete the table with ideas.

---

**Articles wanted!**

**My perfect job**

What makes the perfect job?

Is it being creative, travelling, meeting people, or something else?

How important is it to earn a lot of money?

Tell us what you think!

Write an article answering these questions and we will publish the most interesting articles on our website.

---

| **Paragraph 1** (answer the first question) | |
|---|---|
| **Paragraph 2** (give more details) | |
| **Paragraph 3** (give your opinion about money) | |
| **Useful phrases I can use** | |

**6** Write your article, using your notes from Exercise 5. Write about 100 words.

**7** Check your article and make changes if necessary.

- ☐ Have you answered all the questions and included all the necessary information?
- ☐ Have you used adjectives to make your article interesting to read?
- ☐ Have you expressed a personal opinion?
- ☐ Have you used linking words and phrases?
- ☐ Have you counted your words?

Writing bank

# WRITING PART 2: A STORY

**1** Read the exam task. Which is the best way to continue the story (1, 2 or 3)? Why?

- Your English teacher has asked you to write a story.
- Your story must begin with this sentence:

  *I opened the letter from my cousins in Brazil.*

1 I have three cousins who live in Brazil, and I get on very well with them. They are all very keen on football.

2 They said they were coming to visit me, and they were arriving on the 15th – today!

3 I think Brazil is a really interesting country, and I would love to go there one day. There are lots of amazing wild animals there.

## MODEL ANSWER

I opened the letter from my cousins in Brazil. They said they were coming to visit me, and they were arriving on the 15th – today!

I was really excited. First, I cleaned everything in the flat. Then I went to the supermarket to buy food. After that, I made a cake to make them feel welcome. By evening, I was completely exhausted. I picked up the letter again to check the time of their flight, and that's when I noticed the date. They were arriving on July 15th, but today was June 15th!

We had a wonderful time together in July, and all laughed about the mistake I had made!

*The first paragraph gives background to the story.*

*The second paragraph gives the main events of the story.*

*Time expressions make the order of events clear.*

*Adjectives and adverbs make the story more interesting.*

*The last paragraph ends the story.*

### KEY LANGUAGE AND IDEAS FOR STORIES

**Use past simple verbs for the main events:**
I went to a restaurant.    I found a letter.

**Use past continuous verbs for longer actions in the past:**
I was waiting for the bus.    The sun was shining.

**Use past perfect verbs for background events:**
Unfortunately, I had forgotten my purse.

**Time expressions:**
First    then    later    the next day    finally …

**Adjectives to describe people:**
friendly    kind    tall

**Adjectives to describe places:**
busy    quiet    modern

**Adjectives to describe feelings:**
excited    angry    delighted

**Adverbs to describe how someone does something:**
quickly    slowly    carefully

**Adverbs to comment on what happened:**
luckily    fortunately    unfortunately

**2** Complete the sentences with the correct form of the verbs in brackets.
Use the past simple, past continuous or past perfect.

1 I packed my bags and then ................. (call) a taxi to take me to the airport.
2 Sara ................. (wait) for me when I got to the restaurant.
3 I could finally relax because I ................. (pass) all my exams!
4 I found an old key while I ................. (walk) along the beach.
5 James was late because he ................. (forget) to set his alarm.
6 I opened the door and then quickly ................. (close) it again.

**3** Choose the correct time expressions in *italics*.

I was really scared when my car broke down near the forest. (1) *Then / First*, I tried starting the car, but that didn't work. (2) *Finally / Then*, I tried to call a friend, but I had no signal on my phone. (3) *Next / After*, I decided to wait for another car so I could ask for help. (4) *An hour later / Before an hour*, I was still sitting there! Suddenly, I heard the sound of another car. (5) *Finally / After*, someone came to help me and I got home safely.

**4** Complete the sentences with adjectives from the box.

> curly   disappointed   entertaining   messy
> smart   spicy

1 She introduced me to a tall young man with ................. hair.
2 She was wearing a very nice, ................. jacket and skirt.
3 He cooked some delicious, ................. food for us.
4 The show was fun and very ................. .
5 The room was ................. and not very clean.
6 I was very ................. when she didn't call me.

**5** Read the exam task. Before you write your story, complete the table with ideas.

- Your English teacher has asked you to write a story.
- Your story must have this title: *A day at the zoo.*
- Write your **story** in about **100** words.

**Paragraph 1** (the background to the story)

**Paragraph 2** (the main events)

**Paragraph 3** (the ending)

**Language I can use**

**6** Write your story, using your notes from Exercise 5.
**7** Check your story and make changes if necessary.
☐ Does your story have a clear beginning, middle and ending?
☐ Have you used verbs in the past simple, past continuous and past perfect?
☐ Have you used time expressions to order the events?
☐ Have you used adjectives and adverbs to make your story interesting?
☐ Have you counted your words?

Writing bank

# Speaking bank

## SPEAKING PART 1

🎧 **1** **Listen to Maria answering the questions. Does she use full sentences in her answers?**
1. What's your name?
2. What's your surname?
3. Where do you come from?
4. Do you work, or are you a student?

🎧 **2** **Listen to Maria answering more questions. Notice how she adds extra information.**
1. What did you do yesterday evening?
2. Do you think that English will be useful to you in the future?
3. Tell us about a place you would like to visit in the future.
4. Can you describe your house or flat?
5. What do you enjoy doing in your free time?

### KEY LANGUAGE AND IDEAS FOR PERSONAL QUESTIONS

**Use frequency adverbs to talk about habits and routines:**
I usually have breakfast …
I often watch TV …

**Use the past simple and time expressions to talk about the past:**
Yesterday I watched …
Last weekend I visited …

**Use *be going to* and time expressions to talk about future plans:**
Next summer, I'm going to travel to …

**Talk about future hopes:**
I'd like to visit …
I want to get a job …
I hope I'll work …

**Add extra information:** actually  and  also

**Add contrasting information:** but …

**Add reasons and results:** because  so  That's why …

**Add examples:** For example, …
For instance, …

🎧 **3** **Complete Maria's answers with the words in the box. Listen again and check.**

> actually   also   and   because
> but   for example   often   so

1. I .................... watch films with my friends.
2. I hope I'll travel to different countries with my job, .................... I'm sure I will need English.
3. I'd love to go to New York one day .................... it looks such an exciting city.
4. ...................., my uncle lives there.
5. The kitchen is very small, .................... the living room is quite big.
6. ...................., it's got a balcony.
7. I'm quite into sport, .................... I do quite a lot of sport in my free time.
8. ...................., I sometimes go running in the evenings.

**4** **Complete the table with the time expressions from the box.**

> always   last night   last weekend
> next weekend   sometimes   tomorrow
> tonight   usually   when I was younger

| present simple | past simple | be going to |
|---|---|---|
|  |  |  |

152

**5** Match the questions (1–5) with the answers (a–e). Then choose one extra piece of information (f–j) to add to each answer. Listen and check.

1 Tell us about your English teacher.
2 Would you like to live in a different country?
3 Can you tell us about your home town?
4 How do you usually travel to university or work?
5 What did you do last weekend?

a My home town is Barcelona. ……..
b His name's Mr Adams. ……..
c On Saturday I played football. ……..
d I wouldn't like to go for long. ……..
e I usually catch the bus. ……..

f It's on the coast.
g We usually have a match every Saturday.
h I'd miss my family and friends at home.
i He's really funny.
j I'd prefer to walk.

**6** How does the student introduce extra information? Complete the sentences. Listen again and check.

1 I like him ………………… he always makes our lessons interesting.
2 I'd like to visit different countries, ………………… the United States or maybe Australia.
3 There are lots of beautiful buildings ………………… are very famous.
4 I'd prefer to walk, ………………… it's too far for me.
5 We usually have a match every Saturday. …………………, we didn't win last week.

**7** Practise answering the questions. Use a range of tenses, and add extra information.

- What's your name?
- What's your surname?
- Where do you come from?
- Do you work, or are you a student?

- What did you do yesterday evening?
- Do you think that English will be useful to you in the future?
- Tell us about a place you would like to visit in the future.
- Can you describe your house or flat?

- What do you enjoy doing in your free time?
- Tell us about your English teacher.
- Would you like to live in a different country?
- Can you tell us about your home town?
- How do you usually travel to university or work?
- What did you do last weekend?

Speaking bank 153

# Speaking bank

## SPEAKING PART 2

🎧 **1** Listen to Pablo describing a photo. What guesses does he make about the people?

**KEY LANGUAGE AND IDEAS FOR DESCRIBING A PHOTO**

**Say what you can see:**
The picture shows …     I can see …     There's a …

There are some …     but you can't see …     She's got …     He has …

**Describe where things are in the picture:**
at the front     in the background     on the left     on the right     in the middle
behind     in front of     next to

**Use the present continuous:**
He's wearing     She's running …

**Talk about the people:**
tall     long/short hair     young     old

**Talk about the place:**
indoors     outdoors     attractive     comfortable     safe

**Talk about the weather:**
sunny     cloudy     wet

**When you don't know the word for something:**
It's a kind of …     It looks like a …

**Make guesses**
He looks like …     He seems to be …     I guess he's probably …
I think maybe …     It might be …

**2** Look at the photo. Choose the correct words in *italics* to describe where the people are.

1 There are two young women *at the front / in the background* of the picture.
2 There's an old man with a beard on the *right / left*.
3 There's a young couple on the *left / right*, further back in the bus.
4 You can see someone's legs *behind / next to* the old man, but you can't see their face.
5 *In the background / At the front*, you can see a man standing up.

**3** Look at the photo again. Complete the sentences with the correct present continuous form of the verbs in brackets. Listen and check.

1 The picture shows some people who ………………… (travel) by bus.
2 There are two women at the front of the picture. They ………………… (smile).
3 One woman ………………… (show) the other one something on her phone.
4 The older man on the right ………………… (look) forwards. Maybe he ………………… (think) about where to get off the bus.
5 In the background, there's a man ………………… (stand) up. I think he ………………… (talk) to another passenger.

Speaking bank  155

**4** Look at the photo. Complete the sentences with words from the box.

> guess   looks   might   probably   seem

1 I think they're .................. father and son.
2 They .................. be watching TV.
3 They're eating something from a box. It .................. like pizza.
4 They .................. quite relaxed.
5 I .................. they're probably having a relaxing evening at home.

**5** Look at the photo again. Practise describing it. Then listen and compare your ideas.

**6** Practise describing the photos on this page and page 158.

Speaking bank

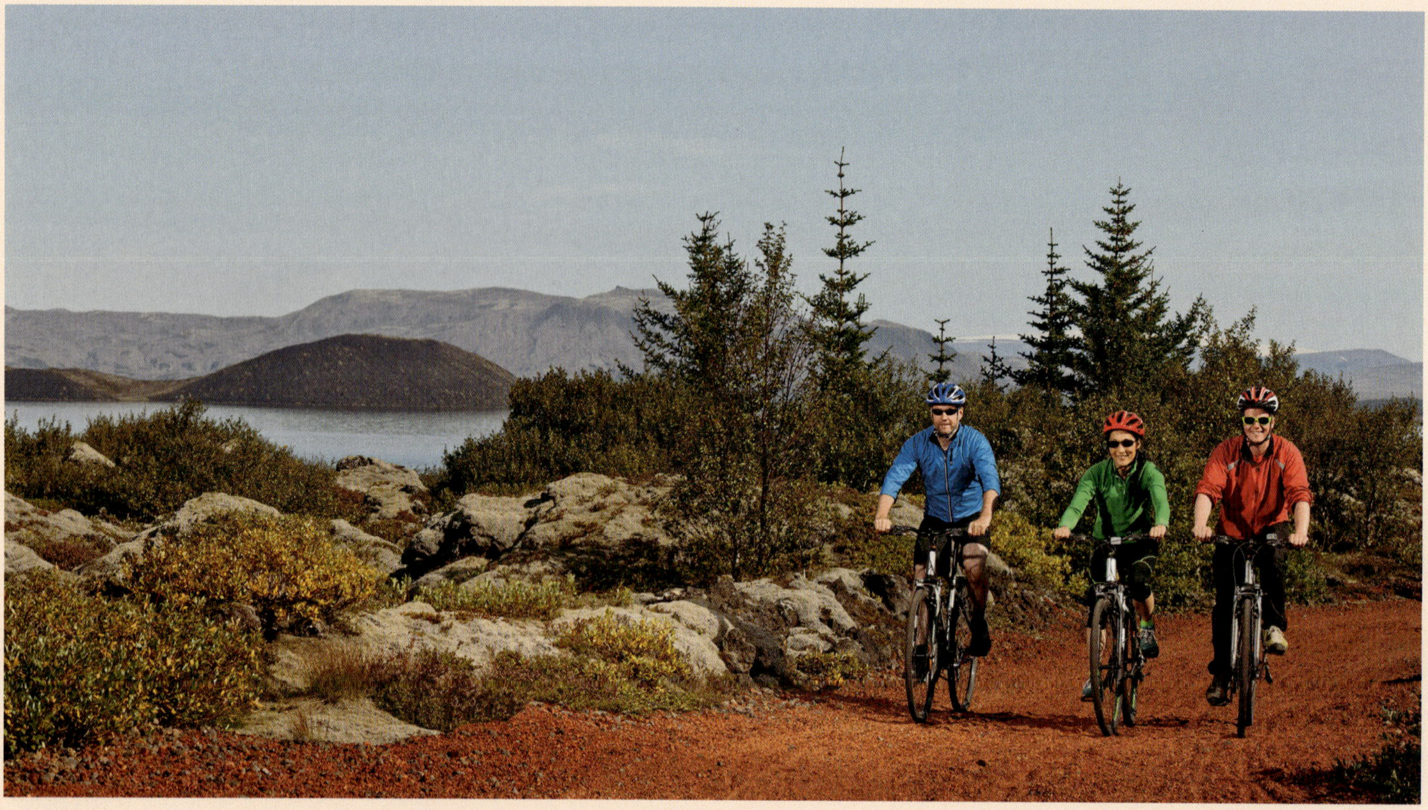

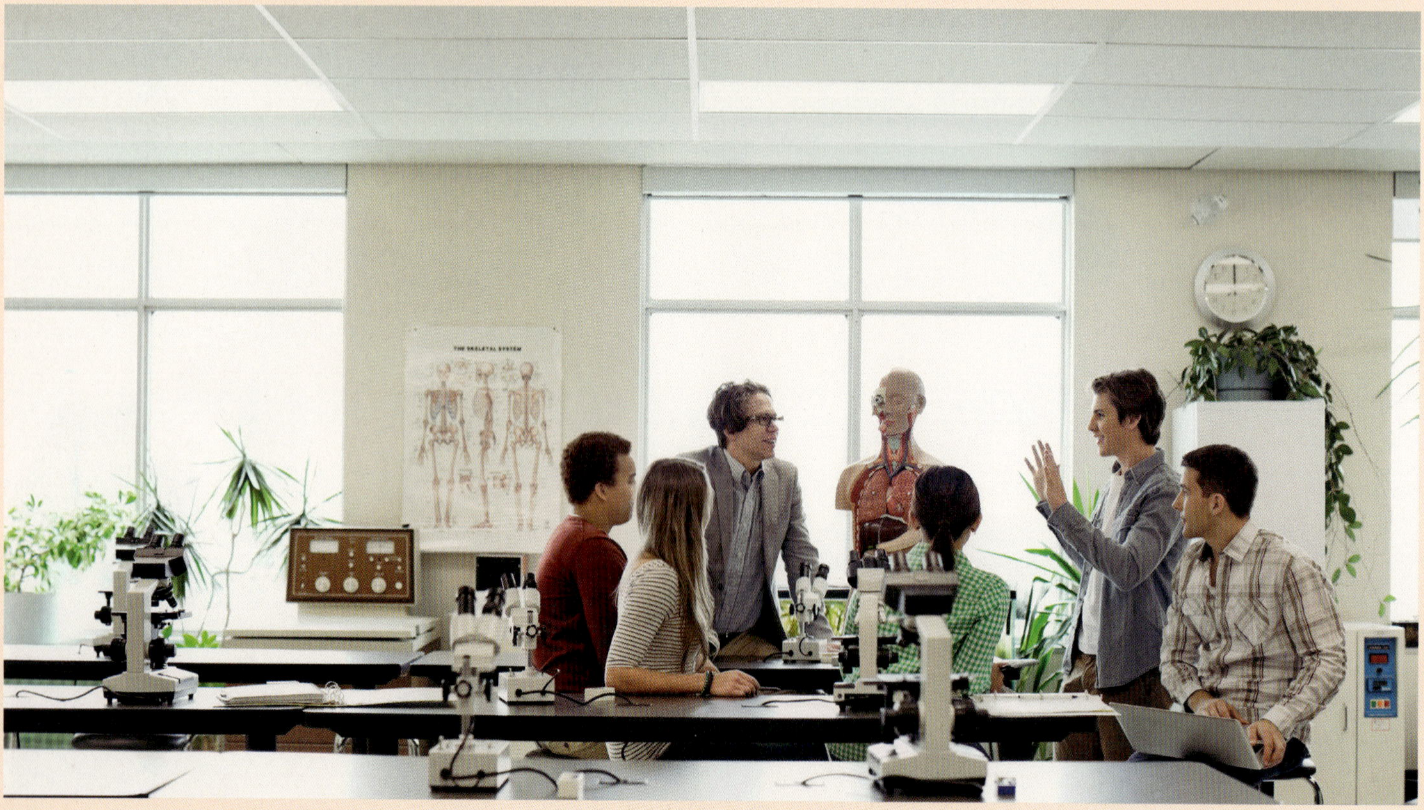

# Speaking bank

## SPEAKING PART 3

**1** Listen to two students doing the task below. Do they talk about all the options? Which present do they agree on?

It is your friend's birthday soon, and you would like to buy her a present. Here are some ideas.

Talk together about the different presents you could buy, and say which would be the most suitable.

### KEY LANGUAGE AND IDEAS FOR DISCUSSING OPTIONS

**Making suggestions:**
What about … ?    What do you think about … ?    Would … be a good idea?

**Responding to suggestions:**
That's a great idea.    Yes, good idea.    I'm not sure.

**Giving your opinion:**
I think …    In my opinion, …

**Asking someone's opinion:**
What do you think?    Do you agree?

**Agreeing:**
That's true. I agree (with you).    Yes, I think you're right.    OK, so …

**Disagreeing:**
I don't agree with you because …    I'm not sure about that because …

**Considering alternatives:**
… might be a better choice. What if we … ?

**Reaching agreement:**
It's time to decide.    Are you OK with that?    We'll go for that one, then.

Speaking bank

**2 Complete the discussion with words from the box. Then listen again and check.**

> agree  go  idea  OK  opinion  so  sure  think

**A:** What do you (1) .................... about that idea?
**B:** I'm not (2) .................... . It's difficult to choose a book for someone else.
**A:** I (3) .................... with you. And I don't think flowers are a good idea, because they're a bit boring in my (4) .................... .
**B:** Would a T-shirt be a good (5) .................... ? Most people wear T-shirts.
**A:** Well, I don't really like it when people buy me clothes, because I prefer to choose them myself.
**B:** OK, (6) .................... not a T-shirt.
**B:** Maybe we should choose the cinema tickets. Are you (7) .................... with that?
**A:** Yes, good idea. We'll (8) .................... for that one, then.

**3 Match the beginnings and endings of the sentences.**

1 That's a          a agree with you.
2 Do you           b be a better choice.
3 I don't           c to decide.
4 Flowers might    d great idea.
5 It's time         e you're right.
6 Yes, I think      f agree?

**4 Work in pairs. Do the task below. Then listen and compare your ideas.**

Two friends are discussing how their class should celebrate the end of exams. Here are some ideas. Talk together about the different ideas and say which would be the most fun.

160

# Speaking bank

## SPEAKING PART 4

**1** Listen to two students answering the questions. Which things do they do?
- give reasons for their answers
- interrupt each other
- ask for each other's opinions
- disagree with each other
- use an expression to allow time to think about the answer

> 1 Who do you most enjoy buying presents for?
> 2 Which people in your family are the most difficult to choose presents for?
> 3 Do you like receiving money instead of presents?

### KEY LANGUAGE AND IDEAS FOR DISCUSSING IDEAS

**Talking about likes/dislikes/preferences:**
I like/love + -ing    I prefer to ...    I enjoy ...

**Talking about habits:**
I sometimes/usually/always ...

**Giving your opinion:**
I think ...    In my opinion, ...

**Asking someone's opinion:**
What do you think?    Do you agree?

**Agreeing:**
That's true.    I agree with you.    Yes, I think you're right.

**Disagreeing:**
I don't agree with you because ...
I'm not sure about that because ...

**Giving yourself time to think:**
That's an interesting question.
That's a difficult question.    Let me see.

**2** Choose the correct words in *italics*.
1 I enjoy *to buy / buying* things for my nephew.
2 It *sometimes is / is sometimes* nice to receive money.
3 I *usually get / get usually* money from three or four relatives.
4 I prefer *get / to get* money from people who don't know me very well.
5 I love *get / getting* presents.

**3** Complete the dialogues with phrases from the box.

> Do you agree?    That's an interesting question.
> That's true.    What do you think?

**A:** I think surprise presents are the best presents. (1) ..........................
**B:** Yes, I do. I love opening presents when I have no idea what they are!
**A:** I think money is sometimes the most useful present to get.
**B:** (2) .......................... Because then you can use it to buy something you really need.
**A:** In my opinion, men are the most difficult people to buy presents for. (3) ..........................
**B:** Yes, I think you're right. I never know what to buy for my dad or my uncle.
**A:** Do you think that some people spend too much money on presents?
**B:** Hmm. (4) .......................... I think most people spend as much as they can afford.

**4** Work in pairs. Discuss these questions together.

> 1 Would you like to have more social events with your English class?
> 2 Do you think watching sports events can be more fun than taking part?
> 3 Do you prefer cooking a meal for friends or eating out in a restaurant?

**5** Listen and compare your ideas.

# Extra resources

## Unit 3
### Prepositions of place

## Unit 4
### Comparative and superlative adjectives

a True. The population of Canada is approximately 37 million. The population of Tokyo is 9 million.
b False. The longest country is Chile. It's 4,270km long.
c True. There is about 83 cm of rain every year in Rome. There is about 62 cm of rain every year in Paris.

## Unit 8
### Writing Part 2

| | |
|---|---|
| capital letter | • the first letter of a sentence: **F**ootball is very popular in Britain.<br>• for countries, nationalities, languages, names of people, places, trademarks, days, months: **P**ortugal, **R**ussian, **L**ego, **M**rs, etc.<br>• for titles of books, films, etc.: **S**tar **W**ars, **S**hrek<br>• for abbreviations: **UNICEF, WWF, FIFA** |
| full stop UK/ period US | • the end of a sentence: I'm going for a walk. |
| comma | • between items in a list: I need some peas**,** butter**,** sugar and eggs.<br>• to show a pause in a long sentence: If I lost my phone**,** I'd go to the police station.<br>• when you want to add information: The woman**,** who I'd met last week**,** waved as she went past. |
| apostrophe | • for missing letters: don**'**t, I**'**ll, it**'**s<br>• for possessives: Paul**'**s bike |
| hyphen | • to join two words: good**-**looking, hard**-**working |

## Unit 9
### Starting off

Add up the points from your answers.

| | | |
|---|---|---|
| 1 A=0 | B=1 | C=2 |
| 2 A=1 | B=0 | C=2 |
| 3 A=0 | B=1 | C=2 |
| 4 A=2 | B=0 | C=1 |
| 5 A=0 | B=2 | C=1 |
| 6 A=0 | B=1 | C=2 |

**Your total score =** ..........................

**Your total score = 0–4**

You're not keen on exercise, are you? By not getting a minimum 30 minutes of activity a day, you're missing a great way to feel less stressed, sleep better and get more energy. As it's all new to you, start with a little at first. Remember you can do parts of your half-hour at different times, so why not walk to work, clean the house, go for a swim – anything that stops you sitting on the sofa, really. You don't have to run 40 kilometres to improve your fitness.

**Your total score = 5–8**

You could be fitter. You're quite relaxed and, while taking it easy can be a good idea, it shouldn't take too much extra effort to do the recommended 30 minutes a day, five times a week. You enjoy spending time with your friends, so why not take up an activity together? It can be anything – from a street dance class to basketball. Or if you don't fancy organised classes, go out dancing instead of sitting around doing nothing.

**Your total score = 9 or more**

Well done! You're fit and active. Half an hour of activity a day is a minimum for you. While keeping active now means you feel great, you can also look forward to a healthy future. You shouldn't have to worry if you stay active. As you enjoy being fit, make sure you do all the activities you can: from hill walks to rock climbing.

# Answer key

## Unit 1 My life and home

### Starting off
**1**
1 sitting room/living room, balcony, bathroom, kitchen
2–5 Students' own answers.

### Listening Part 2
**1**
Students' own answers.
**2**
2 a man talking to his friend, changing jobs
3 a woman talking about a trip to the beach
4 two friends, the town where they live
5 two friends, comparing shops
6 two friends, their homes
**3**
1 C   2 B   3 C   4 A   5 B   6 C

**Track 2**
**Narrator:** For each question, choose the correct answer. One. You will hear two friends talking about the kind of flat they would like to live in.
**Man:** Wouldn't it be great to live right at the top of that block of flats, with views across the city?
**Woman:** Nice views are fine but I'm not very keen on lifts. I think I'd rather be on the ground floor. It'd be good to live in a building that's not far from a bus stop, too.
**Man:** Or an underground station.
**Woman:** Right. But the most important thing for me would be to have my own room, so it'd have to be a three-bedroom apartment.
**Man:** I don't mind sharing, so two would be enough for me.
**Narrator:** Two. You will hear a man telling his friend about changing job.
**Woman:** I haven't seen you for a long time. How do you feel now about your new job?
**Man:** Well, before I moved at the beginning of January, I thought it'd be difficult to make friends with people in my new office, but they've given me a really warm welcome. Of course I'm a bit sad that I don't see anyone from my previous company, but there's nothing I can do about that. My work seems to be going better than I'd expected, too, so making the change hasn't been too hard, really.
**Narrator:** Three. You will hear a woman talking about a trip to the beach.
**Man:** How was your day out?
**Woman:** Great! The bus left early on Saturday so I had to get up at 5 a.m., but that meant we got to the beach really early.
**Man:** Did you go for a swim?
**Woman:** Yes, I thought I would enjoy that but it was a bit cold so we hired a little boat instead and sailed round the bay. That was fun too, but not as much as having a game of volleyball. We're going there again in July when it'll be too hot for beach sports, but swimming in the sea will be wonderful!
**Narrator:** Four. You will hear two friends talking about the town where they live.
**Woman:** It's quite a good place to live, isn't it? Although I sometimes think it would be nice if more people lived here.
**Man:** Well, it might be livelier, but I think the size is about right, actually. In bigger places there are problems like street crime, especially at night, but here you feel safe anywhere, really.
**Woman:** That's true, although everywhere you go the roads are really busy, and it's the same here. All that noise and pollution is horrible early in the morning.
**Man:** I know. I wish people would walk or go by bike instead.
**Narrator:** Five. You will hear a man talking to a friend about shops.
**Woman:** I don't really know this part of town. Where's the best place to do a bit of shopping?
**Man:** The little shop on the corner isn't bad. The range of things there is a bit limited, but just about everything is amazingly good value, especially if you compare it to the local supermarket.
**Woman:** The one opposite the station?
**Man:** Yes, you can find almost anything you want there, but it always seems to be really crowded, with lots of people waiting to pay because it's short of staff.
**Woman:** Thanks. I'll definitely avoid that one.
**Narrator:** Six. You will hear two friends talking about their homes.
**Man:** I like my room, though I haven't got much space for my things.
**Woman:** Mine's about the right size really, but I know what you mean. My cupboards and shelves are far too small.
**Man:** At least mine's got big windows, so I get plenty of sunshine.
**Woman:** I do too, though it's a pity I can't turn the central heating up in winter.
**Man:** Does it get noisy? It can do at my place, especially in the morning rush hour.
**Woman:** My flatmate complains about traffic noise waking her up too! But I'm on the inside of the building, so I hardly notice it.

**4**
Students' own answers.

### Prepositions of time
**5**
1 in   2 In   3 at   4 in   5 on
**6**
**at:** 5 o'clock, bedtime, half past four, night
**in:** 2020, July, the afternoon, the holidays, winter
**on:** 25 May, my birthday, Sundays, weekdays
**7**
Students' own answers.

### Grammar
**Frequency adverbs**
**1**
Students' own answers.
**2**
1 be + frequency adverb   2 before   3 at the end of a sentence
**3**
2 I check my phone for messages every two hours.
3 I'm never late for my English lessons.
4 I sometimes write emails to friends.
5 I don't always have lunch at home.
6 I'm sleepy in the morning almost every day.
7 I hardly ever go out on Monday nights.
8 I stay in bed late most weekends.
**4 & 5**
Students' own answers.

### Reading Part 5
**1**
Students' own answers.
**2**
1 An article
2 D
3 Emilia does lots of interesting things.
Her education takes place on the boat.
Living on a boat has some disadvantages.
She sometimes meets her friends.
**3**
1 D   2 B   3 D   4 C   5 A   6 C
**4 & 5**
Students' own answers.

### Grammar
**Present simple and present continuous**
**1**
2 d   3 a   4 b   5 c

Answer key 163

**2**
2 am/'m sitting   3 has   4 am/'m looking   5 love   6 stay   7 go
8 is/'s getting   9 leave   10 is blowing   11 are/'re having
12 don't want
**3**
1 What does 'habit' mean?
2 Do any buses stop in your street?
3 Who watches the most TV in your house?
4 Do you prefer to get up early or late?
5 Is everyone talking to their partners at the moment?
6 What colour clothes are you wearing today?
7 Is anyone sitting behind us in class right now?
8 What do you sometimes forget to do?
**4 & 5**
Students' own answers.
**6**
/s/: forgets, likes, speaks, thinks, walks, wants, works
/z/: does, goes, lives, loves, plays, prefers, sees, studies, wears
/ɪz/: changes, chooses, finishes, passes, practises, uses, washes
**7 & 8**
Students' own answers.

## Vocabulary
**House and home**
**1**
Students' own answers.
**2**
(Suggested answers)
Living room: armchair, cushions, rug, sofa
Bathroom: bath, cupboards, mirror, taps, toilet, towels
Kitchen: cooker, cupboards, dishwasher, fridge, microwave, sink, taps, washing machine
Bedroom: blankets, chest of drawers, cupboards, duvet, mirror, pillow, wardrobe

**Countable and uncountable nouns**
**3**
furniture
**4**
[U] tells you the noun is uncountable.
[C] is the symbol for a countable noun.
**5**
Students' own answers.

## Grammar
*a few, a bit of, many, much, a lot of* and *lots of*
**1**
1 countable   2 uncountable   3 uncountable   4 countable
**2**
1 a bit of, much
2 much, a few
3 a few, a lot of
4 a lot of, lots of
5 much, a bit, a lot
6 much, many
**3**
Students' own answers.

## Speaking Part 1
**Prepositions of place**
**1**
1 at   2 in   3 at   4 on   5 at   6 on
**2**
Students' own answers.
**3**
at (college etc.)
in (a city, etc.)
on (the coast, etc.)
**4**
2 b Where do you live?
3 d What do you do in Recife?
4 e Do you like having English lessons?
5 a Will you use English in the future?

164

**5**
Students' own answers.
**6**
2 in   3 in   4 on   5 are you   6 at   7 do you get   8 in   9 in   10 do you like   11 in   12 at

> **Track 3**
> **Hugo:** Where do you come from, Sara?
> **Sara:** I live in Vigo, a city in Galicia. That's in north-west Spain, on the Atlantic coast.
> **Hugo:** Do you work or are you a student?
> **Sara:** I'm a second-year student at the University of Vigo. I'm studying Economics.
> **Hugo:** How do you get there in the mornings?
> **Sara:** The university isn't in the city so I usually take the bus, but in summer I often ride there on my bike.
> **Hugo:** And where do you like to go in the evenings?
> **Sara:** Sometimes I go out with my friends, but most evenings I stay at home studying. I've got exams soon!

**7**
Students' own answers.

## Writing Part 1
**1**
2 an email, plus four notes that you have made.
3 an email in reply
4 Alex's boss will let her/him have time off work; very pleased.
5 which would be the best month for her/him to visit; when he/she can come and why that would be the best month
6 what your home is like
7 which things he/she should bring
**2**
1 four
2 Brilliant! – first, Say when and why – second, Describe – third, Suggest – fourth
3 two
4 *at* my place, *in* a three-bedroom flat, *on* the fifth floor, *in* a quiet neighbourhood; *in* August, *at* weekends, *in* the summer; *usually* away in August, *sometimes* have barbecues, *hardly ever* rains in July
**3–5**
Students' own answers.

# Unit 2 Making choices

## Starting off
**Life choices**
**1**
A get some work experience B take a gap year   C retire early
D quit your job   E apply for a job
(Possible order)
1 take a gap year   2 get some work experience   3 apply for a job
4 quit your job   5 retire early
**2**
Students' own answers.

## Reading Part 6
**1**
Students' own answers.
**2**
(Suggested answers)
1 relative pronoun   2 preposition   3 verb   4 preposition   5 pronoun
6 preposition   7 article   8 linker
**3**
1 who/that   2 to   3 are   4 with   5 their   6 and
**4 & 5**
(Suggested answer)
some unusual university courses
**6**
1 about   2 are   3 an   4 as   5 who   6 from
**7 & 8**
Students' own answers.

## Vocabulary

*fail, pass, take, lose, miss, study* and *teach*

**1**
2 pass  3 fail  4 miss  5 lose  6 learn  7 teach  8 study
**2**
2 lose  3 teach  4 learn  5 miss  6 study  7 teach  8 fail
**3**
Students' own answers.

## Grammar

**Past simple**

**1**
(Suggested answers)
Life in St. Andrews is very quiet – it is a very small town and there isn't much to do, while Mexico City is an enormous city with many people and there is a lot to see and do.
**2**
The city – Mexico City, a very large city
Shops and entertainment – shopping centres, museums, large cinemas with a choice of films, restaurants with food from all over the world.

### Track 4
**Interviewer:** Emily Cale's finishing her degree in chemistry right now. She's here with us today to talk about the nine months she spent abroad when she left school. Hello, Emily.
**Emily:** Hi!
**Interviewer:** So, where did you go?
**Emily:** I went to Mexico for nine months and I worked in a laboratory.
**Interviewer:** Young people often go straight to university in their own country when they leave school. Why did you decide to work abroad?
**Emily:** When I left school, I wanted to get some work experience to be sure that I really wanted to study chemistry and I wanted to improve my Spanish. Mexico City's the capital, of course, and it's also the largest Spanish-speaking city in the world!
**Interviewer:** How did you find a place in the laboratory?
**Emily:** My dad contacted an agency and they found me a place to do work experience in a research centre.
**Interviewer:** Where did you stay?
**Emily:** I stayed with Alicia and her family in Mexico City. Alicia's around my age and we got on really well.
**Interviewer:** Did you speak Spanish before you went?
**Emily:** Yes, I did. I studied French and Spanish at school and I thought I was good at languages. But when I got to Mexico I couldn't say anything. It was awful.
**Interviewer:** How did you feel when you first arrived?
**Emily:** To tell you the truth, when I arrived, I was scared. Mexico City is so different from my home town. It's enormous! And of course, I didn't know anyone.
**Interviewer:** Did you like the city?
**Emily:** I liked it a lot. You see, there's so much to see and do unlike Saint Andrews, my home town. There are shopping centres, museums, large cinemas with a choice of films and then there are restaurants with food from all over the world.
**Interviewer:** Did you enjoy the experience?
**Emily:** Oh yes, I did. I loved working in the laboratory. My Spanish also got better and I even began to dream in Spanish. I made so many really good friends and Alicia is coming to stay with me very soon.
**Interviewer:** Thank you, Emily … and if you'd like to know more about getting work experience abroad, contact …

**3**
2 Why did you decide to work abroad?
3 How did you find a place in the laboratory?
4 Where did you stay?
5 Did you speak Spanish before you went?
6 How did you feel when you first arrived?
7 Did you like the city?
8 Did you enjoy the experience?
**4**
2 wanted  3 contacted; found  4 stayed  5 studied  6 arrived; was  7 liked  8 loved

**5**
Regular verbs: wanted, contacted, stayed, studied, arrived, liked, loved
Irregular verbs: went, found, was
**6**
1 /ɪd/  2 /d/  3 /t/

### Track 5
1 I wanted to improve my Spanish.
2 I stayed with Alicia and her family.
3 I liked the city a lot.

**7**
/d/: arrived, enjoyed, loved, studied
/t/: helped, liked, watched, worked
/ɪd/: contacted, decided, invited, needed, wanted

### Track 6
| /d/ | arrived | enjoyed | loved | stayed | studied |
| /t/ | helped | liked | watched | worked | |
| /ɪd/ | contacted | decided | invited | needed | wanted |

**8**
Students' own answers.
**9**
1 My friends and I ~~plaied~~ **played** football yesterday.
2 In our first English lesson our teacher ~~teached~~ **taught** us some new words for sports.
3 When I went to university, I ~~studyed~~ **studied** very hard.
4 Last weekend, I ~~founded~~ **found** a very good restaurant in my town.
5 When I ~~arribed~~ **arrived** at work, my colleagues weren't there.
6 My friend Sara ~~bringed~~ **brought** her dog to class one day.
7 I'm reading a book that my English teacher ~~recommend~~ **recommended** to me.
8 We ~~puted~~ **put** all our things in the car and we set off on holiday.
**10**
2 spent  3 chose  4 wanted  5 left  6 was  7 felt  8 said  9 looked after  10 ate  11 saw  12 made
**11**
Students' own answers.

## Grammar

**Past simple and past continuous**

**1**
Students' own answers.
**2**
She saw a group of dogs.

### Track 7
**Emily:** It was in my second week. The sun was shining and I was feeling good. I was walking to work with Alicia when we saw a group of dogs. We were frightened and we didn't know what to do.

**3**
(Possible answer)
They started shouting for help.

### Track 8
**Emily:** Suddenly a woman appeared from nowhere and she started screaming at the dogs. The dogs ran off. We said 'Gracias!' and went to work.

**4**
1 No, they were three separate actions which happened one after the other. The dogs ran off last.
2 We don't know when the sun started shining or if it stopped shining.
3 No, they didn't. They saw the dogs on their walk to work.
**5**
2 past continuous  3 past simple  4 past continuous (or 3 past continuous / 4 past simple)  5 past simple  6 past continuous
**6**
2 went  3 was talking  4 stopped  5 said  6 was feeling  7 didn't know  8 helped  9 were setting off  10 shouted  11 took off  12 started

Answer key  165

### Track 9
**Emily:** One morning, Alicia woke up early and went to the kitchen where I was talking loudly to my flatmate. We stopped talking and I said, 'Look outside! There's twenty centimetres of snow on the ground. We'll have to ski to the town centre.' Alicia was feeling excited and nervous at the same time. Snow in Mexico City is very rare and she didn't know how to ski. I helped her to put on the skis. As we were setting off, one of the neighbours shouted, 'Everything is closed, even the shops!' We took off our skis and started throwing snowballs.

**7 & 8**
Students' own answers.

## Listening Part 1
**1**
2 <u>What time</u> does Stuart need to be <u>at work</u>?
3 <u>Where</u> does <u>Jack live</u>?
4 <u>Where</u> did the man <u>find</u> his <u>football boots</u>?
5 <u>What</u> did Julia <u>eat before she came home</u>?
6 <u>What</u> are the two friends going to <u>buy Paul</u> for his birthday?
7 What is the <u>weather</u> forecast for <u>tomorrow</u>?

**2**
(Suggested answers)
1 A a large camera, B a packed lunch for a trip, C a water bottle
2 A it's eight thirty or half past eight, B it's eight fifty or ten to nine, C it's nine or nine o'clock
3 A A house next to a swimming pool, B A house next to a pizza restaurant, C A house next to a cinema
4 A a sports bag, B a kitchen, C a cupboard
5 A a burger, B a sandwich, C a chocolate cake
6 A a thriller, B a book about surfing, C a book about music / a pop group or band
7 A rain, B sun, C clouds

**3**
1 C   2 B   3 B   4 A   5 C   6 A   7 B

### Track 10
**Narrator:** Part 1. For each question, choose the correct answer. One. What do the people need to bring for the cycling trip?
**Woman:** Just before you leave. Ssh! Listen carefully. Don't forget it's our annual day out tomorrow and the office will be closed. For those of you on the cycling trip, we're meeting outside the train station. Lunch will be provided so you don't have to bring any food but don't forget a water bottle. It may be hot. Please don't bring any large items like heavy bags or cameras as you won't be able to carry them.
**Narrator:** Two. What time does Stuart need to be at work?
**Woman:** Stuart! It's ten past nine.
**Stuart:** I know, I'm late again. You see, I left my mobile at home so I went back for it. Then I missed the bus and the next one was at half past eight. There was a terrible traffic jam so I got off the bus and ran the rest of the way.
**Woman:** Yes but the shop opens at nine. I can't manage everything on my own. You should really be here by ten to nine.
**Stuart:** I'm sorry.
**Narrator:** Three. Where does Jack live?
**Jack:** Hi it's Jack. Do you still fancy going to the swimming pool later? George lives near the pool so he might want to come too. Shall we meet outside the cinema? You know, the one near where I used to live. And if you like, we can get a take-away afterwards and have it at my house. They've opened a great pizza place next door to us. Let me know what you think. Bye!
**Narrator:** Four. Where did the man find his football boots?
**Man:** Have you seen my football boots anywhere? I brought them home from training yesterday. They were wet so I left them in the kitchen to dry and now I can't find them.
**Katie:** We were tidying up this morning. Have you looked in the cupboard in the hall?
**Man:** Yes, but they weren't there. Wait a minute. What's in that bag over there? Oh, they must be my boots.
**Narrator:** Five. What did Julia eat before she came home?
**Man:** Hi Julia. How was your day? I'm just having a cheese sandwich. Would you like one?

**Julia:** No thanks. I'm not hungry. You know Nigel at work, don't you? It was his birthday today and he brought in a homemade chocolate cake. It was delicious.
**Man:** I guess you don't want dinner, then.
**Julia:** Oh yes, I do! What are you making?
**Man:** It's my special burgers tonight. They should be ready by about eight.
**Narrator:** Six. What are the two friends going to buy Paul for his birthday?
**Man:** It's Paul's birthday next weekend. We should get him something. We got him a book about his favourite band last year.
**Woman:** Oh yeah, that's right but his sister had bought him the same one so he took it back to the shop. He got a book about surfing instead, didn't he?
**Man:** Yes, that's right. I know! My brother's reading a new spy thriller. It's set in Italy and he says it's really exciting. Let's get him that.
**Woman:** OK.
**Narrator:** Seven. What is the weather forecast for tomorrow?
**Joe:** Best of luck with the tennis competition, Vicki! It's tomorrow, isn't it?
**Vicki:** Thanks, Joe! They might have to cancel it. It hasn't stopped raining all day today and we're playing outdoors.
**Joe:** Have you looked it up on the internet? It says on this page that it's going to be cloudy but dry. It won't be sunny though.
**Vicki:** That's OK. I don't like playing when it's hot but I'll take my sun cream just in case.

## Grammar
**used to**
**1**
used to, didn't use to
**2**
1 No   2 We write *didn't use to* (NOT *didn't used to*) and *did you use to* (NOT *did you used to …?*)   3 the infinitive
**3**
(Model answer)
I think my life was easier ten years ago because I used to live at home and I didn't use to do any housework. I was still at school so I used to see my friends at school every day and we used to make plans for the weekend. I didn't use to have to phone them to meet them. However, I used to do a lot of homework and we used to do lots of exams, which I didn't enjoy.

## Vocabulary
*do, earn, make, spend, take* and *win*
**1**
2 earn   3 take   4 spend   5 take   6 take / do   7 do   8 win
**2**
Students' own answers.

## Speaking Part 3
**1**
1 quiz night, weekend trips, cooking classes
2 a team meal, a running group, yoga and relaxation
3 a team meal

### Track 11
**Tanya:** Have you got a moment, Gareth?
**Gareth:** Err, yeah, go on!
**Tanya:** Well, you know our boss wants us to vote on a new social activity at work. Can we talk about the choices first?
**Gareth:** Sure!
**Tanya:** Shall we start with the quiz night?
**Gareth:** OK, go on.
**Tanya:** Don't you think it would be a great idea? Quizzes are such fun and I love competitions, you know.
**Gareth:** Umm… I don't think many of our colleagues would agree with you. How about a team meal? In my sister's company, each department has lunch together once a month so that they can get to know each other better.
**Tanya:** Good point. Let's talk about another one. Then we can decide. Perhaps we could go on a weekend trip and try new sports or activities together.
**Gareth:** Do you really think that's a good idea? Some of our colleagues have families and they can't go away at the weekend.

> **Tanya:** That's a good point. I often go round to my grandma's house on Saturdays anyway.
> **Gareth:** I think it'd be better to start something like a running group where we meet at lunchtime twice a week and go for a run together for about forty minutes.
> **Tanya:** I don't agree. Some of us hate running. What's left on the list? Let's see. What about cooking classes? Did you see *MasterChef* on TV last night?
> **Gareth:** I'm not sure about that one.
> **Tanya:** Nor am I.
> **Gareth:** Yeah. I'd prefer to do yoga and relaxation, to be quite honest. Then we would all feel less stressed.
> **Tanya:** That's true but I still think a team meal is the best option.
> **Gareth:** So do I. Let's go for that.

**2**
Nor am I; So do I
We use 'so' to agree with positive sentences and 'nor' to agree with negative sentences.
**3**
1 start   2 about   3 point   4 agree   5 sure   6 Let's

> **Track 12**
> 1 **Tanya:** Shall we start with the quiz night?
> 2 **Gareth:** How about a team meal?
> 3 **Tanya:** Good point. Let's talk about another one.
> 4 **Tanya:** I don't agree. Some of us hate running.
> 5 **Gareth:** I'm not sure about that one.
> 6 **Gareth:** Let's go for that.

**4**
Suggesting: How about
Agreeing: Good point
Disagreeing: I don't agree, I'm not sure
Deciding: Let's go for that
**5**
Students' own answers.

## Writing Part 2
**1**
1 an article   2 What makes a great place to work? Is it the people or the facilities or something else? What kinds of social activities should a great place to work offer its employees?
**2**
(Suggested answer)
staff; facilities (office space, furniture, kitchen, canteen etc.); working day, location and views; technology; career opportunities etc.

**3 & 4**
(Suggested answers)
A great place to work
• Staff: a fair boss who encourages us, interesting colleagues, easy to get on with
• Facilities: a large bright office with space is more pleasant to work in
• Working day: workers can choose their hours, one afternoon off a week, lots of holidays
• Social activities: a place to work should offer different activities so we can get to know each other
**5**
Yes, Charlotte has completed the task well.
**6**
Students' own answers.

## 1 Vocabulary and grammar review
**1**
2 in   3 on   4 in   5 in   6 at   7 In   8 at/on   9 in   10 at   11 in   12 on
**2**
2 a bit of   3 a lot   4 much   5 time   6 much   7 a bit of   8 a few
**3**
2 Hello, I call **I'm calling** to ask if you want to go out somewhere tonight.
3 Why do you stand **are you standing** here in the rain at this time of night?
4 I'm tired usually **usually tired** in the morning.
5 I'm never believing **I never believe** anything that newspaper says.
6 I every day water the plants on the balcony **water the plants on the balcony every day**.
7 How do you often **often do you** have a bath?
8 I get normally **normally get** home at about half past five.

**4**
2 sofa   3 fridge   4 cooker   5 dishwasher   6 microwave   7 duvet
8 chest of drawers   9 wardrobe   10 washing machine

## 2 Vocabulary and grammar review
**1**
2 do   3 learned   4 pass   5 earning   6 made   7 taking   8 did
**2**
2 I think I lefted **left** my bag at your house last night.
3 Our teacher was kind. She teached **taught** us very well.
4 I woke up very early because I was planing **planning** to go to the lake.
5 My dad only payed **paid** €75 for his mobile phone.
6 While my sister was riding her bike, she felt **fell** and injured her leg.
7 When I was younger, I prefered **preferred** to take the bus everywhere.
8 I met Holly a very long time ago. We were studing **studying** at the same university.
**3**
2 were chatting, was writing   3 were having, rang   4 was buying, saw
5 thought, was   6 began, was walking   7 sat (or was sitting), broke
8 watched, understood   9 went, enjoyed   10 was feeling, went
**4**
2 use   3 give   4 used   5 didn't

# Unit 3 Having fun
## Starting off
**Leisure activities**
**1**
2 taking   3 going   4 riding   5 watching   6 playing   7 posting   8 visiting
**2 & 3**
Students' own answers.

## Listening Part 4
**1**
Students' own answers.
**2**
1 a reason   2 an opinion   3 an opinion   4 feelings   5 an opinion   6 advice
**3**
1 B   2 B   3 C   4 A   5 C   6 A

> **Track 13**
> **Narrator:** You will hear a radio interview with the Instagram photographer Marc Pasqual. For each question, choose the correct answer.
> **Interviewer:** Today I'm talking to photographer Marc Pasqual, who posts all his pictures on Instagram. Marc, what made you want to do that full-time?
> **Marc:** I was an international tour guide, visiting some amazing countries. I was also doing wedding photos as a hobby, but I was finding that pretty boring and was keen to try something more creative, even though I felt it unlikely I'd earn much money from it. I noticed my favourite people on Instagram, like the chef Lauren Bath, had given up interesting careers to concentrate on photography, so I decided to make the change, too.
> **Interviewer:** How did you become such a good photographer? With a good teacher?
> **Marc:** I did have some lessons with an experienced photographer. He encouraged me to think about how I wanted my photographs to look before I actually took them. That works for some people but not others, and personally, whenever I arrive somewhere new I start taking photos, such as drops of rain on a flower, or the sun shining through a small window. Not everyone notices these little things and it can really improve your pictures.
> **Interviewer:** Did you make any mistakes?
> **Marc:** Well, some beginners can't help posting lots of selfies on Instagram, but I avoided doing that. However, only uploading weekly, as I did at first, means people soon forget you. I saw those ads for expensive apps that promise to make you an Instagram star in a week, but fortunately I ignored them.
> **Interviewer:** What's the best thing about your work?
> **Marc:** I love getting messages on Instagram and replying to them, or working with other photographers, because I get lonely if I'm by myself. But nothing gives me quite as much pleasure as having the memories of all the fantastic places I've travelled to. Taking photos means I'll never forget them.

Answer key  167

**Interviewer:** What do you most want to do next?
**Marc:** I've thought of studying photography at university and that would be great, but it'd probably be more useful for someone aiming to start a career in a large organization. I'd rather read lots about it since its invention in the 19th century, and still be able to work on my own.
**Interviewer:** What would you say to new Instagram photographers?
**Marc:** Make sure people on Instagram notice your work. Research shows that it doesn't really matter whether you post on weekdays or weekends, so do so whenever you like. Some photographers say you shouldn't add any text, but I disagree. I tell the story of each picture, saying why and how I took it and people like that. Also, add a link to your blog or Facebook page and upload some of your photos there, though keep your best ones for Instagram.

**4**
Students' own answers.

## Vocabulary
**Prepositions of place**
**1**
See page 162.

### Track 14
**Kirsty:** Hi Jack, I forgot I'm playing tennis later and I've left all my things at home! Can you find them for me? And could you bring them with you later?
**Jack:** Sure, I'll go and look for them in your room now. Where's your racket?
**Kirsty:** You'll see that as soon as you walk in. It's lying on the floor just in front of the wardrobe.
**Jack:** Right, I'm just opening the door… yes, there it is.
**Kirsty:** Great. Now there should also be some tennis balls, four I think, on the shelf that's opposite the window. Can you see it?
**Jack:** Yes, I can.
**Kirsty:** They're actually behind the clock there.
**Jack:** Yes, all four are there. I'll bring those too. What else?
**Kirsty:** My trainers. Do you see the small table next to my bed? Well, they're under that.
**Jack:** I've got them. Is that everything?
**Kirsty:** Just one more thing. Could you get my T-shirt?
**Jack:** Sure. Where is it?
**Kirsty:** If you look inside the wardrobe, on the right, you'll see it on the shelf above the one where my jeans are. And that's all.
**Jack:** OK, if I can find a big enough bag, I think I can carry everything!
**Kirsty:** Thanks, Jack.
**Jack:** No problem, see you later.

**2**
2 Her tennis balls are on the shelf opposite the window, behind the clock.
3 Her trainers are under the small table, next to the bed.
4 Her T-shirt is inside the wardrobe on the right, on the shelf above her jeans.

## Reading Part 3
**1**
Sand sculptures; students' own answers.
**2**
D
**3**
1 Because she saw some on the beach near where she lives.
2 She felt determined to try harder to build it.
3 That people don't realise that even lightly touching a sand sculpture can damage it.
**4**
1 D  2 B  3 C  4 A
**5**
Students' own answers.

## Grammar
**Verbs followed by *to* or *-ing***
**1**
*-ing*: 2, 3; *to*: 1, 4
**2**

| verb + *-ing* | verb + *to* |
|---|---|
| avoid, enjoy, fancy, feel like, finish, keep, mind, miss, practise, suggest | agree, decide, hope, learn, manage, promise, seem, want, would like |

**3**
something you have to do: 2, 3
a memory of something in the past: 1, 4
**4**
2 I hope ~~see~~ **to see** you soon!
3 I really enjoyed ~~to help~~ **helping** at a music festival.
4 Do you fancy ~~to come~~ **coming** out with us?
5 When we finished ~~to eat~~ **eating** I went home.
6 I'll never forget ~~to visit~~ **visiting** New York last year.
**5**
2 listening  3 to do  4 going  5 to bring  6 to do
**6**
1 /ŋ/  2 no  3 no

### Track 15
1 Where do you fancy going this evening?
2 What kind of music do you enjoy listening to at home?
3 What are you planning to do at the weekend?
4 Do you remember going away on holiday when you were younger?
5 Do you ever forget to bring anything to your English lesson?
6 What would you like to do tomorrow?

**7**
Students' own answers.
**8**
(Possible answers)
1 I'm learning to play the drums.
2 I can't afford to buy a new computer.
3 I decided to stop spending too much last week.
4 I must remember to phone my best friend tomorrow.
5 I'll finish doing this exercise soon.
6 I shouldn't forget to watch that film on TV next weekend.

## Vocabulary
**Phrasal verbs**
**1**
1 hang on  2 run out of  3 look after
**2**
2 give up  3 look forward to  4 take up  5 go off  6 go on  7 sign up for  8 put (your name) down  9 set off
**3**
1 sign up for, look forward to
2 put (your name) down
**4**
2 went off  3 take up  4 put … down  5 gave up  6 go on  7 looking forward to

### Track 16
**Chris:** Hi, Ava. Are you and Megan going away on holiday soon?
**Ava:** Yes, on Saturday. We want to set off very early in the morning.
**Chris:** Are you going to the coast?
**Ava:** No, we went off beach holidays a long time ago. There are always too many people. We've decided to take up skiing instead. We're off to the Alps.
**Chris:** Do you know how to ski?
**Ava:** Err, not really. That's why I'm going to put my name down for lessons.
**Chris:** I tried skiing once, but I found it really difficult. After three days I gave up and went home!
**Ava:** Well, the lessons go on until late afternoon every day, so I hope I can improve quickly. I'm really looking forward to trying, anyway!
**Chris:** Yes. I'm sure you'll have a great time.

**5**
Students' own answers.

## People's hobbies
**6**

| hobby | person | equipment |
|---|---|---|
| 1 cycling | cyclist | bike, helmet |
| 2 painting | painter | brush, paint |
| 3 cooking | cook | cooker, oven |
| 4 chess | chess player | board, pieces |
| 5 photography | photographer | camera |
| 6 music | musician | instrument |
| 7 camping | | tent, backpack |

**7**
(Suggested answers)
cycling: wheels, seat, chain, lock, ride
painting: landscape, frame, picture, oils
cooking: recipe, saucepans, frying pan, boil, roast, bake
photography: digital, zoom, close-up
music: practise, performance, notes, keys
camping: sleeping bag, fire, campsite
**8**
Students' own answers.

## Speaking Part 2
**1**
A acting   B sightseeing   C camping
**2**
He is talking about photo C. He talks about all of them.
**3**
2 is wearing   3 looks like   4 It seems   5 In the background
6 appears to be   7 looks

### Track 17
**Eduardo:** In this picture I can see two people in the countryside and they're camping there. The woman on the left is wearing a green jacket, grey trousers and walking boots, and the other is wearing a red jacket and hat, blue trousers and boots. It looks like they're cooking some vegetables in a, err, a frying pan on a small gas cooker, perhaps in the evening. Behind them is their yellow tent, where they're going to spend the night. It seems they are backpackers because there is a big bag for carrying things on the left of the photo, and another one on the right. In the background there's a high mountain and a forest, with some trees quite close to their tent. It appears to be winter because there's some snow on the mountain, and although the weather looks dry, I think it's probably very cold there.

**4**
1 We use *look like* with a noun to describe an activity (it *looks like* they're cooking) and *look* (without *like*) with an adjective to give a physical description (the weather *looks* dry).
2 He uses *In, on, behind, on, In*
**5–7**
Students' own answers.

## Writing Part 2
**1**
1 Yes, you are.   2 first person
**2**
b 1   c 3   d 2   e 1
**3 & 4**
Students' own answers.

# Unit 4 On holiday

## Starting off
**Holiday activities**
**1**
(Suggested activities)
1 look around a market / buy gifts/souvenirs
2 go snowboarding
3 hire a bike
4 take photos / go sightseeing
5 hang out with friends / relax on the beach
6 go snorkelling

**2**
Marrakesh – go sightseeing, take photos, look around markets, buy gifts

### Track 18
**Joe:** Where did you go on holiday, Sonia?
**Sonia:** Well, I went to Marrakesh with my cousin.
**Joe:** Marrakesh? Where's that?
**Sonia:** It's a city in Morocco, North Africa.
**Joe:** What did you do there?
**Sonia:** Well, you know my cousin. She loves to see everything so we went sightseeing almost every day.
**Joe:** Did you see a lot of things?
**Sonia:** Yeah! We looked around so many palaces, mosques and museums and of course I took lots of photos. You've seen them, haven't you?
**Joe:** I think so. Do you like visiting museums?
**Sonia:** It's OK, but I prefer going shopping and wow, in Marrakesh the *souks* are amazing.
**Joe:** What's a *souk*?
**Sonia:** It's an open-air marketplace where you can buy almost everything.
**Joe:** So, did you buy anything?
**Sonia:** Oh yes! I bought some little gifts for my friends and I got a couple of scarves.
**Joe:** I'm not sure I'd enjoy that kind of holiday.
**Sonia:** What do you mean?
**Joe:** When I go on holiday, I prefer hanging out on the beach. It's much more relaxing.

**3**
Students' own answers.

## Reading Part 1
**1**
(Suggested answer)
Read the text, decide what it says and then choose the correct option.
**2**
(Suggested answers)
It's a sign. The weather is bad, the time is the same, the day is 'tomorrow' and the food is still lunch.
**3**
lunch – refreshments
same time tomorrow – time / day
**4**
C
**5**
2 C   3 A   4 A   5 B
**6 & 7**
Students' own answers.

## Vocabulary
*travel*, *journey* and *trip*
**1 & 2**
1 trips   2 trip   3 travelled   4 trip   5 journey
**3**
Students' own answers.

## Grammar
**Comparative and superlative adjectives**
**1**
a true   b false   c true
**2**
1 c   2 b
**3**  1 deeper   2 safer   3 noisier   4 bigger   5 worse   6 noisiest
7 biggest   8 most beautiful   9 best   10 worst   11 most   12 least
**4**
1 I don't like living in the countryside even if it is ~~more safe~~ **safer** than cities.
2 That's the ~~worse~~ **worst** joke I have ever heard in all my life.
3 In the centre is the ~~bigest~~ **biggest** market in Europe.
4 Portugal is the ~~hotest~~ **hottest** country I have ever visited.
5 This town is ~~more quiet~~ **quieter** than the town I used to live in.
6 My best friend is ~~taler~~ **taller** than me and better looking too!

Answer key   169

**5**
(Suggested answers)
- For short adjectives, add -er or -est
- For short adjectives ending in a vowel + a consonant, double the last letter and add -er or -est
- For short adjectives ending in -e, add -r or -st
- For two-syllable adjectives ending in -y, change the y to i and add -er or -est
- For longer adjectives, or two-syllable adjectives not ending in -y, put more (less), most (least) in front of the adjective.

**6 & 7**
1 C   2 A   3 the most dangerous, B   4 lighter, A
5 noisier, C   6 the slowest, A   7 faster, C   8 the busiest, C
9 the deepest, A   10 drier, C

### Track 19
**Lucas:** And here are the answers to the quiz. We all know that Asia is the biggest continent in the world, followed by Africa, but did you know that North America is the third largest continent in the world? This means that it's bigger than South America.
**Abby:** And of course, at 17 million square kilometres, Russia is the largest country in the world. That's twice the size of Canada, which is the second largest country.
**Lucas:** And now for the animal facts. The most dangerous animal on the planet is not the snake or the shark but the tiny mosquito because it carries diseases. The African elephant can weigh up to eight thousand kilos so it is the largest and heaviest land animal, but the blue whale is the heaviest living animal. It can weigh around 150 tonnes – that's 150,000 kilos. I wouldn't like to share my home with a howler monkey. They're much louder than parrots or lions. In fact they are the noisiest animals on Earth – you can hear them from up to five kilometres away. The slowest-moving fish is the sea horse. It would take this fish about an hour to move 15 metres. As for the fastest fish, tunas are one of the fastest fish. Some tunas can swim at 80 kilometres per hour while the killer whales can swim at 55 kilometres per hour. Great white sharks can swim at 40 kilometres per hour, so they're faster than dolphins, which can swim at 30 kilometres per hour. You've got some answers about places, haven't you, Abby?
**Abby:** Yes, I have. Did you know that the busiest train station in the world is in Tokyo, Japan? Around one million people travel through Shinjuku station every day. And, if you like diving then you should go to Y40 Deep Joy in Italy. Its deepest point is nearly 40 metres, which makes it the deepest diving pool in the world.
**Lucas:** And finally, Antarctica is the coldest, driest and windiest continent. On the 21st July 1983, the temperature was minus eighty-nine degrees centigrade. That's the lowest temperature ever! And it only rains or snows two hundred millimetres a year there. The second driest continent is Australia where it rains six hundred millimetres a year. That's all for now.

**8 & 9**
They aren't stressed in conversation and they are pronounced /ə/ (schwa).

### Track 20
1 I wouldn't like to share my home with a howler monkey. They're much louder than parrots or lions.
2 Great white sharks can swim at 40 kilometres per hour, so they're faster than dolphins, which can swim at 30 kilometres per hour.

*a bit, a little, slightly, much, far, a lot*
**10**
2 An African elephant's brain is much / far / a lot heavier than a human's brain.
3 Arica is much / far / a lot drier (or dryer) than Death Valley.
4 Atlanta International Airport is much / far / a lot busier than Heathrow Airport.
5 Cherrapunji is a bit / a little / slightly wetter than Tutendo.
6 Cheetahs can run much / far / a lot faster than elephants.

*(not) as ... as*
**11**
1 as ... as   2 not   3 no
**12 & 13**
Students' own answers.

## Vocabulary
**Buildings and places**
**1 & 2**
A Camp Nou football stadium in Barcelona
B The Statue of Liberty
C The Mall of the Emirates in Dubai
D The Trevi Fountain in Rome
Students' own answers.
**3**
2 wide   3 low   4 old   5 clean   6 ugly   7 dull (accept quiet)
8 interesting   9 dangerous   10 cheap   11 quiet   12 near
**4**
Students' own answers.

## Grammar
*big* and *enormous*
**1**
1 B   2 C   3 A
very, extremely and quite: tall and large;
absolutely and totally: enormous
**2**
(Suggested answers) 2 small   3 hot   4 cold   5 bad   6 tiring
7 interesting   8 good
**3**
1 absolutely   2 extremely   3 absolutely   4 quite   5 very
**4**
1 Katikati, New Zealand   2 it's an open-air gallery, it never gets crowded, it's safe, easy to get into the countryside   3 quite boring, I'd like to live somewhere bigger with nightlife, cinemas, shopping centres and sports centres.

### Track 21
**Ani:** Err… I come from New Zealand, I live in Katikati which is a town about six hours away from the capital, Wellington. There are only about 4,000 people there – It's tiny. My town is amazing because it's also an open-air gallery. There are paintings on the walls, sculptures everywhere and other artwork. Katikati is a very nice place to live because it never gets too crowded and because it's a small town, it's extremely safe. It's also very easy to get into the countryside to go walking, fishing or even hunting. Sometimes I find living here quite boring. I'd like to live somewhere bigger, with a more lively nightlife and with more cinemas, shopping centres and sports centres.

**5**
Students' own answers.

## Listening Part 3
**1**
Students' own answers.
**2**
1 place   2 noun (something you can sleep in)   3 noun (type of food)
4 noun (something you use to predict the weather)   5 email address or name   6 number
**3**
1 station   2 hut   3 rabbit   4 clouds   5 justyna / Justyna / JUSTYNA
6 01773442256

### Track 22
**Narrator:** You will hear a woman talking to a group of people about the bushcraft courses she organises. For each question, write the correct answer in the gap. Write one or two words or a number or a date or time.
**Justyna:** I'm here to tell you about our bushcraft courses. Since 2007, we've been teaching people the necessary skills to stay alive in the wild by using the things around them.
So, what are weekend courses like? On Saturday morning, your guide will pick you up for your adventure in front of the station and drive you to our main office. There, you'll need to repack your backpack with just the essential equipment and then it's time to walk to the forest camp.
The first lesson is how to use the equipment, for example you'll learn how to use a knife properly so that you don't hurt yourself or others. The next job is building your own hut. It doesn't need to be beautiful but it will be your place to spend the night as it will get cold. But don't worry, your guide will have an emergency tent for the group to sleep in if necessary.

170

> You'll learn how to catch a rabbit, although I can't promise you'll be lucky enough to get one. If you do, I'll show you how to prepare it and we'll have it for lunch. We'll also go fishing in the river, but whatever we catch there, we will have to put back into the water. Those are the rules in this area.
> Over the rest of the weekend you'll learn how to make drinking water, use the stars and moon to find your way and check the clouds for rain or a change in temperature.
> Please visit our website for more details but if you have any questions, please email me on Justyna at bushcraftskills dot com, that's J-U-S-T-Y-N-A. Or if you prefer, you can telephone us. Our number is zero one, double seven, three, double four, double two, five, six. There's someone in our office from Monday to Friday from 10 to five.

**4**
Students' own answers.

## Writing Part 1
**1**
1 an email  2 the notes – a reaction to your friend's news, describe the city, say the most popular time of year, and recommend other places to visit
**2**
Johannesburg
**3**
The answer is 'yes' to all the questions.
**4–6**
Students' own answers.

## Speaking Part 3
**1**
a cruise

> **Track 23**
> **Maria:** Someone from work has just got back from an absolutely fantastic holiday in Paris. They stayed in an apartment in the city centre and did loads of sightseeing. He said the art museums were amazing, better than the museums here. Why don't we all go to Paris for our next holiday?
> **Nathan:** Maria! Not more museums! And don't you think Paris will be really crowded? I'd like to go somewhere quieter. We could hire a campervan and go camping. My friend Dan went to a park in the USA and he says it's one of the most beautiful places in the world.
> **Pete:** Not camping again, please! We got really wet last time. That was the worst holiday of my life! What about trying a new sport, like surfing or snorkelling? It would be so much fun. Yeah! Let's do that!
> **Charlie:** Um… But snorkelling is as dangerous as surfing. I'm not sure I fancy doing either of those two sports.
> **Maria:** OK. What do you suggest, Charlie?
> **Charlie:** Well, how about a cruise?
> **Maria:** Why do you think we should choose that?
> **Charlie:** Because there's so much to do and we don't need to plan where we're going to stay or what we're going to do. It's all done for you.
> **Maria:** What can you do on a cruise? I really think a city break would be more interesting than a cruise.
> **Charlie:** No, not at all! There are loads of different things to do. There are swimming pools and gyms, cinemas and organised entertainment. And then when you wake up in the morning, you're in a new place! I think that's a lot more exciting than other types of holiday.
> **Pete:** That sounds perfect!
> **Nathan:** I agree!
> **Maria:** OK.

**2**
1 and 2: yes, they do.
**3**
2 like  3 most  4 really  5 about  6 do  7 much
**4**
2 R  3 R  4 R  5 S  6 S  7 R
**5**
Students' own answers.

## 3 Vocabulary and grammar review
**1**
2 near  3 above  4 in front of  5 under  6 inside

**2**
2 e  3 a  4 h  5 b  6 g  7 d  8 f
**3**
2 A  3 A  4 C  5 B  6 B
**4**
2 to do  3 to take  4 to buy  5 spending  6 to borrow  7 to see  8 spending  9 to send  10 to do

## 4 Vocabulary and grammar review
**1**
2 great  3 wettest  4 coldest  5 freezing  6 lively  7 huge  8 boring
**2**
2 than  3 very  4 far  5 travel  6 library
**3**
2 It is more easy **easier** for you to walk to my house.
3 That's the worse **worst** restaurant we've ever been to.
4 I like living in the city much more that **than** the countryside.
5 Those days on holiday were the happier **happiest** days of my life.
6 Hotels are more cheaper **cheaper** here than the hotels in the city.
**4**
2 than  3 most  4 best/most  5 as  6 in

# Unit 5  Different feelings

## Starting off
**Feelings**
**1**
Someone rock climbing, a happy family, someone throwing rubbish (a banana skin) out of a car window, a rich young man in an expensive sports car, a flood in a rural area; Students' own answers.
**2**
angry – anger; happy – happiness; jealous – jealousy; sad – sadness
**3**
2 anger  3 fear  4 happiness  5 jealousy
**4**
(Possible answers)
2 say nothing to them / tell them it's OK / shout at them
3 a bit nervous / absolutely terrified / completely relaxed
4 laugh and jump around / smile a little / do nothing because you knew you would pass
5 say they're very lucky / say they don't deserve it / take no notice and say nothing
**5**
Students' own answers.

## Listening Part 2
**1**
2 disappointed  3 nervous  4 confident  5 embarrassed  6 bored
**2**
1 how a woman felt after a singing contest
2 the advice that the man gives the woman
3 how the student feels
4 who a young woman had most fun with
5 the reason a man decided to go to work by bike
6 who annoyed the woman yesterday
**3**
1 B  2 B  3 C  4 B  5 B  6 A

> **Track 24**
> **Narrator:** For each question, choose the correct answer. One. You will hear a woman talking about taking part in a singing contest.
> **Man:** What did you think of the judges' scores?
> **Woman:** Well, I thought I'd sung pretty well, certainly nothing to be ashamed of, but I must admit they were lower than I'd expected. I knew then that I had little chance of beating the others, but at least I'd done my best. For me that's the most important thing.

Answer key  171

**Man:** Yes, definitely. So do you think you'll try again in next year's contest?
**Woman:** Yes, if I can. I might not win, but I think I could do better than this year.
**Narrator:** Two. You will hear two friends talking about camping.
**Woman:** I'm going camping in the mountains on Friday.
**Man:** That'll be great fun, especially with the hot weather we're having right now, but the temperatures there can really drop at night, even in summer. You'd better put a jacket and a thick sweater in your backpack instead of lots of things to eat. You can always get a tasty meal in one of the local villages. Where exactly will you be going?
**Woman:** Up by the lake.
**Man:** It's beautiful there, isn't it? But perhaps it'd be best to put your tent up somewhere else. At this time of year the mosquitoes there are awful. They never stop biting!
**Narrator:** Three. You will hear a student talking to his friend about a literature exam.
**Woman:** You've got that literature exam next week, haven't you? How's the revision going?
**Man:** I thought I'd be tired of it by now, but your suggestion that I should watch films of the books we have to study has made it more interesting and I understand the stories better. Usually just before an important exam like this one I feel really worried about what could go wrong on the day, but this time it's quite different.
**Woman:** That's great to hear. I'm sure you'll do really well on Monday morning. Good luck.
**Narrator:** Four. You will hear a young woman telling a friend about studying abroad.
**Man:** Did you enjoy your month abroad?
**Woman:** Yes, I was in a small town in the countryside. The lessons were good, even though the rest of the class were younger than me and we didn't have much in common. I had a lovely room in the house where I was staying with a couple. They were kind to me but they had a busy social life and I hardly saw them. So I went to the main square where all the shops and cafés are and made friends there. We had a great time hanging out and chatting.
**Narrator:** Five. You will hear a man telling his friend about how he travels to work.
**Woman:** I see you're using your bike every day now, instead of coming to work in your friend's car.
**Man:** Yes, I've been doing that for a couple of months. Actually, he still goes right past our office on his way to work, so it's not about protecting the environment, spending less on petrol or anything like that. It's just that I realised I was spending nearly all my time sitting down, in the office and at home, and I thought I'd better do something about it.
**Woman:** That's a good idea. Maybe I should do the same.
**Narrator:** Six. You will hear a woman talking to a friend about going shopping.
**Man:** So, how was your shopping trip yesterday? I imagine the city centre's pretty crowded on a Saturday morning at this time of the year.
**Woman:** Yes, there were lots of people walking in the streets and the department store was full of customers, too. I don't mind that, but I wasn't happy about having shop assistants trying to sell me stuff when all I wanted to do was look at things. I noticed they were bothering other customers, too. If they carry on like that, their shop won't be full much longer.

## Grammar

*can*, *could*, *might* and *may*

**1**
1 *might not* is negative
2 *not* goes after the modal verb
3 *can't* and *couldn't*
4 the infinitive without *to*

**2**
1 We can ~~to go~~ **go** to the cinema next weekend.
2 I know it may ~~seems~~ **seem** strange.
3 Sorry but tomorrow I ~~not can~~ **can't** go.
4 What ~~we could~~ **could we** do?
5 We can ~~doing~~ **do** a lot of sports here.
6 ~~It's~~ **It** could be quite boring for you.
7 We could ~~met~~ **meet** at 8 o'clock near the cinema.

**3**
1 can, couldn't  2 may/might/could

**4**
2 can  3 might  4 can't  5 can  6 could

**5**
Students' own answers.

## Speaking Part 4

**1**
Students' own answers.

**2**
1 Who, to  2 How, usually  3 When, to  4 What, about

### Track 25

**Daniel:** Who do you most enjoy chatting to?
**Wen:** To my friends. Especially my best friend An, who lives in another city now. We always have so much to say to each other! How about you?
**Daniel:** Yes, to friends too. And also to my cousin Ricardo. He's about the same age as me and we get on really well so we spend a lot of time talking to each other. How do you usually chat? By phone?
**Wen:** Quite often, but sometimes we text. Especially when it's difficult to talk aloud, for instance if I'm at work. And you?
**Daniel:** Mostly on Instagram, if I've got an internet connection of course. And it doesn't cost anything to post messages, which is great. I can't do that at work, though. When can you chat to people?
**Wen:** In the evenings, mainly. After I get home from work and I can relax. I think that's the best time. What about you?
**Daniel:** Oh I can't wait that long. I check my messages and reply as soon as I get out of the office! It's usually to make plans for the evening, or just to catch up with what's going on. What do you most like chatting about?
**Wen:** Sorry, could you say that again?
**Daniel:** Sure. What do you most like chatting about?
**Wen:** Well, An and I often give each other advice. For example, if I'm worried about something, I ask her what I should or shouldn't do and she might tell me what I could do. I think that's very important. Do you **agree**?
**Daniel:** Yes I do. That's what friends are for. But other times they tell me about something funny that's happened and we laugh and I think that's good too. What do you think?
**Wen:** Oh yes, definitely. It's not good to be serious all the time!

**3**
1 about  2 And  3 about  4 agree  5 think

**4**
Students' own answers.

## Grammar

**Modals for advice, obligation and prohibition**

**1**
ought to, shouldn't

**2**
2 B  3 A  4 C

**3**
2 have to  3 don't have to  4 must  5 shouldn't

**4**
2 must  3 mustn't  4 don't have to  5 have to / must

**5 & 6**
Students' own answers.

### Track 26

**Leah** can **take** a **taxi**.
**Jack** should **go** to **work**.

**7**
1 names  2 nouns  3 main  4 articles  5 prepositions  6 modal

**8**
1 b, d, f; yes  2 n't; no  3 a, c, e; no

### Track 27

a I can buy another one.
b I can't afford that one.
c I could meet you at 5.30.
d I couldn't live without my phone!
e I should get up earlier on Sundays.
f I shouldn't go to bed so late.

**9**
Students' own answers.

## Vocabulary
**Adjectives and prepositions**
**1**
with
**2**
1 with   2 of   3 about
**3**
1 of   2 with   3 about
**4**
1 about   2 with   3 of   4 of/with   5 of/about

**Adjectives with -ed and -ing**
**1**
1 He wanted to contact the woman he met (and needed her details / phone number).
2 They met again and got married.
**2**
boring; it drops the final -e and adds -ing
**3**
bored; We use -ing if it describes something; -ed if it tells us how someone feels about it.
**4**
2 relaxed   3 surprising   4 embarrassing   5 amused   6 annoyed
7 disappointed   8 interested   9 amazed   10 excited
**5 & 6**
Students' own answers.

## Reading Part 4
**1**
Students' own answers.
**2**
paragraph 2: lifestyle changes
paragraph 3: changing work habits
paragraph 4: using technology to reduce stress
paragraph 5: amusing things
**3**
2 F   3 H   4 A   5 E
**4**
Students' own answers.

## Vocabulary
**Adjectives and their opposites**
**1**
funny/serious   generous/mean   miserable/cheerful
negative/positive   nervous/relaxed   simple/complicated   strange/ordinary
**2**
Students' own answers.

## Writing Part 2
**1**
1 the first line   2 third person   3 read, message, friend, smiled
**2**
1 in an airport / in two airports, a Friday evening
2 Olivia and Ellie; friends
3 They live in different countries and Ellie intends to visit Olivia.
4 Fog is preventing Ellie's flight from taking off.
5 The sky eventually clears.
6 At last they meet, and are very happy to see each other.
**3**
excited, disappointed, miserable, delighted
**4**
1 the first line   2 third person   3 excited, waited, train
**5 & 6**
Students' own answers.

# Unit 6 That's entertainment!

## Starting off
**Television programmes**
**1**
A sports   B wildlife documentary   C cooking show   D cartoon
**2**
Nick watches quite a lot of TV. His favourite types of programme are comedy series, wildlife documentaries and cooking shows.

> **Track 28**
> **Nick:** Did you see that new comedy series on TV last night?
> **Clare:** No, I didn't. I don't watch TV very often. How much TV do you watch?
> **Nick:** Quite a lot, actually. When I get up, I often watch a bit of a series while I'm having breakfast and then I also watch something when I get home.
> **Clare:** Really? Have you got more than one TV in your house?
> **Nick:** No, I don't, but I don't need more than one. I mainly watch TV on my mobile or on my tablet.
> **Clare:** Do you usually watch TV on your own?
> **Nick:** No, not always. I watch sports programmes on the TV in the living room with my flatmates or at my dad's because the screen is much bigger there, but for everything else, I watch it online and often alone.
> **Clare:** What sorts of things do you watch?
> **Nick:** A little bit of everything but I really like comedy series, wildlife documentaries, cooking shows, that sort of thing. I'm not very keen on films or drama.
> **Clare:** No? Do you ever go out to the theatre or to the cinema?
> **Nick:** Not really. To be honest, I find plays and films a bit dull.
> **Clare:** You're joking! I love seeing plays and films, much more than staying in and watching TV in fact.

**3**
How much TV do you watch?
Have you got more than one TV in your house?
Do you usually watch TV on your own?
What sorts of things do you watch?
Do you ever go out to the theatre or to the cinema?

## Reading Part 2
**1**
Tom and Ian have a free afternoon but neither of them like crowds. They're interested in theatre and exhibitions, but they don't have much money.
**2**
B
1 D is a musical (theatre) but you have to pay for a ticket.
2 G has long queues for everything and neither of them like crowds.
**3**
2 E (First performances this week, family discounts at our restaurant, two-minute walk from the underground)
3 G (comic market celebrates Japanese animation, fans can meet other fans, buy rare comics)
4 H (he uses traditional words from his own country, snacks will be available)
5 F (Marco Morelli has fallen in love with a rich young woman. However, one of the family's servants is also in love with her, Italian opera with amazing singing and real classical music)
**4**
Students' own answers.

## Vocabulary
**Going out**
**1**
(Suggested answers)
Film: screen, subtitles
Play: None
Concert: live music
Film and play: acting
Play and concert: interval, stage
Concert and film: None
All three: book early, perform, refreshments, reviews, ticket

Answer key 173

**2**
2 subtitles   3 book early   4 refreshments   5 live music   6 ticket
7 stage   8 acting
**3**
Students' own answers.

## Grammar
**Present perfect**
**1**
Go to Bella's house, watch a film and have pizza.

> **Track 29**
> **Bella:** Have you seen *The Lion King* yet?
> **Eliza:** Do you mean the musical?
> **Bella:** Yeah! We've got a spare ticket for the Friday show. Fancy coming?
> **Eliza:** Um …
> **Bella:** Please! We've been good friends for three years but we haven't been to a show together since last summer.
> **Eliza:** Yes, I know, but I've already seen it. I saw it with my cousins last month but I'd love to do something else with you. How about Saturday? I haven't seen the new Robin Hood film yet. Everyone's talking about it and it's on at the cinema near us. Have you seen it?
> **Bella:** Afraid so. I saw it last night with my flatmate. Let's have a look at the guide to see what else is on. Oh, what about *Carmen*? It says here that it's an incredible show with dancing and live music. Sounds good.
> **Eliza:** *Carmen*? Fantastic idea. I've just learnt how to play one of the songs on the violin and my sister is learning to sing one of them too.
> **Bella:** Oh no! It's not an opera, is it? I don't fancy that!
> **Eliza:** Why don't you come round to my house on Saturday and we can watch a film?
> **Bella:** Great! And why don't I get a pizza on my way to your house?

**2**
1 seen   2 seen   3 seen   4 learnt
**3**
The present perfect, has/have + past participle. To connect the past with the present. It usually describes something with a connection in the present, something that continues in the present, or an experience that happened at an unspecified time in the past.
**4**
1 just   2 already   3 yet
**5**
2 My brother hasn't (has not) found a new job yet.
3 But he's (has) started a course in computing.
4 My flatmate has just won a prize in a photography competition.
5 Have you seen the new *Star Wars* film yet?
6 I've already seen it three times.
7 Have you taken your driving test yet?
**6**
1 since   2 for
**7**
1 for   2 since   3 since   4 For   5 since
**8**
(Suggested answers)
2 How long have you been in that club?
3 How long have you taken that class?
Students' own answers.

**Present perfect or past simple?**
**1**
He's a DJ and his single *Animals* is famous.
**2**
Present perfect: 's been, 's toured
Past simple: was born, was, became
We normally use the expression in bold with the past simple.
**3**
the present perfect – already, since 2010, this week, today, yet
the past simple – at 8 o'clock in the morning, last year, two months ago, yesterday

**4**
2 yet; Have (you) read   3 three months ago; saw
4 last year; won   5 for three months; haven't swum
6 last night; did (you) go   7 since; have (you) taken
**5 & 6**
Students' own answers.

## Vocabulary
***been/gone, meet, get to know, know* and *find out***
**1**
1 Paul is at his friend's house.
2 Sophia is at home (she's returned from the cinema).
3 *Been* means go and come back. *Gone* means hasn't come back yet.
4 Lucas and Nick became friends years ago at university.
5 They see each other, often on Saturday afternoons.
6 Lucas sometimes sleeps at Nick's house.
7 No, he didn't.
8 The neighbours.
**2**
1 been   2 gone   3 known, meet   4 stay   5 getting to know   6 find out
**3**
Students' own answers.

## Listening Part 1
**1**
2 2A, B or C   3 1A or C   4 1C   5 3A   6 1B
**2**
(Suggested answers)
1 What would the woman like to try on? A a plain sweater with a round neck, B a plain sweater with a V-neck, C a striped sweater with a round neck
2 Where has Matt left his keys? A in his coat pocket, B in the front pocket of his rucksack, C in his jeans' pocket
3 What did Karen buy last weekend? A a dress, B a top, C a skirt
4 Which one is Sarah's cousin? A a girl with short hair and no earrings, B a girl with long hair and no earrings, C a girl with long hair with huge earrings.
5 Where did the man get the trainers that's he's wearing now? A in a sports shop, B on a website, C on a market stall.
6 What's the latest time visitors can buy a ticket today? A half past five, B a quarter to six, C a quarter to seven
7 What sort of TV programmes does the girl like watching? A a football match, B a comedy, C a wildlife documentary
**3**
1 A   2 B   3 C   4 B   5 B   6 A   7 C

> **Track 30**
> **Narrator:** For each question, choose the correct answer. One. What would the woman like to try on?
> **Woman:** Excuse me. Could I try on one of the jumpers in the window please?
> **Shop assistant:** Sure. Do you mean one of the striped ones? They'd look good on you.
> **Woman:** I was actually thinking of a plain one. Have you got it in a small?
> **Shop assistant:** I think so. I'll check. Did you want it with a V-neck?
> **Woman:** I'd rather have a round one.
> **Shop assistant:** OK. I'll just get it for you to try on.
> **Narrator:** Two. Where has Matt left his keys?
> **Matt:** Ava, I think I've lost my keys, have you seen them? I thought I'd put them in my jeans' pocket a minute ago but they're not there now.
> **Ava:** Not again! You were wearing your coat just now. Have you checked all the pockets? You usually leave your keys there.
> **Matt:** I've looked in all the pockets. Was I carrying my backpack when I came in?
> **Ava:** I think so. I bet they're in there.
> **Matt:** You're right again, Ava!
> **Narrator:** Three. What did Karen buy last weekend?
> **Man:** Did you have a good weekend, Karen?
> **Karen:** Yes, I did, thanks. On Saturday I went to the new shopping centre with my aunt. She wanted to get a dress for the summer.
> **Man:** Did she buy one?

**Karen:** They were all the wrong size. Then she tried on loads of tops.
**Man:** What about the red one you're wearing?
**Karen:** Isn't it lovely! She didn't like the colour, so I got it instead.
**Man:** So, she didn't buy anything but you did!
**Karen:** That's right! It'll look good with that skirt I got for my birthday.
**Narrator:** Four. Which one is Sarah's cousin?
**Man:** Sarah, did you manage to get your cousin something for her birthday?
**Sarah:** Don't ask! We got her some earrings in the end, but then we found out that she never wears jewellery.
**Man:** Oh no! I thought that girl over there with long hair and huge earrings was your cousin.
**Sarah:** That's my sister, but they look alike, don't they? They even used to have the same length hair.
**Man:** Has she had it cut?
**Sarah:** Yeah, but she says she's going to grow it long again.
**Narrator:** Five. Where did the man get the trainers he's wearing now?
**Woman:** Nice trainers! Have you just been to that new sports shop?
**Man:** Yeah! It's a great store with some amazing bargains. I bought some trainers there last week, but they weren't the right size so I had to take them back. Then one of my friends suggested looking in the market, so I did and found these. They fit perfectly.
**Woman:** My flatmate keeps telling me to look on the web. She buys everything there.
**Man:** She's right! You know the boots I wore to the party? I got them online.
**Woman:** They're really cool! Were they expensive?
**Narrator:** Six. What's the latest time visitors can buy a ticket today?
**Man:** You have reached Lansdown Art Museum. We're sorry that there's no one to take your call right now. If you are interested in seeing the Photographer of the Year exhibition, the ticket office is open from nine a.m. to half past five. You need to leave the museum at quarter to seven, but remember that last admission to the gallery is at quarter to six. Thank you for calling.
**Narrator:** Seven. What sorts of TV programmes does the woman like watching?
**Connor:** You look tired. Did you go to bed late last night after the football?
**Laura:** I think my flatmate was watching the match in his bedroom. I don't even care who won it, to be honest! I watched this comedy instead, about two men who get lost in a department store.
**Connor:** I saw that! I haven't laughed so much for years. Wasn't the ending good?
**Laura:** Well, I'd kind of lost interest by then. I'd much rather watch a wildlife documentary.
**Connor:** Oh? I didn't think you liked those sorts of programmes.

**4**
Students' own answers.
**5**
Oh? I didn't think you liked those sorts of programmes. = The man didn't know this about the woman.
Oh? I didn't think you liked those sorts of programmes. = I knew that other people liked serious stuff but I didn't know that the woman liked serious stuff.
Oh? I didn't think you liked those sorts of programmes. = I knew that the woman liked a certain sort of TV programme but I didn't know she liked that sort.

### Track 31
1 Oh? I didn't think you liked those sorts of programmes.
2 Oh? I didn't think you liked those sorts of programmes.
3 Oh? I didn't think you liked those sorts of programmes.

**6**
Students' own answers.

## Speaking Part 3
**1**
The different events the university could organise and which would be most popular.
**2**
Students' own answers.

**3 & 4**
1 ✓  2 ✗ (students should discuss their ideas with their partner in this part)
3 ✓  4 ✓
5 ✗ (If they only talk about one picture then they may not complete the task successfully. Ideally the students should talk about as many of the pictures as they can, but they won't lose marks if they don't talk about all of them.)
6 ✗ (They should aim to reach an agreement towards the end of the two minutes.)
7 ✓ (Ideally they should carry on speaking until the examiner asks them to stop – this is what happens to Noa and Greta).

### Track 32
**Examiner:** Now, in this part of the test you're going to talk about something together for about two minutes. I'm going to describe a situation to you. A university would like to celebrate its 25th anniversary with a special event. Here are some events the university could organise. Talk together about the different events the university could organise, and say which would be most popular. All right? Now, talk together.
**Noa:** Let's start with the photography exhibition. I think it would be a great idea. The university could collect pictures and photos from now and the past. It would be really interesting.
**Greta:** I agree. Students could see how things have changed.
**Noa:** Yeah. For example, my mum showed me a picture of her university library with loads of old books all over the desks. My mum used to spend hours in the library looking for information. Now we can go online and do most of our research there. Another difference is that there used to be more men than women.
**Greta:** That's right! Let's talk about another one. What about a concert? Everyone loves music and everyone could take part. What do you think?
**Noa:** I'm not sure about that one. Some people like rock music and other people hate it. And have you thought about the noise?
**Greta:** Perhaps you're right. Shall we talk about the student fashion show?
**Noa:** OK. I think the student fashion show is a great idea. Past and present fashion students could show the clothes they've designed.
**Greta:** Um… I'm not very interested in fashion, I'm afraid. We haven't talked about the bike ride yet. Do you think it's a good idea?
**Noa:** Perhaps, but if it rains, they won't be able to go very far, don't you think?
**Greta:** Yes, I agree. That leaves the talent show and the disco. Well, you know lots of people love dancing but do you think everyone would enjoy it?
**Noa:** I don't think so. I can't stand discos. How about the talent show then?
**Greta:** I'm not sure I understand. How would it work?
**Noa:** Yes, you know, groups of friends perform something different. One group could sing and do a dance, for example.
**Greta:** Oh I see! But remember that some people don't like dancing.
**Noa:** You're right. Well, what do you think? Shall we choose the photography exhibition?
**Greta:** Yes, I think that's the best idea. Do you…
**Examiner:** Thank you.

**5**
Shall we talk about the fashion show?
We haven't talked about the bike ride yet. Do you think it's a good idea?
**6**
Students' own answers.

## Writing Part 2
**1**
The festivals are Chinese New Year and the Venice Carnival; Students' own answers.
**2**
Students' own answers.
**3**
(Suggested answer)
a celebration in your country, What people wear, What people do, Why special, article, answering questions, about 100 words.
**4**
The second answer is better. She has written an article and not a story. The first answer is a story and not an article.

Answer key 175

5
Yes
6
The answer is 'yes' to all the questions.
7 & 8
Students' own answers.

## 5 Vocabulary and grammar review
1
2 of   3 with   4 on   5 of   6 about   7 about   8 about   9 of   10 of
2
When I was tidying my room last Sunday, I found some surprising things. Among all the ~~bored~~ **boring** exercise books from my school days, there was something ~~amazed~~ **amazing** – my diary, from when I was eight years old. It was really ~~interested~~ **interesting** to read my thoughts from back then, though at times I felt a bit ~~embarrassing~~ **embarrassed**, too. For example, I was still very ~~frightening~~ **frightened** of the dark in those days. It was also funny to read how ~~exciting~~ **excited** I was about being nine soon – I thought I would be really grown up then.
3
**Across:** 1 mean   5 anger   6 afraid   8 jealous   9 bored
**Down:** 2 negative   3 sad   4 nervous   6 awful   7 love
4
2 can't   3 should   4 Could   5 don't have to   6 might   7 have to

## 6 Vocabulary and grammar review
1
2 Audiences   3 live   4 reviews   5 performances   6 admission   7 interval
2
2 B   3 A   4 B   5 C
3
2 since = for   3 he's gone = he went   4 gone = been
5 Already I've been = I've already been   6 I looked = I've looked
7 I've never been = I've ever been   8 has given = gave
9 didn't decide = haven't decided
10 has opened = opened
4
2 for   3 have   4 since   5 got   6 already

# Unit 7  Getting around

## Starting off
**Weather**
1
1 hot, sunny, sunshine; 2 cold, foggy; 3 freezing, frost, ice, icy, snowy; 4 lightning, rainy, showers, storm, thunderstorm, windy
2 & 3 Students' own answers.
4 chilly = cold
It's pouring = It's raining
It's boiling = It's very hot
nippy = cold
cleared up = the sky became clear
soaring temperatures = rising temperatures

## Listening Part 4
1
1 Olivia   2 travelling in Italy during the world's heaviest-ever snowfall
3 What Olivia and her friend were doing when the heavy snow began, how she felt when it started to snow heavily, why the car stopped moving, how they tried to keep warm in the car, why they stayed in the car all night, how they travelled to a village the next day.
2 & 3
1 A   2 B   3 B   4 A   5 B   6 C

## Track 33
**Narrator:** You will hear an interview with a woman called Olivia talking about her experience of travelling through a snow-storm with her friend Grace. For each question, choose the correct answer.
**Interviewer:** Today I'm talking to Olivia Richardson, who was with a friend on a skiing holiday in central Italy when over two metres of snow fell in 24 hours. Where were you, Olivia, when that happened?
**Olivia:** Grace and I were near Capracotta, in the mountains. There'd already been some light snow and we stopped for a quick meal before carrying on to a crossroads, but there we took a wrong turning and got completely lost. Then, while we were trying to decide how to return to the main road, some really heavy snow started coming down.
**Interviewer:** Was that frightening?
**Olivia:** At first I was quite certain it wouldn't last long. It was March in Italy, so I wasn't worried. Of course, it was rather annoying we'd gone the wrong way, but I couldn't blame Grace because it'd been my idea. And we were still moving, but not very fast.
**Interviewer:** When did you have to stop?
**Olivia:** Well, it was getting quite difficult to see and we nearly crashed into a parked car. There was more and more snow on the road, so when we tried to go up a steep hill the wheels started going round really fast, but it was so deep the car just wouldn't move forwards. It looked as if we'd be stuck there, but we didn't have much petrol left so we switched off the engine. Grace tried to phone for help but couldn't get through.
**Interviewer:** How did you stay warm? With the car heater?
**Olivia:** That meant having the engine on so we only used it a bit. Instead we got all our jumpers, trousers and socks from our suitcases and wore them all night. We were still frozen, though, and wished we had some coffee or tea with us.
**Interviewer:** So you spent the whole night inside the car?
**Olivia:** Yes, I'd at last managed to contact the emergency services. They knew our location from my phone and they advised us to stay in our vehicle until help could be sent the next day. That's what we did, but by then the snow was starting to cover the car completely so we cleared a space next to the doors in case we needed to get out.
**Interviewer:** How did you get moving again?
**Olivia:** The rescue vehicles didn't get there until the afternoon. They'd called to ask if we needed an ambulance and luckily we didn't, so they just cleared the snow and led us along the road to the nearest village. There we stopped for an enormous hot meal of roast fish and pasta with cheese, the most delicious I've ever tasted!

4
Students' own answers.

## Grammar
*extremely, fairly, quite, rather, really* **and** *very*
1
1 really   2 rather   3 quite
2
Students' own answers.

**too and enough**
1
1 more than you need or want   2 before, *to* + infinitive
3 uncountable, countable   4 as much as   5 before, after, *to* + infinitive
2
1 correct
2 In the streets, there are too ~~much~~ **many** cars.
3 My sister is ~~very~~ **too** young to travel alone.
4 correct
5 We did not have ~~plenty of~~ **enough time** to see the University of Cambridge.
6 I think you are ~~enough old~~ **old enough** to spend this summer with your friends.
3
Students' own answers.

176

## Reading Part 1
**1**
A next to a lake in winter   B on a ferry   C on a bus
D on a phone or tablet screen   E in a street
**2**
1 C   NOTICE, £3, only
2 E   No (+ -ing) – for prohibition
3 A   DANGER
4 B   Leave, Go, Return – use of imperatives
5 D   Sign up, extra credit
**3**
1 C   2 A   3 B   4 A   5 B

## Grammar
**The future**
**1**
2 's going to rain   3 'm meeting   4 leaves   5 'll take

> **Track 34**
> **Mia:** Look at the rain, Owen.
> **Owen:** Yes, I know. I'm hoping it'll stop soon, but I don't think there's much chance of that.
> **Mia:** No, the weather forecast said it's a big storm and it's going to rain for hours. What time do you have to be at the station?
> **Owen:** I'm meeting Jason and Mark there at 8.30, in the café near the main entrance. The train leaves at 8.45.
> **Mia:** It's quite a long walk to the station, isn't it? And it's 8.15 already. Look, I'll take you in the car.
> **Owen:** Thanks!

**2**
b 5 'll take   c 1 'll stop   d 3 'm meeting   e 2 's going to rain
**3**
2 Where are you going to go this evening? I'm going to go to the cinema.
3 When will you take your next English test? I'll take my next test in two weeks' time.
4 Is the Earth going to get hotter? Yes, it's going to get a lot hotter.
5 Do you think it will be cloudy tomorrow? No, I think it'll be sunny.
**4**
2 I'll help you / fix it (if you like).
3 It starts / begins on July 1st (etc.).
4 I think there's going to be a storm soon.
5 I'm going to study French. / I don't know which I'm going to study.

## Vocabulary
**Compound words**
**1**
2 suitcase   3 crossroads   4 backpack   5 signpost   6 overnight
7 campsite   8 sightseeing
**2**
2 guidebook   3 sightseeing   4 campsite   5 backpack   6 suitcase
7 crossroads   8 signpost

> **Track 35**
> **Lewis:** Next week I'm going to Australia! I'm arriving in the north, so first I'm going to stay overnight in Darwin. My guidebook says it's an interesting city, so I think I'll do a bit of sightseeing there. Then I'm getting the train to Alice Springs, right in the middle of the country, where I'll spend the night at a campsite. The next day I'm hoping to get a lift down the main road. I'm taking all my things in a backpack so that I don't have to carry a heavy suitcase around. About 200 kilometres south of Alice, I'll reach a crossroads where there's a signpost that says 'Uluru 247 km'. Uluru is also known as Ayers Rock – one of the most amazing sights in the world.

**3**
He stresses the first part of all words 2–8. Point out that *overnight* is not a compound noun.
**4**
Students' own answers.

## Grammar
**Prepositions of movement**
**1**
2 on   3 on   4 off   5 in   6 out

> **Track 36**
> **Toby:** Hi Leon, Toby here. I'm really pleased you're coming to our new house next week. The quickest way here is by train to the city centre, which takes an hour and is usually on time. Then you can get on the number 64 bus to Edgely, getting off by the stadium. From there it's a fifteen-minute walk. Or, if you don't feel like walking, you could jump in a taxi and ask the driver to take you to the end of Valley Road. When you get out of the taxi, you'll see our place right in front of you. See you soon!

**2**
1 in, out of   2 on, off   3 by, by   4 on
**3**
1 You can get here ~~in~~ **by** plane.
2 correct
3 correct
4 Could you come ~~at~~ **on** time, please?
5 I will travel ~~with~~ **by** train.
**4**
Students' own answers.

## Speaking Part 2
**1 & 2**
Students' own answers.

> **Track 37**
> **Lorenzo:** It's a picture of a railway station, quite a small one I think. There are some trees on the left and I can see some green fields, too, so it might be in the countryside. There's a train coming into the station and it's probably going to stop there. There are some people waiting to get on it, a woman and a man and maybe others. They're very close to the railway lines, on the place where people stand, and maybe they're on their way to work in the morning. The woman has a dark coat on and she's wearing, I mean carrying, a large bag on her shoulder. She's doing something on her mobile phone, perhaps sending a message to someone. The man's wearing a suit and he also has a bag on his shoulder. The front of the train has big windows but they're a bit dark and I can't see the person who is driving it. It looks like quite a sunny day, but I don't think it's hot because the woman is dressed for winter weather.

**3**
2 There's, coming   3 There are, waiting   4 place where   5 I mean   6 also
7 person who
**4**
a too (1); also (6)   b I mean (5)   c There's, coming (2); There are, waiting (3)
d place where (4); person who (7)
**5**
Students' own answers.

## Writing Part 1
**1**
Hi (B), Looking forward to hearing from / seeing you (E), Well, that's all for now (E), All the best (E), This is just a quick message to say (B), It was great to hear from you (B), Give my love to everyone (E), Take care (E), See you soon (E), Don't forget to write soon (E), Sorry I've taken so long to write back (B), Bye for now (E), Dear (B)
**2**
1 Your English-speaking friend Thomas; arranging a trip to a music festival next Saturday
2 Hi, Sorry I've taken so long to write back, All the best
3 I'm going, will be, We'll be, we'll need, will you meet; very
4 a, c, e; you should also agree to go, and say whether you prefer to take your own food or pay for something to eat at the festival.

**3**
1 Yes
2 No problem!: 1st paragraph, Yes, say why: 2nd paragraph, Tell Thomas: 3rd paragraph, Suggest: 4th paragraph
3 a Hi …, See you soon  b really, very  c It'll be, will be, that'll be, will take me, I'll text  d enough time, be enough
**4 & 5**
Students' own answers.

# Unit 8 Influencers

## Starting off
**1**
Students' own answers.
**2**
1 B  2 D  3 A  4 C
**3**
Students' own answers.

## Reading Part 6
**1**
(Suggested answer)
'Someone who affects or changes the way that people behave' from the Cambridge online dictionary.
**2**
(Suggested answer)
She tells her fans what she thinks and supports issues through her social networks.
**3**
1 was  2 when  3 than  4 as  5 to  6 on
**4**
1 She's clever. She's very funny ~~to~~ **too**.
2 We ~~where~~ **were** both young when I first met her in school.
3 He plays soccer very well, ~~an~~ **and** he's the junior world champion in shooting.
4 At first I thought she was shy because she was a very ~~quite~~ **quiet** girl.
5 I love spending time ~~whit~~ **with** him. I can say that he's my best friend.
6 I like to do my homework with Daniela ~~becouse~~ **because** she is intelligent.
**5**
Students' own answers.

## Vocabulary
**Phrasal verbs**
**1**
(Suggested answers)
1 became older  2 started/created
3 take care of a child until it is an adult  4 start doing
**2**
2 runs out of  3 set up  4 take up  5 get on well with
6 make up  7 found out  8 brought up
**3 & 4**
Students' own answers.

## Grammar
**Zero, first and second conditionals**
**1**
Students' own answers.
**2**
(Suggested answer)
1 He should talk to the university and Channel Seven.
2 Students' own answers.

### Track 38
**Ella:** Kristian! Kristian?
**Kristian:** Oh hi, Ella.
**Ella:** Are you OK? What's the matter?
**Kristian:** You know I've always wanted to work in television? Well, Channel Seven have just got in touch. They'd like me to take part in their new reality show.

**Ella:** Wow! What's it about?
**Kristian:** It's a bit of a secret, actually, but the idea is that twelve of us are going to run a youth hostel for twelve weeks.
**Ella:** But that's amazing! Haven't you always wanted to be on TV?
**Kristian:** Err, yes, but filming starts next week. If I take up the offer, I'll have to give up my degree. And if I don't finish my degree, what will everyone say?
**Ella:** I'm sorry? I don't understand.
**Kristian:** I have to give in a project by Thursday and then my exams start next week.
**Ella:** Oh, I see. Have you spoken to your tutor yet?
**Kristian:** No. Why? She's never in her office anyway.
**Ella:** If you spoke to your tutor, I'm sure she'd understand.
**Kristian:** But you know the rules. If you don't hand in your project on time, you can't do your exams. If you don't do your exams, you don't pass the year. And you have to leave if you don't pass the year!
**Ella:** Yes, but this is an incredible opportunity. You can't afford to miss a chance like this. If I were you, I'd talk to the university and also to the people at Channel Seven. There must be a way around this.
**Kristian:** I hope so! Thanks for your support, Ella.

**3**
2 spoke, 'd understand  3 have, don't pass

### Track 39
1 If I take up the offer, I'll have to give up my degree.
2 If you spoke to your tutor, I'm sure she'd understand.
3 And you have to leave if you don't pass the year!
**4**
1 c  2 a  3 b
**5**
Type 0: present, present   Type 1: present, future
Type 2: past, would + infinitive
We use a comma when the conditional sentence begins with the *If* clause (the situation). We don't use commas when the sentence begins with the result.
**6**
2 8  3 5
**7**
2 don't do your exams, you don't  3 were you, I'd talk

### Track 40
1 And if I don't finish my degree, what will everyone say?
2 If you don't do your exams, you don't pass the year.
3 If I were you, I'd talk to the university.
**8**
2 is  3 get  4 won't go out  5 'll buy  6 don't sleep
**9–11**
Students' own answers.

## Grammar
***when**, **if** and **unless***
**1**
2 Hayley
**2**
1 when  2 if/unless  3 unless/if  4 unless
**3**
1 when  2 if  3 unless  4 if  5 unless  6 when

## Listening Part 3
**1**
Students' own answers.
**2**
(Suggested answers)
1 a number  2 a noun  3 an adjective or pronoun  4 a noun  5 a noun
6 a time (e.g. days, weeks, months etc.)
**3**
1 300  2 music  3 yourself  4 channel  5 description  6 years

178

### Track 41
**Narrator:** Part 3. You will hear a man called Ben Richards talking about how to get famous on YouTube. For each question, write the correct answer in the gap. Write one or two words or a date or a number or a time.
**Presenter:** Hi! Ben Richards here. About a billion people around the world use YouTube. While some people just watch videos, others upload around 300 hours of them a minute. That means that by the time I finish this introduction there'll be 500 hours of new videos on YouTube. Have you ever dreamt of becoming a famous YouTuber? Here's my advice to help you get started.
Do your research! Find out what kind of videos people are into right now by searching for 'Popular on YouTube' and then choose your style. Everyone loves watching animals doing funny things – in fact, the first ever video on YouTube was a visit to a zoo – but the ones with the most likes are often music videos.
Next, think about how you can make something bigger, better and different, something that you and the people you know would like to watch. Your audience will also want to get to know you, so avoid being a clown or a film star, just act like yourself.
Practise making very short, high-quality videos first. Tell your friends about your videos and ask them for their opinion. However, aim to upload at least 10 good ones before letting them know about your channel. You'll need to create a video for this which attracts attention.
Make sure you upload new videos with new information at least once a week. Choose a day and let the people who follow you know. To increase the number of people watching your videos, each one should have an unforgettable title and a clear description, but once again, try to be a bit different.
Many people give up after two or three months because nobody's watching, but attracting a large audience takes time, often two or three years. It's hard work, but definitely worth it!

**4 & 5**
Students' own answers.

## Vocabulary
**Describing people**
**1**
B

### Track 42
**Carter:** Hey Will! Is that you?
**Will:** Carter! How's things?
**Carter:** Great! You know I've been creating a new YouTube channel? Well, I'm looking for someone to present it. Would you do it?
**Will:** Me? Sorry, I'm too shy. I'd be terrible. What would your perfect presenter look like?
**Carter:** You know, someone with an interesting face. He should be medium height, look around twenty-five years old with straight hair. He should probably be good-looking, too.
**Will:** Um … there's John. He's got a great voice.
**Carter:** Yeah but I think I'm looking for someone without a beard or moustache.
**Will:** So no beard or moustache, right?
**Carter:** Right!
**Will:** What about Robert? He's got that cool scar on his chin.
**Carter:** He's got blue eyes, hasn't he?
**Will:** That's right and everyone says he's honest and reliable. Do you want his phone number?

**2**
(Suggested answers)
skin: dark, fair, pale
hair: bald, beard, blond(e), curly, dark, fair, grey, long, moustache, red, straight, wavy
build: broad shoulders, medium height, short, slim
other: attractive, beautiful, good-looking, plain, scar

**3**
2 lazy   3 stupid   4 quiet   5 generous   6 polite   7 anxious   8 shy

**4**
impatient, unpleasant, dishonest, unreliable

**5**
2 cheerful   3 beautiful   4 helpful   5 helpless
(*Helpful* means you are useful or willing to help. *Helpless* means you can't defend yourself, for example baby animals are often helpless and can be easily attacked.)

**6**
a In my tennis club, there are two ~~coaches very nice~~ **very nice coaches**.
b My best friend has ~~hair and eyes brown~~ **brown hair and brown eyes**.
c At the beginning of the film, a ~~young handsome~~ **handsome young** man is sitting in a café.
d She is wearing a ~~white beautiful~~ **beautiful white** dress.
e I've made a new friend with ~~black short~~ **short black** hair.
f He lives in a house with a ~~green big~~ **big green** garden.

**7**
Students' own answers.

## Speaking Part 1
**1**
1 Switzerland   2 Tokyo in Japan   3 I work in my mum's shop, but I'd like to go to university.   4 I'm an engineer in a large company.   5 I love it!
6 too often.   7 playing sports.

### Track 43
**Narrator:** One.
**Examiner:** What's your name?
**Chiara:** My name's Chiara.
**Examiner:** Where do you live?
**Chiara:** I live in Italy.
**Examiner:** Do you work or are you a student?
**Chiara:** I'm a student.
**Examiner:** What do you study?
**Chiara:** I'm studying to be a teacher. I'd like to be a primary school teacher.
**Examiner:** Thank you. Do you enjoy studying English?
**Chiara:** I love it!
**Examiner:** Why?
**Chiara:** Because the classes are fun and we've got a really good teacher. And also, as I said, I want to be a teacher and I know that I'll need English for my work.
**Narrator:** Two.
**Examiner:** And what's your name?
**Celine:** My name's Celine.
**Examiner:** Thank you. Where do you come from?
**Celine:** I come from Switzerland.
**Examiner:** Do you work or are you a student?
**Celine:** At the moment, I'm working.
**Examiner:** What do you do?
**Celine:** I'm working in my mum's shop, but I'd like to go to university next year.
**Examiner:** How often do you use a mobile phone?
**Celine:** Sorry, can you say that again, please?
**Examiner:** Do you often use a mobile phone?
**Celine:** Oh yes! My friends say I use it too often. I use it for everything. It's my alarm clock, I check it for messages and I also use my phone for the internet and to watch videos.
**Narrator:** Three.
**Examiner:** What's your name?
**Akihiko:** Akihiko.
**Examiner:** Where do you live, Akihiko?
**Akihiko:** I live in Tokyo in Japan.
**Examiner:** Do you work or are you a student?
**Akihiko:** Err … I work.
**Examiner:** What do you do?
**Akihiko:** I'm an engineer in a large company.
**Examiner:** What do you enjoy doing in your free time?
**Akihiko:** I really enjoy playing sports. I play table tennis and I also like baseball. I also like travelling to new places.

Answer key   179

**2**
1 Yes they do, because they answer the examiner's questions and they give more than one-word answers.
2 Sorry, can you say that again, please?
3 No, he repeats it in a slightly different way: 'Do you often use a mobile phone?'
**3**
(Suggested answers)
**Examiner:** What's your name?
**Enrico:** I'm Enrico / My name's Enrico.
**Examiner:** Where do you live, Enrico?
**Enrico:** I live in Porto, which is in Portugal.
**Examiner:** Do you work or are you a student?
**Enrico:** I work.
**Examiner:** What do you do?
**Enrico:** I'm a journalist for an important newspaper in my country.
**4**
Students' own answers.

## Writing Part 2
**1**
Students' own answers.
**2**
1 **D**ear **S**am**,** **I** had a great time with my friends last weekend too**.**
2 **W**hat about you**?** **W**ho is your best friend**?**
3 **O**n **S**aturday **I** took my cousin**'s** (or cousins**'** if more than one cousin owns the dog) dog to the beach**.**
4 **A**fter that**,** we ate salad**,** chicken and ice cream**.**
5 **H**e loves **E**nglish**.** **H**e thinks that **it's** easy**.**
6 **I'm** looking forward to seeing you soon**.**
**3**
(Suggested answers)
Who? –member family, friend, someone famous
What look like? What like?
Why admire?
article answering questions
about **100** words
**4**
(Suggested answer)
Although Zahra answers the questions well, she doesn't get full marks because she makes several mistakes with punctuation and spelling.
**5**
1 Yes   2 Yes   3 Yes   4 No   5 Yes
**6**
Spelling: 1 with curly dark hair <u>and</u> brown eyes   2 gets on well <u>with</u> him
3 <u>because</u> he's   4 Hasan is hardworking and generous <u>too</u>
5 he set up his own online company <u>which</u> sells
Punctuation: 1 If <u>I</u> had to choose   2 <u>He's</u> medium height
3 he's easygoing<u>,</u> honest and reliable   4 to help an international children's charity<u>.</u>
**7 & 8**
Students' own answers.

## 7 Vocabulary and grammar review
**1**
2 big enough   3 too dark   4 thick enough   5 too sleepy   6 old enough
7 too cold   8 too expensive
**2**
2 'm meeting   3 'll go   4 leaves   5 'll   6 are going
**3**
2 f   3 a   4 b   5 c   6 e
**4**
Across: 1 freezing   4 cold   6 crossroads   7 backpack   8 extremely
9 lightning
Down: 2 guidebook   3 sightseeing   5 foggy

## 8 Vocabulary and grammar review
**1**
2 B   3 A   4 C   5 D   6 B   7 A   8 C   9 D   10 C

**2**
1 I only go shopping if I have to ~~becouse~~ **because** most of the shops are expensive.
2 I've just received your email. You ask me ~~wich~~ **which** film stars I like.
3 Since ~~than~~ **then** we have been very good friends.
4 You asked me if ~~i~~ **I** had fun last weekend.
5 On ~~friday~~ **Friday**, my family and I got on a boat to the island.
6 I think you ~~now~~ **know** him. He is called Patrick.
**3**
(Suggested answers)
2 I feel tired / I'll be tired tomorrow
3 I'd take it to the police station
4 you don't come too
5 I'll start learning French
6 I lost my mobile phone
7 I'll go to the beach
8 I would live in Australia.
**4**
2 with   3 a   4 up   5 for   6 to

# Unit 9 Stay fit and healthy

## Starting off
**1–3**
Students' own answers.
Key to quiz: How fit and active are you?
Question 1: A 0 B 1 C 2
Question 2: A 1 B 0 C 2
Question 3: A 0 B 1 C 2
Question 4: A 2 B 0 C 1
Question 5: A 0 B 2 C 1
Question 6: A 0 B 1 C 2

**0–4** You're not keen on exercise, are you? By not getting a minimum 30 minutes of activity a day, you're missing a great way to feel less stressed, sleep better and get more energy. As it's all new to you, start with a little at first. Remember you can do parts of your half-hour at different times, so why not walk to work, clean the house, go for a swim – anything that stops you sitting on the sofa, really. You don't have to run 40 kilometres to improve your fitness.
**5–8** You could be fitter. You're quite relaxed and, while taking it easy can be a good idea, it shouldn't take too much extra effort to do the recommended 30 minutes a day, five times a week. You enjoy spending time with your friends, so why not take up an activity together? It can be anything – from a street dance class to basketball. Or if you don't fancy organised classes, go out dancing instead of sitting around doing nothing.
**9 or more** Well done! You're fit and active. Half an hour of activity a day is a minimum for you. While keeping active now means you feel great, you can also look forward to a healthy future. You shouldn't have to worry if you stay active. As you enjoy being fit, make sure you do all the activities you can: from hill walks to rock climbing.

## Listening Part 2
**1**
1 a conversation about running 20 kilometres, a woman and her friend, the reason she decided to run in the race
2 a conversation about a film after two people watched it, two friends, what they agree about
3 a conversation about a bicycle, two friends, the reason he wants to sell it
4 a conversation about a concert one of the speakers went to, two friends, his opinion of it
5 a conversation about an illness, a man and his friend, how he feels now
6 a conversation about a sports centre, two friends, what they agree about
**2**
1 B   2 A   3 B   4 A   5 C   6 B

> **Track 44**
> **Narrator:** For each question, choose the correct answer. One. You will hear a woman telling her friend about running in a 20-kilometre race. Why did she decide to run in the race?
> **Man:** Why did you run in that 20-kilometre race over the weekend? To get fit?

**Woman:** Well, as you know, I do a lot of athletics training most weeks, so a single race wouldn't really make any difference. But my friend Julia, who keeps fit by running in other races like this, told me the winner gets £500. I thought if I could somehow manage to come first, I'd be able to give that to a good charity, so I went online, found the website and registered for it straight away.
**Man:** Did you win?
**Woman:** I came second. But I still made £200 for charity.
**Narrator:** Two. You will hear two friends talking about a film they have just watched.
**Woman:** So what did you think of the film?
**Man:** It was pretty good, I thought. It was quite long, but it was certainly more interesting than the last one we watched here.
**Woman:** Well, I found it rather slow and a bit hard to follow in places. And I noticed a lot of people in the seats around us left before it ended.
**Man:** Yes they did, and it was a shame because they missed the best bit in the last few minutes. I really didn't expect it to finish like that.
**Woman:** That was quite a shock, wasn't it?
**Narrator:** Three. You will hear a student telling his friend about his bicycle.
**Female student:** I think I've just seen an ad on the notice board for your bike. Are you really selling it?
**Male student:** Yes. It's in great condition and I should get a good price for it. Then I can get a brand-new phone.
**Female student:** I'm really surprised. I often see you riding it when I'm going to university, even on cold winter mornings.
**Male student:** Yes, I know. I'll miss it, but I can't afford to replace it with a new one as well as buy a phone. The screen on the one I've got is just too small and it's damaged, too.
**Narrator:** Four. You will hear a young man telling his friend about a concert he went to.
**Woman:** I heard you went to the concert in the park on Saturday night. How was it?
**Man:** Well, I know normally you'd pay a lot of money to see a top band like that so it was good in that way, but it was still a bit of a disappointment. They didn't play any of their big hits, just a load of new songs from their latest album and they seemed to go on for hours. Like a lot of other people there, I went home quite a while before the end because it wasn't interesting. The only good thing really was that the concert was free.
**Narrator:** Five. You will hear a man telling his friend about his illness.
**Woman:** I saw you were off work at the end of last week and someone said you were ill. What was the matter?
**Man:** Yes, I had a nasty cough, a sore throat and a stomach ache, but fortunately that's gone now.
**Woman:** So, do you feel better today?
**Man:** I've still got a bit of a headache and I don't have any energy at all, maybe because I wasn't eating properly until today. But at least I've got rid of the fever I had.
**Woman:** Good. Remember to keep warm and have plenty of drinks, especially hot ones.
**Narrator:** Six. You will hear two friends talking about their local sports centre.
**Male student:** There are definitely lots of things to do at that new sports centre next to the park.
**Female student:** If you like team sports or racket sports, yes, but they need things like athletics and gymnastics, too.
**Male student:** Their swimming pool's a really good size, though, and there's a reduced admission fee for students.
**Female student:** That's true. Actually, I should go more often because it's only about ten minutes by bus from my place.

**Male student:** And even less from mine. Actually, I could walk there instead and save a bit of money.
**Female student:** If we have time, let's go next weekend!

## Vocabulary
**Illnesses and accidents**
**1**
1 Phonetic script for underlined words: cough: /kɒf/; sore: /sɔː/; throat: /θrəʊt/; stomach: /stʌmək/; ache: /eɪk/
2 Meanings: cough: make air come out of your throat with a short sound; sore throat: pain inside the throat; stomach ache: pain in your stomach

### Track 45
I had a nasty cough, a sore throat and a stomach ache.

**2**
**illnesses:** earache, fever, flu, high temperature
**accidents:** bruise, cut, fracture, sprain, wound
**treatments:** aspirin, bandage, medicine, operation, pill, plaster, plaster cast, test, X-ray
**3**
2 cut   3 bruise   4 cough   5 sprain
**4**
1 parts of the body   2 illnesses   3 treatments
**5**
Students' own answers.

## Grammar
**Relative clauses**
**1**
1 that   2 who   3 which   4 when   5 that   6 whose   7 where   8 that
**2**
2 who   3 that/which   4 which/that   5 when   6 where   7 whose
**3**
2 who   3 where   4 which/that   5 whose   6 when
**4**
(Suggested answers)
2 I watch TV / I listen to music
3 I hate / I really like
4 I stay in bed late / I go swimming
5 always helps you / listens to you
6 name is the same as mine / best friend works in the same place as me
**5**
1 which   2 which is very healthy   3 yes   4 no
**6**
2 you met, works at the hospital.
3 we hired a boat, is in the next valley.
4 sister is a teacher, is my best friend.
5 I was 19.
6 is popular in my country.
**7**
1 I want to know ~~who~~ **which** sport is your favourite.
2 I can play my favourite sport, ~~that~~ **which** is tennis.
3 They filmed students ~~which~~ **who/that** were playing football.
4 This is the book ~~who~~ **which/that** my best friend Joey gave me.
5 One sport ~~who~~ **which/that** I think is good is swimming.
6 I want to learn more about tennis, ~~that~~ **which** is my hobby.

## Vocabulary
**Sports**
**1**
1 A   2 C   3 B
**2**
do: Taekwondo; go: surfing; play: volleyball
**3**
do: athletics, gymnastics
go: climbing, cycling, jogging, mountain biking, rollerblading, running, skateboarding, skiing, swimming
play: baseball, basketball, football, golf, ice hockey, tennis, volleyball

**4**
1 play   2 go   3 do
**5**
1 I ~~practise~~ **go** horse riding twice a week.
2 You can ~~make~~ **do** a lot of sports and activities.
3 In winter you can ~~make~~ **go** snowboarding.
4 We have ~~done~~ **played** table tennis.
5 At first, we ~~made~~ **did** aerobics.
6 We ~~played~~ **went** windsurfing.
**6**
(Suggested answers)
on a court: tennis, squash, basketball, volleyball, etc.
in a gym: gymnastics, aerobics, martial arts, etc.
on a pitch: football, rugby, hockey, baseball, etc.
in a stadium: football, rugby, baseball, etc.
on a track: athletics, running, cycling, etc.
**7**
(Suggested answers)
Clothes: boots (football, rugby, skiing, etc.); gloves (boxing, football goalkeeper, ice hockey, skiing, etc.); helmet (horse riding, motorcycling, baseball, etc.); trainers (running, jogging, tennis, etc.)
Equipment: bat (baseball, cricket, table tennis, etc.); racket (table tennis, squash, badminton, etc.); net (tennis, table tennis, volleyball, etc.)
**8**
2 score   3 draw/lose/win
**9**
Students' own answers.

## Reading Part 3
**1 & 2**
Students' own answers.
**3**
1 A   2 D   3 C   4 C   5 B
**4**
Students' own answers.

## Grammar
**Past perfect**
**1**
1 *had* + past participle, *had not* + past participle   2 the first action
**2**
2 I had/'d walked all the way home
3 arrived at the stadium, the match had started
4 had/'d left my trainers at home, I couldn't run in the race
**3**
(Suggested answers)
2 … I went to hospital.
3 … had left their trainers there.
4 … the film had (already) started.

## Writing Part 2
**1**
1 title   2 first person   3 story, title, frightening, experience, my
**2**
b 1   c 3   d 3   e 3   f 1
**3**
1 went (go) snowboarding   2 , who is a champion snowboarder   3 it had started; she had disappeared; had she gone; I'd gone; she'd heard; she'd found
**4**
1 the first line   2 first person   3 I, nervous, game, began
**5**
(Model answer)
I felt nervous when the game began. Fifty thousand people were watching me in the stadium, as well as a television audience of millions. I had always dreamt of playing football for my favourite team, and at last I had my chance.
For the first hour, everything went fine. We were playing well and I had started to feel less nervous. Then, suddenly, it all went horribly wrong: I made a terrible mistake and the other team scored. I felt awful. Then I thought back to what the coach had said to me, about never giving up, and I knew that I had to win the match for my team. So, in the last few minutes, I scored the two most important goals of my life.

## Speaking Part 4
**1**
2 sure   3 totally   4 so   5 way   6 all   7 true   8 too

**Track 46**
1 You _may_ be _right_, but …
2 I'm not really _sure_ about that.
3 Yes, I _totally_ agree with you.
4 I don't _think_ so because …
5 That's not the way _I_ see it.
6 I don't agree at _all_.
7 That's _true_.
8 I think so _too_.

**2**
a agree: 3, 7, 8
b disagree strongly: 5, 6
c disagree politely: 1, 2, 4
**3 & 4**
As Exercise 1 audioscript.
**5**
Students' own answers.

# Unit 10  Looks amazing!

## Starting off
**1**
A Carbohydrates   B Fruit and vegetables   C Milk and dairy products   D Protein   E Fats, e.g. chocolate, crisps and cake
**2**
Students' own answers.

## Reading Part 2
**1**
(Suggested answer)
Choose the most suitable street food stall for each group of people.
**2**
(Suggested answers)
1 try something new on Tuesday, Both of them really like fish, a hot drink with their meal
2 some of the stalls have won prizes, vegetarian main meal, short of money
3 light lunch together on Saturday, are not willing to pay very much, sit down to eat
4 meal on Sunday, doesn't want to walk too far, proper meal, wants a dessert
5 trying a spicy vegetable dish, won't have much time, need to take away their dessert
**3**
(Suggested answers)
1 tea, coffee or hot chocolate
2 they don't want to eat meat or fish
3 not expensive, reasonable, cheap
4 near the entrance or front door
5 Jack: a complete meal, a heavy meal, main dish; Sara: a sandwich, salad or snack
**4**
1 B   2 G   3 F   4 E   5 H
**5**
Students' own answers.

## Vocabulary
*course*, *dish*, *food*, *meal* and *plate*
**1**
1 d   2 a   3 e   4 c   5 b
**2**
(Suggested answer)
They are all countable but food can be both countable and uncountable. We know by the *C* and *U*.
**3**
2 meals   3 plate   4 courses   5 dish

## Grammar
**Commands and instructions**
**1 & 2**
(Suggested answers)
1 Mexico: tortilla, rice, beans, lettuce, tomato, meat, avocado
2 Japan: rice, seaweed, fish, carrots, avocado, cucumber
3 India: pancake, potatoes, curry, spice

### Track 47
1 On today's programme, we're going to learn how to make chicken burritos from Mexico. First of all, mix the chicken together with salt, pepper and chilli and then fry it. Don't cook it on a high heat or the burrito will be rather dry. Next, boil some rice until it is just soft. Then prepare the other ingredients.
2 Everyone loves Japanese sushi and this is actually something you can make at home quite easily. Wash one and a half cups of sushi rice and then boil it for twelve minutes. Next, decide on your ingredients. Use cucumber, carrot and tuna for your first sushi rolls and then try other things.
3 Masala dosa is a vegetarian breakfast dish from South India. To make it at home, buy the dosa from an Indian supermarket and fill it with spicy boiled potato. Don't forget to serve your dosa with lassi, an Indian yoghurt drink.

**3**
2 Don't cook   3 Wash   4 Use, try   5 Buy   6 Don't forget
**4**
We use *wash*, *use*, *try*, etc. (infinitive without *to*) to tell people what to do. We use *don't cook*, *don't forget*, etc. (*don't* + infinitive without *to*) to tell people what not to do.
**5 & 6**
Students' own answers.

## Listening Part 1
**1**
2 bottle of water   3 bar of chocolate   4 cups   5 crisps
**2**
Students' own answers.

### Track 48
**Narrator:** One. What will Natalie buy for the picnic?
**Natalie:** Have we got everything we need for the picnic, Sam?
**Sam:** Hang on! I'll check. You know what? We haven't got any bread.
**Natalie:** You're joking! I'll get some from the bakery on our way there. No, I've got a better idea. I'll cycle down to the supermarket now to get some and I'll buy another bottle of water. I'll also get some crisps while I'm there.

**3**
B

### Track 49
**Sam:** Great! But please don't get any more snacks or chocolate. We've got plenty. We need some cups though. Could you buy some?
**Natalie:** Sure.

**4**
(Suggested answers)
2 What did the <u>woman</u> <u>take</u> to the party?
Did she take A two pizzas, B some homemade biscuits or C a cake?
3 What food will the <u>man try</u>?
Does the man try A a plate of steak and chips, B a plate of mixed fried fish or C a bowl of soup?
4 <u>Where</u> did <u>the woman go yesterday</u>?
Did she go to A the cinema, B the theatre or C a concert?
5 What do they need to <u>bring</u> for <u>training</u> tomorrow?
Do they need to bring A a tracksuit, B a helmet or C a pair of gloves?
6 What activity did the man do for the <u>first time</u> on <u>holiday</u>?
Did the man try A waterskiing, B diving or C windsurfing?
7 Where has the woman <u>been</u>?
Has she been to A a jewellery shop, B a gallery or C a bookshop?

**5**
2 A   3 B   4 A   5 A   6 A   7 B

### Track 50
**Narrator:** For each question, choose the correct answer. Two. What did the woman take to the party?
**Man:** Hi Katy! How was the party? Did everyone like the biscuits you made?
**Woman:** I didn't make them in the end. I baked a cake instead. But then, I phoned Mark to see what time his party was and he mentioned that he had already made a huge chocolate one. I didn't know what to do. So I bought a couple of pizzas on the way and we ate those at the party.
**Man:** What a shame! Perhaps we can have it for dessert today.
**Narrator:** Three. What food will the man try?
**Presenter:** And I've just got a few minutes left to tell you about a new programme where we send our presenters around the world to try local dishes. Today, Paul's in Milan, Italy, where his favourite food, *fritto misto de pesce*, is on the menu. This is a plate of mixed fried fish, and will make a change from his usual favourite of steak and chips! Then next week his sister's going to Granada, Spain to try *gazpacho*, a cold soup made with tomatoes, peppers and cucumber.
**Narrator:** Four. Where did the woman go yesterday?
**Man:** Hi. Are you doing anything later? We're going to the early-afternoon performance of that new spy film. The reviews are incredible. Do you want to come?
**Woman:** Oh! I saw it yesterday with my cousin. He wanted to see a play but I didn't fancy it. I heard it was very long with no interval.
**Man:** Would you recommend the film, then?
**Woman:** Oh yes! It's brilliant, but I don't think I want to see it again. Are you going to the concert tomorrow? It's going to be amazing.
**Narrator:** Five. What do they need to bring for training tomorrow?
**Trainer:** Shh! Great work today guys! Now listen carefully, because as you know, tomorrow we're going to train at the sports centre on their indoor climbing wall. Remember to wear comfortable clothes. A tracksuit is much better than shorts. The sports centre will provide you with a helmet and a pair of climbing shoes. Your hands may get a bit sore, I'm afraid, but it isn't really a good idea to wear gloves because you might slip on the wall.
**Narrator:** Six. What activity did the man do for the first time on holiday?
**Woman:** You're looking well. How was your trip to Egypt?
**Man:** Great, we've just got back. We had an amazing time. We went diving on the first day and we took some beautiful underwater photos.
**Woman:** But you've done that before, haven't you?
**Man:** Yeah, that's right! Then my friend persuaded me to try waterskiing. I'd never done that before and by the end I was quite good at it. It was fun, but my favourite watersport is still windsurfing. Do you remember when we both tried that for the first time at university?
**Narrator:** Seven. Where has the woman been?
**Woman:** Sorry I'm late. I've been trying to find a present for Mum. I was on my way to the bookshop, but then I remembered it's closed today.
**Man:** What did you get her in the end?
**Woman:** Well, I went to the art gallery to see if they had a nice picture in a frame for her, but I didn't really like any of them and they were quite expensive. I'm going tomorrow to get her some earrings or a necklace from that new jewellery shop on the corner.

**6**
(Suggested answer)
The consonant sound at the end of a word connects with the vowel sound at the beginning of the next word.

### Track 51
I'm going tomorrow to get her some_earrings_or_a necklace from that new jewellery shop_on the corner.

**7**
1 I baked_a cake_instead.
2 This_is_a plate_of mixed fried fish.

### Track 52
1 I baked_a cake_instead.
2 This_is_a plate_of mixed fried fish.

**8**
Students' own answers.

Answer key   183

## Vocabulary

**Shops and services**

**1**
Students' own answers.

**2**
(Suggested answers)
1 dentist, garage and hairdresser's
2 bakery, bookshop, butcher's, chemist, garage, hairdresser's, supermarket
3 library
4 travel agent's
5 dentist, garage, dry cleaner's
6 [probably in all the places]

**3**
1 hairdresser's   2 garage   3 dry cleaner's

> **Track 53**
> **Narrator:** One.
> **Madison:** What have you done to your hair, Layla?
> **Layla:** Oh don't. I normally have my hair cut at Gabrielle's but I wanted something different, so I went to that new place on the High Street.
> **Madison:** Oh no! Was it very expensive?
> **Narrator:** Two.
> **Andrew:** Are you coming to the party tonight, Lewis?
> **Lewis:** I can't. I need to save up some money.
> **Andrew:** Why's that?
> **Lewis:** I had a little accident on my scooter. All my fault, I'm afraid.
> **Andrew:** What about your scooter? You only got it last week.
> **Lewis:** That's why I can't afford to go out. I'm having the scooter repaired and I'm going to have to look for another job to pay for it.
> **Narrator:** Three.
> **Vicki:** Oh no, Charlie! That's cola you've spilt down my dress.
> **Charlie:** Sorry, Vicki. It was an accident.
> **Vicki:** My sister's going to go mad. I borrowed this dress from her and I had it cleaned last week for this party. The cleaning wasn't cheap, either!

**4**
Students' own answers.

## Grammar

**Have something done**

**1**
1 somebody does for us   2 informal

**2**
1 Polly   2 Ginny   3 Polly   4 Ginny   5 Ginny   6 Polly   7 Polly   8 Ginny

**3**
2 having my flat cleaned.
3 had my hair cut.

**4**
1 *have* (*get* is not possible here because the situation is formal)
2 *have* and *get*

**5**
2 I can't finish this report because I'm having my laptop mended at the moment.
3 My bike is broken again and I had it repaired a week ago.
4 Jack isn't at work. He's having his teeth checked today by the dentist.
5 Keith and Pete are going to a New Year's Eve party. They had their suits cleaned last week.

**6**
Students' own answers.

## Speaking Part 2

**1**
Photo 1. She describes all five things.

> **Track 54**
> **Examiner:** Now I'd like each of you to talk on your own about something. I'm going to give each of you a photograph and I'd like you to talk about it. Luna, here is your photograph. It shows people shopping on a rainy day. Lidia, you just listen. Luna, please tell us what you can see in your photograph.

> **Luna:** Uh-huh. In this picture, I can see a lot of people outside. It's a rainy day and the people are shopping. The street is quite crowded. I can see many shops, for example, a mobile phone shop and a shoe shop. In the middle of the picture, there are two women. One of them is carrying something. I can't remember the word for this object. It's used for the rain … we open it when it rains. She's wearing a long black coat, and black shoes. The other woman is wearing a coat and a red scarf, grey jeans and boots. On her back, she's got … a … it's something like a bag. In front of them, there's another woman. She's wearing a blue coat. She's got a … a … two bags. One is on her back. It's made of leather. The other bag is black and it's enormous. It looks heavy. In the background, I think I can see some flags, I'm not sure …
> **Examiner:** Thank you.

**2**
1 It's used for   2 it's something like

> **Track 55**
> 1 One of them is carrying something. I can't remember the word for this object. It's used for the rain … we open it when it rains.
> 2 On her back, she's got … a … it's something like a bag.

**3 & 4**
Students' own answers.

## Writing Part 2

**1**
(Suggested answers)
<u>Where</u> do <u>you and your friends</u> go <u>shopping</u> nowadays?
Do you <u>prefer</u> going to <u>indoor shopping centres</u> or to <u>town centres</u>?
Or perhaps you'd <u>rather</u> do all your <u>shopping online</u>?
<u>Answer these questions</u> and we will publish the best articles in our next magazine.
Write your <u>article</u> in about <u>100 words</u>.

**2–5**
Students' own answers.

## 9 Vocabulary and grammar review

**1**
2 d which   3 f when   4 a who   5 b where   6 e whose

**2**
2 In summer, when the weather is good, we play tennis.
3 Stevie, whose team won, was the best player of all.
4 In the city centre, where we live, there is a lot of pollution.
5 My brother, who had an accident, is feeling better now.
6 Volleyball, which is a team sport, is played on a court.

**3**
2 had practised   3 felt   4 had/'d brought   5 had/'d put   6 was
7 had/'d rained   8 didn't seem   9 was   10 had left   11 started
12 realised   13 had/'d played   14 was   15 slipped   16 fell   17 knew
18 had/'d injured   19 went   20 had not/hadn't broken   21 wore

**4**
2 sore   3 beat   4 bat   5 athletics   6 pill   7 bruise

## 10 Vocabulary and grammar review

**1**
2 complain   3 book   4 borrow   5 repair/mend

**2**
2 D   3 B   4 D   5 A   6 D

**3**
2 have it cut   3 had it taken   4 have them cleaned   5 had it repaired

**4**
2 ago   3 had   4 have   5 had   6 were

# Unit 11 The natural world

## Starting off

**The environment**

**1**
1 2 Packaging creates waste that harms the environment.
3 Destroying rainforest by cutting down trees. Many animals and plants then have nowhere to live and disappear forever.
4 Air pollution, often the result of too many cars. People's health badly damaged.
5 Cruelty to animals. Poor-quality food.

184

2 2 – A Buy fruit without packaging in your local market (and take it home in non-plastic bags).
3 – E Use less paper and reduce the need for wood, for instance by getting paperless bills sent online.
4 – B Drive an electric car and reduce air pollution where you live.
5 – C Buy free-range chicken and eggs, from animals that can move freely and lead healthy lives.

3
(Suggested answers)
2 Avoid buying items packed in plastic, paper, etc. Recycle packaging.
3 Save data on a memory stick, not paper. Use cloth handkerchiefs you can wash, not paper tissues.
4 Use public transport. Work from home to avoid travelling into the city.
5 Buy cheese, eggs, meat, etc. from local farmers or markets.

2
Students' own answers.

## Listening Part 4
1
(Suggested answers)
1 polar bears, gorillas, rhinoceros, monarch butterflies, bluefin tuna. Deforestation, urbanisation, road-building, hunting, overfishing, water/air pollution.
2 Species becoming extinct, loss of animals and plants that depend on them, overpopulation of other species, loss of food – especially fish – for local people, fewer types of plant available to develop new medicines.
3 Stop the destruction of the places where they live (habitats), control fishing, stop illegal hunting, end ivory trade. Increase their numbers by creating safe areas in the countryside.

2
1 B   2 A   3 A   4 C   5 A   6 B

### Track 56
**Narrator:** You will hear a young woman called Ellie talking about a trip to southern Spain to see the Iberian lynx. For each question, choose the correct answer.
**Interviewer:** With me today is Ellie Johnson, who went to Spain with her university friend Marta to see the beautiful Iberian lynx, one of the world's rarest wildcats. So, Ellie, which location did you choose, and why?
**Ellie:** A place with a stream next to the forest, with plenty of rabbits. The huge fall in the number of rabbits is the main reason why the lynx is so rare, because an adult lynx needs to eat three rabbits a day. Marta knew the area but I didn't until I saw on TV photos of a lynx taken there a few days before.
**Interviewer:** How easy was it to get there?
**Ellie:** Well, it was summer and temperatures were really high during the daytime, so it made sense to set off really early – at five a.m. in fact, when it was still cool. The moon was bright, and we were pleased about that because it's easy to go in the wrong direction in the dark. The track was really challenging in places – it went up and down a lot. We didn't actually find it too exhausting, but it did mean we got to the stream later than we'd expected. Once we were there, we looked for somewhere to hide.
**Interviewer:** Where did you hide?
**Ellie:** There was an empty hut nearby but it was locked, so it looked like the best place was behind some large rocks. There was no shade there, though, so instead we lay down just inside the forest and waited. In fact, we waited there for ages. I was going to suggest leaving, when suddenly we heard something running through the bushes.
**Interviewer:** What was it?
**Ellie:** Well of course we hoped it'd be a lynx and we both grabbed our cameras, but it was just a frightened-looking little rabbit. Just then, though, another creature appeared, running after it. It was grey and brown, about the size of a small cat: it was a young lynx!
**Interviewer:** I can imagine your excitement! What did it do?
**Ellie:** Well, by then the rabbit was far away and the lynx's chance of catching it had gone so it stopped and looked around, though it didn't notice us. We were so busy taking photos of that cute little animal that we didn't see a much larger one approaching. It was an adult female, and clearly the little one was hers. That was why it had stopped.
**Interviewer:** How long did you stay there?
**Ellie:** The sun had almost set, but we stayed another hour, taking photos of them until we couldn't see anything. Marta wanted to stay overnight to see them again at sunrise, but we didn't have a tent, so we set off, reaching the hostel just before midnight.

3
Students' own answers.

## Vocabulary
**Noun suffixes**
1
1 locate, excite, direct; 2 (suffixes are underlined) loca<u>tion</u>, direc<u>tion</u>, excite<u>ment</u>; 3 location drops the final 'e' from the verb form locate; because the suffix begins with a vowel

2

| -ment | -ation | -ion |
|---|---|---|
| announcement | admiration | attraction |
| development | confirmation | celebration |
| disappointment | examination | collection |
| enjoyment | exploration | completion |
| entertainment | information | connection |
| improvement | invitation | creation |
| movement | relaxation | discussion |
| replacement | reservation | education |
|  |  | invention |
|  |  | pollution |
|  |  | prevention |
|  |  | protection |
|  |  | translation |

**3 & 4**
2 exploration   3 information   4 movement   5 disappointment
6 improvement

### Track 57
**Presenter:** Scientists in Antarctica have used a new invention to help them study penguins close up: a tiny robot on wheels that looks like a baby penguin. The robot, similar to those used in the exploration of the moon and Mars, provided lots of exciting new information about the birds. Scientists, working some distance away, controlled every movement the robot made and it was immediately accepted by penguin families as one of them. The adults even sang to it, though to the penguins' great disappointment the 'baby' didn't reply. The scientists are now working on a new model with one important improvement – it will be able to play penguin songs.

5
(underlinings show word stress)
2 explor<u>a</u>tion   3 infor<u>ma</u>tion   4 <u>move</u>ment   5 disapp<u>oint</u>ment
6 impr<u>ove</u>ment
Patterns: the stressed syllable is normally before the suffix, or the *a* in the case of *-ation* (although there are exceptions, e.g. adver<u>tise</u>ment, <u>ar</u>gument).
Exception in Exercise 2 table: de<u>ve</u>lopment

6
(underlinings show word stress)
admir<u>a</u>tion, ann<u>oun</u>cement, att<u>rac</u>tion, celebr<u>a</u>tion, coll<u>ec</u>tion, compl<u>e</u>tion, confirm<u>a</u>tion, conn<u>ec</u>tion, cre<u>a</u>tion, de<u>ve</u>lopment, disapp<u>oint</u>ment, disc<u>u</u>ssion, educ<u>a</u>tion, enj<u>oy</u>ment, entert<u>ain</u>ment, exam<u>in</u>ation, explor<u>a</u>tion, impr<u>ove</u>ment, inform<u>a</u>tion, inv<u>en</u>tion, invit<u>a</u>tion, <u>move</u>ment, poll<u>u</u>tion, pre<u>ven</u>tion, prot<u>ec</u>tion, relax<u>a</u>tion, repl<u>ace</u>ment, reserv<u>a</u>tion, transl<u>a</u>tion

## Grammar
**The passive**
1
1 A and C are active; B and D are passive.
2 C and D describe an event in the past.
3 B and D
4 A: subject – this new technology; object – air pollution. B: subject – air pollution; agent – this new technology (using *by*)
5 C: subject – guides; object – tourists. D: subject – tourists; no object
6 information not in sentence D: *who* allowed the tourists to take photos (the guides)

**2**
2 passive  3 active  4 active  5 passive  6 by
**3**
3 was closed  4 was spoilt  5 is blamed  6 weren't / were not noticed
**4**
2 Two giraffes were seen near the trees.
3 The moon was hidden by one small cloud.
4 Cars aren't / are not allowed in the national park.
5 Rice is grown in the east of the country.
6 A poem was written about this waterfall.
7 The forest was partly destroyed by fire.
**5**
In the past, bears and wolves were considered a danger to both people and farm animals so their numbers <u>were reduced</u>, often to zero. Nowadays, however, a lot more <u>is understood</u> about how they form an essential part of nature, and some years ago international agreements <u>were made</u> to bring back these magnificent creatures. A lot of money <u>was spent</u>, large areas where they could move freely across borders <u>were created</u>, and they <u>are</u> now <u>protected</u> by law. In Europe, bears and wolves <u>are</u> once again <u>found</u> in many countries, from Spain to Scandinavia, where they <u>are allowed</u> to live in places with few people. They <u>are</u> sometimes <u>seen</u> in mountain areas or forests, but usually they prefer to keep away from humans. So if we keep well away from them, we are not in any danger.
Infinitives: consider, reduce, understand, make, spend, create, protect, find, allow, see
**6**
The main verb is stressed. The weak form of the auxiliary verb is used: /wə/

> **Track 58**
> … bears and wolves were considered a danger to both people and farm animals.

**7**
Students' own answers.

> **Track 59**
> 1 A lot of electricity is wasted by those machines.
> 2 Two giraffes were seen near the trees.
> 3 The moon was hidden by one small cloud.
> 4 Cars aren't allowed in the national park.
> 5 Rice is grown in the east of the country.
> 6 A poem was written about this waterfall.
> 7 The forest was partly destroyed by fire.

## Reading Part 5
**1**
2 west  3 South  4 Pacific  5 Ecuador  6 unique  7 hard  8 weight  9 tail  10 wings
**2**
1 a news report in a local paper
2 San Cristóbal Island, one of the Galápagos Islands
3 They will work on environmental projects for free (volunteer work).
4 the environment and the wildlife there are unique
5 see the countryside, study the wildlife, sailing and diving
**3 & 4**
1 D (team)  2 A (include)  3 B (prevent)  4 D (part)  5 C (explore)  6 A (surrounded)
**5**
Students' own answers.

## Grammar
### Comparative and superlative adverbs
**1**
1 Students should underline: comparative adverbs: more quickly, more quietly, worse; superlative adverb: most beautifully
2 by adding *more* in front of the adverb
3 worse  4 than  5 by adding *most* in front of the adverb

**2**

| adverb | comparative | superlative |
| --- | --- | --- |
| quietly | more quietly | (the) most quietly |
| carefully | more carefully | (the) most carefully |
| slowly | more slowly | (the) most slowly |
| easily | more easily | (the) most easily |
| fast | faster | (the) fastest |
| badly | worse | (the) worst |
| hard | harder | (the) hardest |
| well | better | (the) best |
| early | earlier | (the) earliest |

**3**
2 harder  3 more brightly  4 (the) most frequently  5 most heavily  6 worse
**4**
Students' own answers.

## Speaking Part 4
**1**
(Suggested answers)
A She hasn't turned the tap off. She should turn it off when she isn't using the water.
B Using a lot of water to wash the car. They could wash it by hand using a bucket and sponge.
C He's using a dishwasher for just a few plates when he could wash them by hand or wait until he has enough for a full wash.
**2**
Have a quick shower instead of a bath.
When you're brushing your teeth, turn off the tap when you're not actually using any water (and when washing your hair).
Check taps are completely turned off (especially in places like college).

> **Track 60**
> **Ethan:** Well, there's lots you can do to save water. At home, for instance, you can have a quick shower instead of a bath. I read in an article that having a bath uses 80 to 100 litres of water.
> **Lily:** Right. And when you're brushing your teeth, let's say, you should turn off the tap when you're not actually using any water. And do the same when you're doing other things, such as washing your hair.
> **Ethan:** Good idea. And it's important to check the taps are completely turned off, especially in places like our college. The article said that a tap which loses just one drop a second, for example, wastes 20 litres a day!

**3**
2 let's say  3 such as  4 like  5 for example
**4 & 5**
Students' own answers.

## Writing Part 1
**1**
1 She says 'It was great to hear from you'.
2 visit her city
3 Agree with Chloe's suggestion that you should go to the countryside. Say whether you'd prefer to go by bus or bike. Say what wildlife you'd like to see there. Tell Chloe whether you want to go for a day or a weekend.
**2**
1 *Good idea:* 1st paragraph, *Tell Chloe:* 3rd paragraph, *Suggest:* 4th paragraph, *Say which and why:* 2nd paragraph.
2 polluteion – pollution (Sp), the weekend whole – the whole weekend (WO), drive – ride (V), find – are found (G)
3 walk – (get around) on foot, Saturday and Sunday – weekend, wildlife – animals, rather – prefer to
**3 & 4**
Students' own answers.

# Unit 12 Express yourself!
## Starting off
**Collocations: using your phone**
**1 & 2**
Students' own answers.

## Reading Part 4
**1**
1 Becky has to live without her smartphone for a week.
2 & 3 Students' own answers.

186

**2**
No, she didn't.
**3**
B, because the pronoun *them* is plural. In A, the pronoun *her* is singular.
**4**
1 B   2 G   3 E   4 F   5 C
**5 & 6**
Students' own answers.

## Vocabulary

*ask, ask for, speak, talk, say* and *tell*
**1**
1 ask   2 ask for   3 speak   4 talk   5 tell   6 Say   7 tell   8 say   9 tell
**2**
1 speak   2 told   3 ask for   4 tell   5 talk   6 asked
**3**
1 talk   2 speak   3 say   4 tell   5 ask   6 ask for
**4**
1 help   2 hello   3 joke   4 languages   5 problems   6 lie
**5 & 6**
Students' own answers.

## Grammar

**Reported speech**
**1**
Adam: an event like a street party   John: a football match
Nina: a technology-free day

### Track 61
**Helen:** Shh! Be quiet! Close the door, Paul! Thanks. Sonia, can you take notes today?
**Sonia:** Oh, is it my turn to be secretary? OK.
**Helen:** Right. As you know, we have to decide what event we're going to organise for the charity weekend. Any ideas? Yes, Adam?
**Adam:** OK. Last year we organised a street party to collect money. We can organise a similar event again.
**Helen:** But the weather was awful and very few people came.
**Adam:** We don't have to hold it outside. We could decorate the gym in the sports centre and have the party there.
**Helen:** Mmm … That sounds expensive to me. Has anyone else got any other ideas? John?
**John:** Yeah, I've thought about organising a football match.
**Helen:** Another football match? Can't we do something different?
**John:** In my sister's town, groups of friends are going to play against each other.
**Helen:** But how are we going to raise money?
**John:** Everyone will have to pay to play.
**Helen:** Still not sure. Anyone else? Nina?
**Nina:** Yes. Look at everyone! We're all using our phones right now. How about something like a technology-free day?
**Helen:** A technology-free day? How does that work?
**Nina:** The idea is to have a day where we can't use any technology. We won't be able to use any screens, internet or phones.
**Helen:** And the money?
**Nina:** People will give us money not to use technology. We'll hold some old-fashioned, traditional events instead, like story-telling or a picnic if the weather is good.
**Helen:** Thanks. Right. Think about the suggestions. And don't forget the meeting tomorrow. We'll take a vote then.

**2 & 3**
1 had organised a street party
2 could organise a similar event again
3 didn't have to hold it outside
4 had thought about organising a football match
5 were going to play against each other
6 were all using their mobile phones
7 would hold

### Track 62
**Lisa:** Hi Sonia. Sorry I didn't get to the meeting yesterday. What did you decide?
**Sonia:** Oh, hi Lisa. There's going to be another meeting today at one p.m. to take a vote. We have to think about the three suggestions.
**Lisa:** What three suggestions? Did anyone take notes?
**Sonia:** Yeah! I was the secretary. I've got them written here. Let me see. Oh yes, Adam said that they had organised a street party to collect money the year before and they could organise a similar event again.
**Lisa:** But the weather was really bad last year and very few people went.
**Sonia:** Yes, that's what Helen said, but Adam then said that they didn't have to hold it outside. They could use the gym in the sports centre.
**Lisa:** Good idea!
**Sonia:** Helen thought it sounded expensive. Then John said he had thought about organising a football match.
**Lisa:** Not another football match.
**Sonia:** Kind of. He said in his sister's town, groups of friends were going to play against each other.
**Lisa:** Mmm … You said there were three suggestions, didn't you?
**Sonia:** Yes, the third came from Nina. She said that they were all using their mobiles then. She suggested a day when they wouldn't be able to use technology at all. She said people would give them money not to use technology. They would hold some old-fashioned, traditional events instead.
**Lisa:** Like what?
**Sonia:** Like story-telling, or a picnic if the weather's good.
**Lisa:** I like the sound of that one!

**4**
2 past continuous   3 past perfect   4 past perfect   5 *would* + infinitive
6 *was/were going to* + infinitive   7 *could*
**5**
2 the year before   3 his   4 they   5 then
**6**
2 (that) someone had left their phone in the kitchen at the party.
3 (that) he was having a great time there.
**7**
Students' own answers.

**Reported commands**
**8**
2 to close the door   3 to think about the suggestions   4 to forget the meeting
**9**
1 to keep in touch   2 not to be late   3 not to bring more pizza
4 not to forget to download Season 3

## Listening Part 3
**1**
(Suggested answers)
You need to apply online. There are challenges with a subject. There is a judge called Fran Maddison. There are prizes. Food and drink will be provided. The next competition will be held in Prague.
**2**
(Suggested answers)
1 date   2 noun (the subject of the challenges)   3 noun (name of book)
4 noun (prize)   5 noun (what you should bring)   6 noun (name of place)
**3**
A singular noun because of the *a* before the gap
**4 & 5**
1 first/1/1st   2 communication   3 are me   4 (unbelievable) trip   5 laptop
6 Grand Hotel

### Track 63
**Narrator:** You will hear a woman called Catherine Bryant talking about a competition on the radio. For each question, write the correct answer in the gap. Write one or two words or a number or a date or a time.
**Catherine:** Let me tell you about an app design competition which will take place in Lisbon, Portugal from the sixth to the seventh of June. All you need to do is fill in an online form by the first of June. If your application is accepted, you should hear from us before the fourth of June.
On the day, you can take part alone or join one of the teams. You'll need to choose one of the challenges from a list of four and create an app which solves a problem. Last year's challenges were connected to the environment. For example, one of the challenge winners created an app which finds the nearest recycling bin for the rubbish you want to throw away. All I can say about this year is that the challenges have something to do with communication. The rest is a secret!

Answer key   187

The competition judge is blogger Fran Maddison, that's M-A-D-D-I-S-O-N. She presents the 'Apps Programme' on Channel Seven. Her latest book *Apps are me* will be on sale soon.

There are some amazing prizes. There's €1,000 and a tablet for the best app for each challenge. The four winners will then compete in the final for the first prize, which is an unbelievable trip to California.

You won't be able to bring your own food into the event, but reasonably priced refreshments will be available. You mustn't forget your laptop, but you'll be able to hire headphones and chargers there.

And finally, if you can't make the Conference Centre in Lisbon in June, consider the Grand Hotel in Prague in October. There'll be more information about this event on our website at the end of August.

Now, any questions?

**6**
Students' own answers.

## Grammar
**Reported questions**
**1**
2 Do we need to pay anything to take part?
3 How do we register for the competition?
4 What do we do if we have technical problems?
5 What are the prizes?
**2**
2 Peter   3 Connor   4 Samir   5 Charlotte

### Track 64
**Presenter:** Thank you, Catherine. While you've been speaking, some of our listeners have phoned in with their questions. Would you have a moment to answer them?
**Catherine:** Yes, sure.
**Presenter:** Great! First we have Emily from Manchester. Are you there, Emily?
**Emily:** Can I choose the members of my team?
**Catherine:** Good question. And yes, you can choose up to three other people to join your team. However, each person will need to make a separate application.
**Presenter:** And Peter's in Bristol.
**Peter:** Hi Catherine. I've got a question for you. Do we need to pay anything to take part?
**Catherine:** Oh? Did I forget to mention the cost? Yes, there's a fee of €5 per person. This is to show us that you're really interested in the event.
**Presenter:** Now, here's Connor from Belfast.
**Connor:** Hi! This all sounds brilliant. How do we register for the competition?
**Catherine:** It's easy. As I said before, you can do it all online. Go to our website and fill in the application form.
**Presenter:** And now Samir in London.
**Samir:** Hi! What do we do if we have technical problems?
**Catherine:** Interesting point. If you have problems with applying for the event, please get in touch with us. If you have problems on the day, our team will be available. However, it is up to you to make sure that your laptop is working well before the day of the event.
**Presenter:** And finally Charlotte in Oxford sent us her question by text. I'll read it out: 'What are the prizes?'
**Catherine:** Full details of the prizes are on our website …

**3**
a changes   b changes   c never   d isn't   e don't use
**4**
(Suggested answer)
It's an organiser app which creates a work or study plan. It also reminds you when to take breaks, what to eat and get enough sleep. You can also use it to share information with friends, for example notes and ideas, or ask for help.

### Track 65
**Cindy:** What does the app do, Emily?
**Emily:** Good question, Cindy. It's an organiser app. You put in what you have to do and by when and the app organises the week for you. For example, if you have to give a presentation or hand in a piece of work, you can put in how much time you'll need to do it with the date it's due and the app will create a work plan for you. You can do the same with exams; you put in what you need to study and by when and the app will create a study plan.

**Harry:** That could save some time. Does it do anything else?
**Emily:** Yes Harry, it tells you when to take a break and have something to eat too. It also recommends different types of exercise and the alarm reminds you to get enough sleep. It's a bit like one of those fitness watches, but for work.
**Phil:** Can I use it to share work with colleagues?
**Emily:** Yeah and that's the most useful thing, I think, Phil. You can make groups so that you can ask questions, share notes, tips and ideas and generally help each other.
**Diana:** Fantastic! Where did you get the idea from?
**Emily:** Thanks, Diana. One of the competition challenges was called 'efficient work through communication' and I thought of this idea. I never thought we would win though!
**Lily:** That's amazing, Emily! But will the app do my work for me?
**Emily:** That would be unfair, Lily!

**5**
1 what the app did   2 if it did anything else
3 if he could use it to share work with colleagues
4 where she got the idea from   5 if the app would do her work for her

## Vocabulary
**Negative prefixes**
**1**
1 un   2 in   3 im
**2**
2 unhealthy   3 impatient   4 unsociable   5 inexpensive   6 impossible
**3**
Students' own answers.

## Speaking Part 1
**1**

|   | Anton | Eleni | Victoria |
|---|---|---|---|
| 1 | ✗ | ✓ | ✓ |
| 2 | ✗ | ✓ | ✓ |
| 3 | ✗ | * | ✓ |

* Although Eleni uses a range of vocabulary, her grammar is limited – she only uses 'is' and 'like'.

### Track 66
**Narrator:** One.
**Examiner:** Anton, how do you get to work every day?
**Anton:** 8 o'clock.
**Examiner:** Do you walk to work every day?
**Anton:** Bus.
**Examiner:** Thank you.
**Narrator:** Two.
**Examiner:** Eleni, tell us about a good friend.
**Eleni:** Her name is Maria. She's tall. Her hair is long and straight. She is very nice. I like her.
**Examiner:** Thank you.
**Narrator:** Three.
**Examiner:** Victoria, how often do you use the internet?
**Victoria:** I'm sorry, could you say that again, please?
**Examiner:** Do you often use the internet?
**Victoria:** The internet? I use it every day. When I wake up, I check Facebook on my phone to see what my friends have been doing. I often go on the internet to look for information. I use it to buy bus tickets and tickets for the cinema or concerts. I also use the internet to listen to music and to watch films. I couldn't live without it.
**Examiner:** Thank you.

**2**
(Suggested answers)
1 I work about 8 km from here, so I go to work by bus at 8 o'clock every day. My flatmate sometimes gives me a lift when I'm late.
2 Her name is Maria and she's tall with long straight hair. I get on with her because she's very nice and easy-going. Everyone likes her.
**3**
1 your name   2 do you live, do you come   3 you work
4 What do you, What do you   5 Do you often   6 Tell us about
**4**
Students' own answers.

### Track 67

**Examiner:** Good morning. Can I have your mark sheets, please?
**Eleni and Victoria:** Of course. Here you are.
**Examiner:** I'm Janine Rodgers and this is Michelle Johns. She is just going to listen to us. Now, what's your name?
**Victoria:** My name's Victoria.
**Examiner:** Thank you. And what's your name?
**Eleni:** Eleni.
**Examiner:** Thank you. Eleni, where do you live?
**Eleni:** I live in Athens, which is the capital of Greece.
**Examiner:** Do you work or are you a student?
**Eleni:** I'm a student.
**Examiner:** What do you study?
**Eleni:** I'm doing a degree in engineering at the university.
**Examiner:** Thank you. And Victoria, where do you live?
**Victoria:** I live in Montpellier, which is a city in France.
**Examiner:** Do you work or are you a student?
**Victoria:** I work.
**Examiner:** What do you do?
**Victoria:** I'm a teacher in a primary school. My pupils are nine and ten years old.
**Examiner:** Thank you. Victoria, how often do you use the internet?
**Victoria:** I'm sorry, I didn't catch that. Could you say that again, please?
**Examiner:** Do you often use the internet?
**Victoria:** The internet? I use it every day. When I wake up, I check Facebook on my phone to see what my friends have been doing. I often go on the internet to look for information. I use it to buy bus tickets and tickets for the cinema or concerts. I also use the internet to listen to music and to watch films. I couldn't live without it.
**Examiner:** Thank you. Eleni, tell us about a good friend.
**Eleni:** Her name is Maria. She's tall. Her hair is long and straight. She is very nice. I like her.
**Examiner:** Thank you. Now I'd like each of you …

## Grammar

**Indirect questions**

**1**
Students' own answers.

**2**
(Suggested answers)
1 He uses Instagram and Snapchat. He uses Instagram to see what people are doing and for following famous people. He uses Snapchat to send photos to friends.
2 He talks about using a strong password for his social media accounts.

### Track 68

**Journalist:** Good afternoon. I'm a journalist for Channel Thirteen and we're doing some research into communication for a TV programme. I was wondering if I could ask you some questions about how you use social media.
**Bradley:** Sure. What would you like to know?
**Journalist:** Firstly, could you tell me what your name is, please?
**Bradley:** Yes, it's Bradley Jones.
**Journalist:** Thanks, Bradley. I'd like to know how many different kinds of social media you use.
**Bradley:** I don't use as many as most of my friends, or my sister. I suppose I mainly use Instagram and Snapchat.
**Journalist:** Really? Could I ask you what you use each one for?
**Bradley:** Yes, I use Instagram to see what people are up to. It's also great for following famous people. Snapchat is good when you're out somewhere and you want to send a photo to your friends.
**Journalist:** And now for the last question. We're also interested in whether people are worried about others getting into their social media accounts. Do you have any idea if your accounts are safe?
**Bradley:** I think so. I always try to make sure that I use a strong password and I try to use a different password for each account, but I know this is a big problem.
**Journalist:** Thanks for your answers, Bradley. They're all very useful for our research.

**3**
2 your name is   3 you use   4 what you use   5 your accounts are

**4**
1 yes   2 no   3 yes   4 yes   5 no

**5**
As a general rule, in questions with question words, the voice goes down and with yes/no questions, the voice goes up.

### Track 69
1 Could I ask you some questions?
2 What's your name, please?
3 How many different kinds of social media do you use?
4 What do you use each one for?
5 Are your social media accounts safe?

**6**
Generally, where the indirect question is a statement (*I was wondering …*), the voice stays fairly flat and goes down slightly at the end.

### Track 70
1 I was wondering if I could ask you some questions.
2 Could you tell me what your name is, please?
3 I'd like to know how many different kinds of social media you use.
4 Could I ask you what you use each one for?
5 Do you have any idea if your accounts are safe?

**7&8**
Students' own answers.

## Writing Part 2

**1**
Students' own answers.

**2**
1 a story   2 your English teacher

**3**
(Suggested answer)
1 Task 2
2 Because the phone belonged to the teacher and she took her bag with her when she left the classroom.

**4**
They are all true.

**5**
Students' own answers.

## 1 Vocabulary and grammar review

**1**
2 was built   3 seems   4 is rising   5 are washing   6 reaches   7 was completely flooded   8 disappeared   9 is done   10 know   11 were saved   12 was put up

**2**
2 more quickly   3 (the) best   4 more frequently   5 harder   6 (the) worst   7 more heavily   8 more carefully

**3**
2 invitation   3 celebration   4 completion   5 improvement   6 examinations   7 development   8 disappointment

**4**
**Across:** 1 team   6 landscape   7 bee   8 penguin
**Down:** 2 exploration   3 mountain   4 movement   5 discussion   7 bear

## 12 Vocabulary and grammar review

**1**
2 said   3 asked   4 telling   5 ask/asked   6 ask for   7 tell   8 talking   9 speak   10 talked

**2**
2 inexpensive   3 unfair   4 unhealthy   5 impatient   6 impolite

**3**
2 A friend asked me what ~~was my dog~~ **my dog was** called.
3 Marta asked me ~~why didn't I go~~ **why I hadn't gone / didn't go** to the party.
4 My sister asked me ~~why was I~~ **why I was** crying.
5 Nicky asked me what ~~was I going~~ **I was going** to do.
6 Danny asked me what new sport ~~should he~~ **he should** take up.
7 I imagine you are wondering ~~when am I~~ **when I am** going to visit.

**4**
2 they were looking forward
3 she had just bought
4 she was going to invite
5 they had won
6 she was sure they would have

**5**
2 if/whether   3 told   4 the   5 was   6 to

# Grammar reference answer key

## Unit 1

**Prepositions of time**
1
1 on  2 in  3 at  4 on  5 in  6 on

**Frequency adverbs**
1
1 I go to the gym twice a week.
2 I hardly ever spend more than an hour there.
3 I sometimes run for half an hour.
4 I usually listen to music while I'm running.
5 When I get home, I'm always exhausted.
6 I go out with my friends every Friday.

**Present simple and present continuous**
1
1 are taking up  2 helps  3 use up  4 walk  5 go  6 I'm training
7 I'm spending

**State verbs**
1
1 do (you) weigh; prefer  2 helps  3 smell  4 is having  5 costs; think
6 owns; wants

**Countable and uncountable nouns**
1
As well as giving us energy, sugar in our diet makes our food taste better. Sometimes we add sugar to our breakfast cereals. Sugar is also used in biscuits, ice cream, chocolate and many other things we eat. It is also in fruit and vegetables and even in a glass of milk.
2
1 We haven't got **much** time.
2 I drink a **little** water when I wake up.
3 There are **a lot of** / **lots of** things we need to talk about.
4 Can you help? I need some **information** about train times.
5 How **many** friends do you have online?
6 We have a lot of **furniture** in our house.

**Prepositions of place**
1
1 on, in  2 at  3 in, on  4 at

## Unit 2

**Past simple and past continuous**
1
1 was watching  2 often phoned  3 realised
4 was shining; were singing  5 won
2
1 was tidying; found  2 was leaving; realised
3 was watching; was cooking  4 heard; stopped; were doing; walked
5 crashed; was updating

**used to**
1
1 I didn't use to like hot weather (but I do now).
2 My brother used to play football (until he broke his leg).
3 I used to have blond hair / My hair used to be blond (but now it's brown).
4 Did you use to go on holiday with your friends (when you were a child)?
5 When I was younger, I didn't use to get up late.

**So (do) I and Nor/Neither (do) I**
1
1 So did I.  2 Nor/Neither did I.  3 So do I.  4 Nor/Neither do I.
5 So have I. / So do I.

## Unit 3

**Verbs followed by to or -ing**
1
1 going  2 to have  3 going  4 to go  5 doing  6 living  7 to have
8 spending

2
1 ✓  2 ✓
3 ✗ (In A, Ben stopped what he was doing in order to phone. In B, Ben no longer phones his parents.)
4 ✓  5 ✓
6 ✗ (In A, the next thing they told us about was their holiday. In B, they didn't stop telling us about their holiday.)

**Phrasal verbs**
1
1 What should you do if your TV <u>breaks down</u>? c
2 Which of your parents do you <u>take after</u>? d
3 Do you like to <u>dress up</u> when you go to a party? a
4 Who do you really <u>look up to</u>? e
5 Do you ever have to <u>look after</u> anyone? f
6 What do you think about people who <u>show off</u>? b
2
1 I <u>get on (well) with</u> everyone in my family.
2 I've <u>signed up for</u> an English course.
3 I'm <u>looking forward to</u> seeing my friend again.
4 My father has <u>given up</u> eating sugar.
5 My brother's just <u>taken up</u> basketball.

## Unit 4

**Comparative and superlative adjectives**
1
1 the thinnest  2 nicer  3 lazy  4 more comfortable  5 the best
6 worse  7 far
2
1 the wettest  2 the most beautiful  3 heavier  4 better  5 worse
6 further/farther
3
1 Josh isn't as tall as Roman.
2 My new phone is/was much more expensive than my old phone.
3 Fruit is a lot healthier than burgers.
4 Spain is a bit smaller than France.
5 The new shopping centre is far nicer than the old one.

**Gradable and non-gradable adjectives**
1
1 f  2 g  3 e  4 c  5 b  6 a  7 d
2
1 delighted; surprised  2 cold  3 exhausted  4 bad; tired
5 excellent  6 huge

## Unit 5

**Modal verbs: can, could, might and may (ability and possibility)**
1
1 can't  2 could  3 may/might/could  4 might/may/could  5 can
6 couldn't
2
1 d may  2 c can  3 a may  4 e could  5 b can

**Modal verbs: should, shouldn't, must, mustn't, have to, don't have to (obligation and prohibition)**
1
1 mustn't/can't  2 can/must; can't  3 can  4 can't  5 mustn't/can't
2
1 didn't have to  2 could  3 had to  4 had to  5 could  6 couldn't

**Adjectives with -ed and -ing endings**
1
1 interesting; interested  2 relaxed; relaxing  3 annoying; annoyed
4 excited; exciting

## Unit 6

**Present perfect**
1
1 just  2 already  3 already  4 yet  5 yet
2
1 for  2 since  3 since  4 for  5 since

190

**3**
A: Have you heard? My oldest sister's getting married.
B: Who to?
A: A guy called Elliot.
B: Really! How long ~~did she know~~ **has she known** him?
A: Only six months. Apparently ~~they've met~~ **they met** at work.
B: Have you met Elliot ~~already~~ **yet**?
A: No, not yet, but my sister's told me a lot about him.
B: When ~~have you seen~~ **did you see** her?
A: ~~I've seen~~ **I saw** her last week. She drove me to work one day.
**4**
1 went; have just woken up   2 arrived; haven't seen her yet
3 have already seen; saw   4 have ever bought; cost; have never spent
5 Have you ever done; have never done
6 did you go; went; have never visited

## Unit 7

**Adverbs of degree**
**1**
1 I was really cold because I had forgotten my coat.
2 Mia is fairly sure she will pass her exam.
3 The traffic is moving very slowly.
4 Be extremely careful when you cross busy roads.
5 That was a rather difficult question.
**2**
1 too ill   2 too good   3 big enough   4 enough hours
5 enough money; rich enough

**Future forms**
**1**
1 We're going to see   2 I'll be   3 I'm going to go   4 leaves   5 I'll go

**Prepositions of movement**
**1**
1 on   2 by; by   3 on/onto   4 out of   5 by   6 into

## Unit 8

**Conditional sentences**
**1**
1 d   2 g   3 a   4 h   5 c   6 b   7 e   8 f
**2**
2 she spoke English, she could study in Canada.
3 I had enough free time, I'd learn to play a musical instrument.
4 I had enough money, I'd buy a laptop.

**Conjunctions:** *when, if, unless* + present, future
**3**
1 Unless   2 unless   3 If   4 if   5 unless   6 If/When   7 If   8 when

## Unit 9

**Defining and non-defining relative clauses with** *which, that, who, whose, when, where*
**1**
1 whose   2 that/which   3 who   4 that/which   5 that/which
6 where   7 that/which   8 when
**2**
4, 7
**3**
1 The music which Gisela was playing last night was by Mozart.
2 The violin that Gisela was playing in the concert was not hers.
3 James, whose violin Gisela borrowed, is also a music teacher.
4 We've just listened to Gisela's latest recording, which is number 1 in the classical charts.
5 Gisela's mother, who was in the audience tonight, is very proud of her.
6 Tomorrow, Gisela is going back to Vienna, where she plays in an orchestra.

**Past perfect**
**1**
1 had rained; had stopped; was   2 had planned; had to
3 had been; started   4 could not / couldn't; had made   5 went; had seen

## Unit 10

**Commands and instructions**
**1**
1 Do not eat; drink   2 Turn   3 Do not use   4 Be

**Have something done**
**1**
1 Have you had your hair cut?   2 I might have my bedroom painted blue.
3 Has Michael had his bike fixed yet?
4 I get my teeth polished every six months.
5 You should have your computer checked for viruses.
**2**
1 He has had his hair cut and his beard shaved off.
2 She had her car washed yesterday.
3 He's had his shoes cleaned.
4 They're having their house painted.
5 He had his tooth taken out this morning.
6 She'll have her eyes tested tomorrow.

## Unit 11

**The passive: present simple and past simple**
**1**
1 was played; was watched
2 are taken; are driven
3 was written; were predicted
**2**
1 Our cat is seen twice a year by a vet.
2 The roads were closed (by the police) because of the storm.
3 The book was written by a famous author.
4 Cricket is played in Australia.
5 I was taught how to sing by my father.

**Comparative and superlative adverbs**
**1**
1 more clearly   2 the best   3 faster   4 harder
5 more seriously; better   6 the quickest
**2**
1 dances more beautifully   2 writes the best of all
3 the most patiently   4 work harder   5 earlier than you did last night
6 runs faster than me

## Unit 12

**Reported speech and commands**
**1**
2 'I'm sorry but I can't lend you any more money.'
3 'I still feel ill.'   4 'I'm older than you.'
5 'We'll come and see you later.'   6 'I left yesterday.'
7 'Stop worrying!'
**2**
1 He said (that) he was leaving university at the end of the following year.
2 She said (that) she'd got a surprise for me.
3 She told him to shut the door.
4 They said (that) they'd all passed their English exam.
5 He said (that) it was his birthday the next day.
6 She said (that) I was the only person she knew who liked/likes classical music.
7 He told Max not to drink any more coffee.
8 They said (that) they'd gone to / been to Morocco for their holiday the previous year / the year before.

**Reported questions**
**1**
2 'Are you enjoying your new course?'
3 'Has anyone / Have you found my keys?'
4 'What did you do yesterday?'
5 'Can you come to my party this evening / tonight?'
6 'Can you tell us where the station is?' / 'Where's the station?'
7 'Who's your favourite actor?'
8 'Did you try to phone me?' / 'Have you tried to phone me?'

Answer key

**2**
1 My colleague asked (me) why I was wearing my best clothes.
2 My colleague asked (me) where I was going.
3 My colleague asked (me) what I was going to do there.
4 My boss asked (me) if/whether I was going with anyone/someone.
5 My colleague asked (me) if/whether he knew who I was going with.
6 My boss asked (me) what time I'd be back.
7 My colleague asked (me) how I would get back.
8 My boss asked (me) what I would do if I missed the last train.

**Indirect questions**
**1**
1 where you live?
2 if you are doing anything at the weekend.
3 what they did last weekend?
4 what you thought of the film.
5 if/whether my seat number is on this ticket?

# Phrasal verb builder answer key

**Relationships**
**1**
1 bring up   2 get on with   3 get together   4 go out with
5 look after   6 split up with
**2**
1 get together   2 get on   3 brought up   4 look after   5 split up
**3**
Students' own answers.

**Travel**
**1**
1 break down   2 check in   3 get back   4 set off   5 take off   6 turn up
**2**
1 set off   2 broke down; turned up   3 checked in   4 took off   5 got back
**3**
Students' own answers.

**Communication**
**1**
1 call someone back   2 fill in something   3 hang up
4 ring up someone   5 switch something off
**2**
1 switched it off   2 rang up   3 hung up   4 called back   5 fill in
**3**
Students' own answers.

**Daily routines**
**1**
1 get up   2 pick someone up   3 put something on   4 tidy up
5 wake someone up
**2**
1 get up   2 picks me up   3 wake up   4 put on   5 tidies up
**3**
Students' own answers.

# Writing bank answer key

**Making your writing more interesting**
**1**
b 7   c 1   d 5   e 2   f 4   g 6   h 8
**2**

| adjectives | adverbs | linking words | time expressions |
|---|---|---|---|
| beautiful | completely | and | later that day |
| delicious | easily | because | the next day |
| modern | loudly | but | this morning |
| wonderful | quickly | so | yesterday |

**3 (other possible answers in brackets)**
1 suddenly (finally)   2 but
3 early the next morning (the next day; later that day)
4 large (delicious; small)   5 really (very; extremely)
**4**
2 I was very tired, so I went straight to bed.
3 We all went to the party, and everyone had a great time.
4 Paul wanted to come with us, but he couldn't.
5 We all laughed because it was so funny.

## Writing Part 1: An email

**1**
You have to respond to the news, say which month you can go, say which sport you would like to see, and suggest something you should buy as a souvenir.
**2**
1 d R   2 a S   3 b O   4 c P
**3**
1 **I'm** afraid I won't be able to come to your party.
2 Guess **where** I'm going next week?
3 I'm sorry, **but** Dan won't be here when you visit.
4 You'll be pleased **to** hear that I've now finished all my exams!
**4**
1 so   2 also   3 but   4 because   5 and
**5**
You should respond to the idea of a barbecue, say which day you'd like to come, suggest some ideas for food and explain what sport would be best.
**6**
Students' own answers.

**7 (Sample answer)**
Hi Logan,
I think a barbecue sounds like a great idea, and I'd love to come! It will be lovely, especially if the weather's going to be warm and sunny.
Why don't we have some salads and potatoes to go with the meat? Also, make sure you remember that some people in our class are vegetarians, so you'll need some special dishes for them.
I agree that sports are fun after a barbecue. We could play badminton. It's a very easy sport, so everyone can play.
See you on Saturday!
Eva
**8**
Students' own answers.

## Writing Part 2: An article

**1**
The article is about your favourite city. You should say what the city is, why you like it and what makes it so special. You should then explain which city you would love to travel to in the future.
**2**
1 There are many benefits to keeping fit.
2 The internet has changed people's lives in many ways.
3 Teaching is a very difficult job.

### 3

| clothes | films | food | countryside | weather |
|---|---|---|---|---|
| old-fashioned | amusing | delicious | peaceful | freezing |
| tight | frightening | tasty | quiet | stormy |
| *fashionable* | *exciting* | *spicy* | *beautiful* | *hot* |
| *expensive* | *boring* | *salty* | *wild* | *wet* |
| | *horror* | *sweet* | *empty* | *cool* |

### 4
The article is about your perfect job. You should say what makes a job perfect for you. Then give your opinion about how important it is to earn a lot of money in your job.

### 5
Students' own answers.

**6 Sample answer**
For me, an architect is the perfect job because it is interesting, creative and very challenging.
For an architect, every day is different. You might design a modern house, then a new classroom for a school, then change an old factory into flats. So this job is never boring, because every building you work on is different. I think it would also be very satisfying to create beautiful buildings for people to live or work in.
I would say it is important to earn enough money so you don't have to worry about it. But if you enjoy your job, you don't have to be rich to be happy.

### 7
Students' own answers.

## Writing Part 2: A story

### 1
2 is the best because it talks about what was in the letter, and suggests that something is going to happen in the story.

### 2
1 called   2 was waiting   3 had passed / 'd passed
4 was walking   5 had forgotten / 'd forgotten   6 closed

### 3
1 First   2 Then   3 Next   4 An hour later   5 Finally

### 4
1 curly   2 smart   3 spicy   4 entertaining   5 messy   6 disappointed

### 5
Students' own answers.

**6 Sample answer**
A day at the zoo.
The day at the zoo began quite well. I was there with some friends, and the sun was shining.
First, we saw some baby elephants. Then we watched some very funny penguins. By midday, we were getting hungry, so we decided to go for lunch. As we were walking towards the café, we suddenly heard people shouting. A tiger had escaped! We immediately ran to the cafe and shut the door behind us. It was quite scary, but fortunately the tiger was caught quickly and no one was hurt.
Finally, the café offered a free meal to everyone, so the day ended very well.

### 7
Students' own answers.

# Speaking bank answer key and audioscripts

## Speaking Part 1

### 1
Yes, she does.

**Track 71**
**Examiner:** What's your name?
**Maria:** My name's Maria.
**Examiner:** What's your surname?
**Maria:** It's Moretti.
**Examiner:** Where do you come from?
**Maria:** I come from Rome, in Italy.
**Examiner:** Do you work, or are you a student?
**Maria:** I'm a student.

### 2

**Track 72**
**Examiner:** What did you do yesterday evening?
**Maria:** Yesterday evening I went to the cinema with some friends. I often watch films with my friends because we all enjoy the same kinds of films.
**Examiner:** Do you think that English will be useful to you in the future?
**Maria:** Yes, I think it will be very useful. I want to work for an international company, so I hope I'll travel to different countries with my job, and I'm sure I will need English.
**Examiner:** Tell us about a place you would like to visit in the future.
**Maria:** I'd love to go to New York one day because it looks such an exciting city. Actually, my uncle lives there, so I hope I can go and visit him soon.
**Examiner:** Can you describe your house or flat?
**Maria:** My flat is quite small, because I just share it with one friend. The kitchen is very small, but the living room is quite big. Also, it's got a balcony, and I really like sitting there in the evening.
**Examiner:** What do you enjoy doing in your free time?
**Maria:** Well, I'm quite into sport, so I do quite a lot of sport in my free time. For example, I sometimes go running in the evenings and I often play tennis at the weekend. I also like spending time with friends. My friends are very important to me.

### 3
1 often   2 and   3 because   4 Actually   5 but   6 Also   7 so   8 For example

### 4

| present simple | past simple | *be going to* |
|---|---|---|
| always | last night | next weekend |
| sometimes | last weekend | tomorrow |
| usually | when I was younger | tonight |

### 5
1 b + i   2 d + h   3 a + f   4 e + j   5 c + g

### 6
1 because   2 for example   3 which   4 but   5 Unfortunately

**Track 73**
**Examiner:** Tell us about your English teacher.
**Pablo:** My English teacher is called Mr Adams, and he's from Manchester. He's really funny, and I like him because he always makes our lessons interesting. I think he's a really good teacher.
**Examiner:** Would you like to live in a different country?
**Pablo:** I'd like to visit different countries, for example the United States or maybe Australia, to get some experience of what life is like there. But I wouldn't like to for long, because I'd miss my family and friends at home.

Answer key

**Examiner:** Can you tell us about your home town?
**Pablo:** My home town is Barcelona, in the north-east of Spain. It's a big city, and there are lots of beautiful buildings which are very famous. I like it because it's very friendly, and there are lots of cafés where you can meet your friends. Also, it's on the coast, so you can go to the beach in the summer.
**Examiner:** How do you usually travel to university or work?
**Pablo:** I usually catch the bus to work. It takes about half an hour for me to get there. I'd prefer to walk, but it's too far for me to walk every day.
**Examiner:** What did you do last weekend?
**Pablo:** On Saturday I played football for my team. We usually have a match every Saturday. Unfortunately, we didn't win last week. Then on Sunday I met my friends, and we went to the beach because it was very hot.

## Speaking Part 2

**1**
They might be in a car park. They are probably friends.

### Track 74
**Pablo:** The picture shows two teenagers playing basketball outdoors. I think they might be in a car park or something like that. It isn't a very attractive place, because there are no flowers, and there isn't any grass. It's a cloudy day, and it doesn't look very warm because one of the boys is wearing long sleeves. The two boys are at the front of the photo, in the middle, and at the back we can see a basketball net, and some buildings. They look like garages or sheds, something like that. On the left, you can see some houses in the background. The boys aren't actually playing a game, but they're practising. One of the boys is wearing a stripy top, with a hood, and he's holding the ball above his head. He seems to be aiming for the net, which is quite a long way away. The other boy, who's short and has dark hair, is running forwards. I think maybe he's going to catch the ball. I guess the two boys are probably friends because they don't look like brothers.

**2**
1 at the front   2 right   3 left   4 behind   5 In the background
**3**
1 are travelling   2 're smiling   3 is showing   4 is looking; is thinking
5 standing; is talking

### Track 75
**Pablo:** The picture shows some people who are travelling by bus. There are two women at the front of the picture, on the left. They're smiling, and one woman is showing the other one something on her phone. On the right, there's an older man. He's looking forwards. I'm not sure what he's looking at, but maybe he's thinking about where to get off the bus. In the background, at the back of the bus, there's a man. He's standing up and I think he's talking to another passenger.

**4**
1 probably   2 might   3 looks   4 seem   5 guess

**5**

### Track 76
**Maria:** The photo shows two people sitting in a living room in a house, a teenager and an older man. I think they're probably father and son. The teenager, who's on the right, is wearing a pullover and jeans, and the older man is wearing a blue shirt and jeans. He's got grey hair. The sitting room looks quite modern, and the sofa looks very comfortable. In the background, on the left, you can see some photos on a table. On the right, you can see some books. They might be watching TV because you can see that they're looking at something, and there is a remote control, or something like that, on the sofa on the right. They're eating something from a box, some kind of takeaway. It looks like pizza. They seem to be quite relaxed. I guess they're probably having a relaxing evening at home.

**6**
Students' own answers.

## Speaking Part 3

**1**
Yes, they do. They agree on two cinema tickets.
**2**
1 think   2 sure   3 agree   4 opinion   5 idea   6 so   7 OK   8 go

### Track 77
**Maria:** So, shall we start with the book? What do you think about that idea?
**Pablo:** I'm not sure. Some people enjoy reading, but a lot of people don't like it. And it's difficult to choose a book for someone else.
**Maria:** I agree with you. And I don't think flowers are a good idea because they're a bit boring, in my opinion.
**Pablo:** That's true. In my opinion, people buy flowers if they can't think of any other ideas. Would a T-shirt be a good idea? Most people wear T-shirts.
**Maria:** Well, I don't really like it when people buy me clothes, because I prefer to choose them myself.
**Pablo:** OK, so not a T-shirt. Would a concert ticket be a good idea?
**Maria:** Yes, I think that's a great idea. Everyone loves listening to live music.
**Pablo:** No, I disagree. There's only one ticket, and I don't think it would be fun to go to a concert on your own.
**Maria:** Yes, you're right. But there are two cinema tickets, so maybe they might be a better choice.
**Pablo:** Yes, I agree they would be a good choice. So, what else is there? I think a mug is boring, and chocolates seem quite a cheap present. What do you think?
**Maria:** Yes, I agree. And I'm sure she'd love to get a necklace, so that's a possibility.
**Pablo:** OK. So, it's time to decide. What do you think?
**Maria:** Well, I would say either the cinema tickets or the necklace. Do you agree?
**Pablo:** Yes, but the necklace might be too expensive, so maybe we should choose the cinema tickets. Are you OK with that?
**Maria:** Yes, good idea. We'll go for that one, then.

**3**
1 d   2 f   3 a   4 b   5 c   6 e
**4**

### Track 78
**Pablo:** So, shall we talk about the barbecue first? I think it's a good idea. A barbecue is relaxing, and everyone can enjoy it. What do you think?
**Maria:** Yes, I agree with you. The only problem is that someone has to organise everything, like buying the food and cooking it, so it's quite a lot of work. In my opinion, eating in a restaurant would be better, because no one would have to cook.
**Pablo:** Yes, that's a good point. But a meal in a restaurant might be too expensive for some people. What do you think about going to watch a football match?
**Maria:** Well, it would be perfect for me, because I'm a football fan, but I don't think it's a good idea for a class celebration, because not everyone likes football.
**Pablo:** That's true. So, would the beach be a good idea? Everyone likes going to the beach. Do you agree?
**Maria:** I'm not sure. What if the weather's bad?
**Pablo:** Yes, you're right. The beach is great if the weather's good, but it's really boring if it's raining. So, what else is there? I don't think hiking is a good idea, because some people might not be fit enough to enjoy it.
**Maria:** Yes, I agree. What about going to a theme park? I'm sure people would enjoy that.
**Pablo:** Yes, that's a good idea. There are different rides, too, so not everyone has to go on the really scary ones. It's definitely more fun than a boat trip. That would be really boring, in my opinion.
**Maria:** I agree, because on a boat you're just sitting there for a few hours, but I prefer to be active.
**Pablo:** What about the zoo? That could be fun. And there are things to do indoors if it's wet.

**Maria:** Yes, that's true. And everyone loves animals.
**Pablo:** So, it's time to decide. I would choose the theme park or the zoo because I think everyone would enjoy them.
**Maria:** Yes. I think the theme park would be more fun, so I would choose that.
**Pablo:** OK. We'll go for that one, then.

## Speaking Part 4

**1**
They give reasons, ask for each other's opinions, and use an expression to allow time to think about the answer.

### Track 79
**Examiner:** Who do you most enjoy buying presents for?
**Maria:** Let me see. I would say my cousins. One is 14 years old, and the other is 12. I love buying presents for them because there are so many fun things that you can choose for children, like toys or games. What do you think?
**Pablo:** Yes, I agree with you, and it's also fun buying presents for children because they're always so excited when they open them. I've got a cousin who's ten, and I really enjoy buying things for him. He's really into football so it's easy to find things he likes. It's great.
**Examiner:** Which people in your family are the most difficult to choose presents for?
**Pablo:** That's an interesting question. My dad is definitely the most difficult to choose presents for. He never seems to want anything, and he doesn't have any hobbies, so I usually end up buying him something really boring, like socks. Do you agree that it's difficult to buy things for your parents?
**Maria:** Yes, I completely agree. It's much easier to buy things for people your own age, because you know what they like and what they're interested in.
**Examiner:** Do you like receiving money instead of presents?
**Maria:** Hmm, that's a difficult question. It's sometimes nice to receive money, because then you can buy something you really want, or you can save up to buy something bigger, like a new tablet. What do you think?
**Pablo:** Hmm, I'm not sure about that. When it's my birthday, I usually get money from three or four relatives, and it's good because I can use the money to buy something more expensive for myself. But in my opinion it's a bit boring if you don't get any presents on your birthday, just money. Do you agree?
**Maria:** Yes, I do. I love getting presents, but I think when it's relatives who don't know you very well it's better to get money, because sometimes they can give you things you don't really want.
**Pablo:** That's true. I prefer to get money from people who don't know me very well, but it's nice to get presents from people who know what I like.

**2**
1 buying   2 is sometimes   3 usually get   4 to get   5 getting

**3**
1 Do you agree?   2 That's true.   3 What do you think?
4 That's an interesting question.

**4**
Students' own answers

**5**

### Track 80
**Examiner:** Would you like to have more social events with your English class?
**Pablo:** Yes, I think that more social events would be great, because it would be an opportunity to get to know other students in the class better. I would like some trips to the cinema, or maybe visits to other towns and cities. What do you think?
**Maria:** Yes, I agree. I think it would be fun to have more social events, and in my opinion it would also help us to study, because it's easier to study when you're with people that you know, because you're more relaxed. I agree with you that trips to the cinema would be fun, because then we could talk about the films together.
**Examiner:** Do you think watching sports events can be more fun than taking part?
**Maria:** I'm not sure about that. I love sport, and in my opinion it's always more fun to take part than to watch. When you play a game like tennis or football, for example, you really want to win, so it's very exciting and it encourages you to make an effort and do your best. Do you agree?
**Pablo:** Yes, I do. I'm really into sport, too, and I agree that it's exciting when you play a match and you really want to win. But when I watch my favourite football team I also want them to win, so that's exciting too. I also love watching really good players, who are much better than me!
**Maria:** Yes, that's true. It's exciting to watch good players, but I would still prefer to take part.
**Examiner:** Do you prefer cooking a meal for friends or eating out in a restaurant?
**Pablo:** I think it depends. I enjoy cooking, and I often cook meals for a few friends. But if I want to have a big meal with a lot of friends, I prefer to go to a restaurant. What do you think?
**Maria:** Yes, I think you're right. It would be very stressful to cook a meal for 15 or 20 people. But cooking for a few friends is fun, and it's nice because you're at home and you're relaxed.
**Pablo:** Yes, I agree with you. The only problem is that you have to do the washing up.
**Maria:** That's true. I think it's only fun if you have a dishwasher!

Answer key 195

## Acknowledgements

The authors would like to thank Alison Bewsher, Helen Kuffel and Jane Coates personally for all their input, efficiency and good humour.

Emma would like to thank her colleagues and her students at Lacunza – IH San Sebastian for trialling some of the materials. She would also like to thank her family for their patience, support and understanding.

Peter would like to give special thanks to Tek for her patience, support and encouragement.

The authors and publishers would like to thank the following contributors:

Grammar reference: Simon Haines
Writing and Speaking banks: Sheila Dignen

The authors and publishers are grateful to the following for reviewing the material during the writing process:

Spain: Margaret Brown, Kerry Davis, Mario Marcos; Italy: Laura Gerrard; Mexico: Ruben Hernandez.

**The authors and publishers acknowledge the following sources of copyright material and are grateful for the permissions granted. While every effort has been made, it has not always been possible to identify the sources of all the material used, or to trace all copyright holders. If any omissions are brought to our notice, we will be happy to include the appropriate acknowledgements on reprinting and in the next update to the digital edition, as applicable.**

Key: U = Unit, GR = Grammar reference, PVB = Phrasal verb builder, SB = Speaking bank

### Text

**U2:** The Telegraph for the adapted text from 'No-exam university courses fuel rise in first class degrees' by Julie Henry, The Telegraph, 25.11.2012. Copyright © 2012 Telegraph Media Group Limited. Reproduced with permission.

### Photography

The following images are sourced from Getty Images.

**U1:** Mark Segal/DigitalVision; Richard Leo Johnson/Alloy/Getty Images Plus; aooss5/iStock/Getty Images Plus; YinYang/iStock/Getty Images Plus; Ezra Bailey/Taxi; Jose Luis Pelaez Inc/Blend Images; AntonioGuillem/iStock/Getty Images Plus; Westend61; Andersen Ross/Blend Image; duncan1890/DigitalVision Vectors; Nora Carol Photography/Moment; Mika Mika/Moment; the_burtons/Moment; Janos Somodi/Moment; Kilian O'Sullivan/Corbis Documentary; wmaster890/iStock/Getty Images Plus; ViewStock; Gary John Norman/Iconica; Tuul & Bruno Morandi/Photolibrary; monkeybusinessimages/iStock/Getty Images Plus; FG Trade/E+; SensorSpot/E+; Kiyoshi Hijiki/Moment; Erik Rank/The Image Bank; BLUEXHAND/iStock/Getty Images Plus; Kroeger/Gross/StockFood Creative; gerenme/E+; gerenme/iStock/Getty Images Plus; Grassetto/iStock/Getty Images Plus; fatihhoca/E+; shutswis/iStock/Getty Images Plus; dmitriymoroz/iStock/Getty Images Plus; talevr/iStock/Getty Images Plus; Courtney Hale/E+; **U2:** Hinterhaus Productions/Taxi; Jamie Grill/The Image Bank; brinkstock/iStock/Getty Images Plus; DragonImages/iStock/Getty Images Plus; Peter Muller/Cultura; Mike Brinson/The Image Bank; Caiaimage/Paul Bradbury; John Rowley/Stockbyte; Pawel Toczynski/Photolibrary; fitopardo.com/Moment Open; picturegarden/Taxi; Utamaru Kido/Moment; shomos uddin/Moment; Yuri_Arcurs/E+; **U3:** Caiaimage/Paul Bradbury/OJO+; Paul Bradbury/Caiaimage; David De Lossy/Photodisc; JGI/Tom Grill/Blend Images; Newton Daly/DigitalVision; pmcdonald/iStock/Getty Images Plus; Photocellar/iStock/Getty Images Plus; Chris Cross/Caiaimage; Westend61; Tyler D. Rickenbach/Aurora Photos; Caiaimage/Paul Bradbury; Olivia Bell Photography/Moment; Andersen Ross/Blend Images; Ronnie Kaufman/Photodisc; Marc Romanelli/Blend Images; Jacobs Stock Photography Ltd/DigitalVision; Hero Images; GibsonPictures/E+; enjoynz/DigitalVision Vectors; **U4:** Lost Horizon Images/Cultura; Michael DeYoung/Blend Images; TonyV3112/iStock Editorial/Getty Images Plus; Lingbeek/iStock/Getty Images Plus; Anthony Ong/DigitalVision; Stephen Frink/Corbis; webguzs/iStock/Getty Images Plus; joebelanger/iStock/Getty Images Plus; Marco_Piunti/iStock/Getty Images Plus; Jose A. Bernat Bacete/Moment; Nigel Killeen/Moment; Zhang Peng/LightRocket; Manuel Blondeau/Corbis Sport; Merten Snijders/Lonely Planet Images; Chris Jackson/Getty Images News; Sylvain Sonnet/Photographer's Choice; gaspr13/iStock/Getty Images Plus; Massimo Borchi/Atlantide Phototravel/The Image Bank; **U5:** Paul Bradbury/OJO Images; deimagine/E+; Ben-Schonewille/iStock/Getty Images Plus; Kristen Strangwick/EyeEm; a-wrangler/iStock/Getty Images Plus; Sergio Mendoza Hochmann/Moment; XiXinXing; Martin Bernetti/AFP; Arto Hakola/Moment Open; Fred Paul/Photographer's Choice; Ivan-balvan/iStock/Getty Images Plus; Lee Woodgate/Ikon Images; **U6:** Paul Faith/AFP; svetikd/E+; Ron Crabtree/DigitalVision; Jack Hollingsworth/Blend Images; Jay Reilly/UpperCut Images; Plume Creative/DigitalVision; Emma Kim/Cultura; MichaelDeLeon/E+; BJI; Alex Tihonovs/EyeEm; Yuri_Arcurs/DigitalVision; Rudy Sulgan/Corbis Documentary; Francesco Castaldo/Mondadori Portfolio; Andre Vogelaere/Moment; Neil Emmerson/robertharding; David Shvartsman/Moment; **U7:** Kaori Ando/Image Source; Australian Land, City, People Scape Photographer/Moment; Frank and Helena/Cultura; GregorBister/E+; Fabrizio Di Nucci/NurPhoto; Don Farrall/DigitalVision; Issaurinko/iStock/Getty Images Plus; kali9/E+; Guerilla; Ernst Wrba/Picture Press; Guerilla; DavorLovincic; Maskot; VisitBritain/Liz Gander; **U8:** Print Collector/Hulton Archive; Paul Popper/Popperfoto; Shaun Botterill/Getty Images Sport; Christopher Polk/AMA2013/Getty Images Entertainment; R.Tsubin/Moment; Paul Morigi/WireImage; Fabrice Lerouge/ONOKY; pressureUA/iStock Editorial/Getty Images Plus; Rubberball/Alan Bailey/Brand X Pictures; Boogich/iStock/Getty Images Plus; UFO RF; Juanmonino/E+; Emya Photography/Moment; **U9:** AP Dube/Hindustan Times; mediaphotos/iStock/Getty Images Plus; Image Source; funky-data/iStock ; SolStock/E+; Hybrid Images/Cultura; strickke/iStock/Getty Images Plus; jashlock/E+; Kelvin Murray/Taxi; Tracey Lee/Blend Images; Aidon/Photodisc; PhotoAlto/Sigrid Olsson/PhotoAlto Agency RF Collections; Vijay kumar/DigitalVision Vectors; stockstudioX/E+; AndreyPopov/iStock/Getty Images Plus; GOLFX/iStock/Getty

Images Plus; yulkapopkova/E+; Andrew Olney/OJO Images; Bobex-73/iStock/Getty Images Plus; Jakob Helbig/Image Source; Noel Hendrickson/DigitalVision; **U10:** Image Source; Dorling Kindersley; Maximilian Stock Ltd/Photolibrary; Davies and Starr/The Image Bank; alptraum/iStock/Getty Images Plus; Fabrice Lerouge/ONOKY; JGI/Jamie Grill/Blend Images; Dan Dalton/Caiaimage; DAJ; sylv1rob1/iStock/Getty Images Plus; Nikada/iStock/Getty Images Plus; Alexander Spatari/Moment; coldsnowstorm/E+; Cecilia Puebla/CON; Carl D. Walsh/Portland Press Herald; Eye Ubiquitous/Universal Images Group; IndiaPictures/Universal Images Group; Stephen J. Boitano/Lonely Planet Images; Jean-Pierre Lescourret/Lonely Planet Images; Westend61; Digital Vision/Photodisc; 22kay22/iStock Editorial/Getty Images Plus; Artur Widak/NurPhoto; Atlantide Phototravel/Corbis Documentary; monkeybusinessimages/iStock/Getty Images Plus; LeoPatrizi/E+; Eternity in an Instant/The Image Bank; **U11:** Mima Foto/EyeEm; luoman/E+; MariuszSzczygiel/iStock/Getty Images Plus; anouchka/iStock/Getty Images Plus; Krugloff/iStock/Getty Images Plus; Kypros/Moment; Extreme-Photographer/iStock/Getty Images Plus; Blade_kostas/iStock/Getty Images Plus; Socha/iStock/Getty Images Plus; tommaso79/iStock/Getty Images Plus; bgfoto/E+; Robert Pickett/Corbis NX; BernardBreton/iStock/Getty Images Plus; Panoramic Images; Joanne Hedger/Moment; Raimund Linke/Oxford Scientific; Martin Harvey/Gallo Images; Westend61; Paul Franklin/Photodisc; Steve Debenport/E+; Guy Edwardes/VisitBritain; **U12:** bokan76/iStock/Getty Images Plus; JGI/Jamie Grill/Blend Images; Peter Adams/AWL Images; Hero Images; Westend61; Aşkın Dursun Kamberoğlu/DigitalVision Vectors; Vijay kumar/DigitalVision Vectors; Hill Street Studios/Blend Images; Chris Moore - Exploring Light Photography/Moment; **GR:** spyderskidoo/E+; Robert Daly/Caiaimage; Lucidio Studio, Inc/Moment; Betsie Van Der Meer/Taxi; serts/E+; Westend61; monkeybusinessimages/iStock/Getty Images Plus; Michael Dunning/Photographer's Choice; majorosl/iStock/Getty Images Plus; Jeff Greenberg/Universal Images Group; funky-data/iStock/Getty Images Plus; onurdongel/iStock/Getty Images Plus; Pekka Sakki/AFP; Pola Damonte/Moment; Hero Images; Helena Schaeder Söderberg/Moment; Hoxton/Tom Merton; imagenavi; Inti St Clair/Blend Images; RealPeopleGroup/iStock/Getty Images Plus; Sascha Steinbach/Getty Images Entertainment; Caiaimage/Tom Merton/Riser; JaruekChairak/iStock/Getty Images Plus; Jupiterimages/PHOTOS.com/Getty Images Plus; Philippe TURPIN/Photononstop; darioracane/iStock/Getty Images Plus; Roger de la Harpe/Gallo Images; LeoPatrizi/E+; **PVB:** Image Source; narvikk/E+; BJI/Blue Jean Images; Prasit photo/Moment Open; **SB:** NoSystem images/E+; Hero Images; Ronnie Kaufman/Blend Images; Caiaimage/Chris Ryan; shironosov/iStock/Getty Images Plus; filadendron/E+; Henn Photography/Cultura.

**The following images are sourced from other sources.**

U3: © Lauren Bath. Reproduced with permission; Courtesy of Christopher Short.

Front cover photography by Silke Woweries/Corbis/Getty Images; Yagi Studio/Taxi Japan/Getty Images.

**Illustrations**

Abel Ippollito and Amerigo Pinelli

**Audio**

Produced by Leon Chambers and recorded at the SoundHouse studios, London

**Page make up**

Wild Apple Design Ltd and emc design ltd